**PACKER DYNASTY**

# PACKER DYNASTY

BY PHIL BENGTSON

WITH TODD HUNT

---

GARDEN CITY, NEW YORK
DOUBLEDAY & COMPANY, INC.
1969

Library of Congress Catalog Card Number 75-78716
Copyright © 1968, 1969 by Phil Bengtson and Todd Hunt

ALL RIGHTS RESERVED

Printed in the United States of America

# PREFACE

It comes on big and booming, like a circus, a parade, or a medieval pageant:
  The roll of drums . . .
  The fanfare of brass . . .
  The tremors of the crowd . . .
  Flashes of film turn the television screen into a kaleidoscope of mayhem.

Suddenly it is the corrida: fierce bulls charging from the chute, thundering across torn turf, defiantly tossing armor-plated heads, determined not to give ground, resolved to punish and to triumph.

Then, over it all: "From Lambeau Field in Green Bay, Wisconsin . . . CBS Sports presents NFL football. . . . Today, the Green Bay Packers meet . . ."

And the quiet of an autumn Sunday afternoon is interrupted by the throbbing of America's collective heartbeat. Fifty million addicts are submitting to their weekly video injection of adrenelin-sapping hysteria. It is the century-old war game called football, and here it is at its best.

There's been nothing like it since Cecil B. De Mille's rasping voice thrilled millions of radio listeners on Monday nights in the 1940s with "Curtain going up on Lux Radio Theatre." It takes a peculiar combination of excitement, anticipation, tension, and glamor to fuse millions of Americans into one. Professional football of the 1960s, like prewar radio, has that certain something.

## PACKER DYNASTY

Everything about pro football pushes the needle on the audience meter up to Stupendous. The major networks pay over $35 million annually just to televise selected games. (There's an extra pricetag of $2.5 million on the season-capping Super Bowl.) The top collegiate stars don't blush at the notion of haggling over a slice of bacon bigger than their nation's President brings home. It's a slack Sunday when one or more of these handsomely paid gentlemen fails to unleash a fifty-yard field goal, a seventy-five-yard passing "bomb," or a hundred-yard gallop that can be instant-replayed, then spliced into Pro Highlights of the Week . . . the Year . . . and the Decade.

At or near the pinnacle of pro football's loftiest heights for most of the past ten years have been the Green Bay Packers, a team that seemed to be dying in the late fifties when one disastrous losing season followed another. The Packers became to the sports world what the New York Yankees had been before them. The word most often invoked by sportscasters, magazine writers, and the fans was *dynasty*.

Although they have become the most popular banquet speakers, product endorsers, and first-person-magazine article writers in their field, no Packer player or coach has been so bold as to use the word dynasty. They know that such presumptuousness has two drawbacks. It can provide psychological ammunition to the enemy in a contest of wills where such emotions as love, hate, and revenge often provide the balance of power. And it can prove uncomfortable when the fortunes of war change, as they did for the Packers during the 1968 season.

The typical sportswriter, who giveth with one hand and taketh away with the other, was quick to pronounce the Packers dead —victims of old age and their own prolonged success. But men of football are less given to glib pronouncements. Like others who have made the rugged sport their life's work, Packer head coach John Philip (Phil) Bengtson approaches the game with painstaking care and slavish devotion. On the pages that follow, Bengtson offers a coach's view of how the finest team in football's hundred-year history was built and explains how he hopes to keep Green Bay, Wisconsin, on the map forever as Titletown, U.S.A.

TODD HUNT

New Brunswick, N.J.
January 1, 1969

# CONTENTS

Preface ......................................................................... v

PART ONE: THE GOLDEN DECADE

1  Days of Despair .......................................................... 3
2  The New Broom ........................................................... 9
3  A Brand-New Ball Game .................................................. 19
4  What This Team Needs Now . . . ........................................ 28
5  Pretenders to the Crown ................................................ 41
6  Titletown, U.S.A.! ..................................................... 51
7  Being Number Two Is No Fun ............................................. 62
8  Sudden Death, Sudden Life .............................................. 67
9  An Appointment in Dallas ............................................... 93
10 Superchamps! .......................................................... 104
11 Shooting for Three .................................................... 111
12 The Last Ride of Vince Lombardi ....................................... 126

PART TWO: THE MEN, THE MACHINERY, AND THE MYSTIQUE

13 The Biggest Little Major League City in the World .................... 137
14 Superfans: The Packer Backers ......................................... 142
15 The Draft: Playing Football's Stockmarket ............................. 152
16 The Day of Days ....................................................... 162
17 It's Like Going to School Again ....................................... 170
18 Of Muscles and Miseries ............................................... 186
19 Nitschke, and Other Things in My Defense .............................. 195
20 Love, Hate, and Other Useful Emotions ................................. 202
21 "What Men or Gods Are These?" ......................................... 209

| | | |
|---|---|---|
| 22 | The Players' Player: Bart Starr | 215 |
| 23 | Religion and the Green Bay Packers | 220 |
| 24 | What is Vince Lombardi Really Like? | 224 |
| 25 | Sleds, Horns, and Other Toys for Grown Men | 229 |
| 26 | Certain Things You Don't Tamper With | 240 |

PART THREE: WINNING IS THE ONLY THING THAT COUNTS

| | | |
|---|---|---|
| 27 | A Coach without Players | 249 |
| 28 | Football without the Foot | 253 |
| 29 | With a Little Help from Our Friends | 269 |
| 30 | The Pack Will Be Back | 273 |

# PART ONE

# THE GOLDEN DECADE

# 1 · DAYS OF DESPAIR

THE STARBOARD motor of the North Central Airlines' DC-3 came alive, and I shivered at the blast of chilled air that swept through the cabin when we began to taxi. As an assistant coach from 1951 to 1958 with the San Francisco 49ers, one of the National Football League's two West Coast clubs, I had long since received my "100,000 Mile Club" certificate. But on this cold January day at Chicago's Midway Airport, I was apprehensive and tense, wishing I were already in Green Bay. I pulled the beige-and-blue curtain back and looked up toward the overcast sky. It appeared that the sun might soon force its way through.

December had brought days of despair to both Green Bay and San Francisco. After ten years without a winning season, the Packers were limping dejectedly through the last weeks of the worst campaign in their forty-year history. The Wisconsin climate then was considered too harsh for late-season games, and the Packers traditionally had their last two outings with the 49ers and the Los Angeles Rams. After we worked them over 48–21 in one of our few sharp games that year, they were further victimized by the Rams. Their final record was one win, ten losses, and a tie. The hurt was made worse when one sportswriter labeled them the "Conga Team" because all year they had done little more than go 1-2-3-kick, 1-2-3-kick.

Like the Packers, the 49ers were suffering from the hot and cold spells that one California columnist aptly described as the club's "strange malady which seems to overtake it at the strangest times." After the 1954 season, the clubowners fired venerable head coach Buck Shaw, who had hired me to be his line coach. His successor, Red Strader, lasted only the following season. I stayed on through the next coaching shift to assist Frankie Albert. Frankie was one of the original 49ers when San Francisco obtained a franchise in the old All-America Conference, and one of the team's greatest players and leaders.

In his second year, 1957, we thought we would at last go all the way to the NFL title, but we ended up in a divisional tie and lost our playoff game with Detroit. The next year we succumbed to the malady again, despite the presence of the league's leading scorer in kicker Gordy Soltau, one of the all-time great quarterbacks, Y. A. Tittle, along with old warriors like Leo Nomellini and Hugh McElhenny, and promising youngsters such as John Brodie, Abe Woodson, and R. C. Owens. Albert, disappointed with our so-so record after coming so close to championship form, decided to quit coaching. I was shortly to find myself on the job market.

A head football coach must surround himself with assistants who conceive of the game as he does, who are capable of tailoring their teaching efforts to his master program, and who have the personal traits that mesh with his to create an aura of inspiration and leadership for the team. Through three regimes I had fit that mold. But when Howard "Red" Hickey was elevated to the top post at the end of the 1958 season, the chemistry just wasn't there. The day after his appointment was announced I walked into his office, shook his hand, and congratulated him. We stood there, forcing smiles for a few moments, and then finally one or the other of us managed to say what we were both thinking: "It . . . it isn't there . . . it just won't work." When the announcement was made shortly thereafter, I had already cleared my desk. In the pocket of my coat was a sheet from my memo pad with the names and phone numbers of clubs I figured would be in the market for coaches.

A football coach never passes up conference meetings, coaches' sessions, and other professional get-togethers. That fellow who buys him a drink afterward may be his next boss . . . or his next assistant, depending on which way his career is going. Although my long tenure in San Francisco had earned me the rather unenviable nickname of "Old Dad" around the league, I had kept up my contacts just the same. As a Minnesotan, I kept my eye on Green Bay, knowing that eventually it would be nice to be near home. Now was a good time to check it out again.

When my call got through to Packer head coach Ray "Scooter" McLean, I made small talk for a few moments and then broached the subject:

"How's the coaching situation up there?" I asked almost off-handedly, giving him the opportunity to tell me he was in the market for an assistant.

"I have a meeting with the directors this afternoon," he replied unemotionally. "I'll be handing them my resignation." (In the basket upset that resulted, McLean went to the Detroit Lions as backfield coach, and the man he succeeded came to the Packers in the same capacity.)

When the next morning's sports page confirmed the vacancy in Green Bay, I wired the club's president, Dominic Olejniczak, and let him know I was available. Suddenly I was bidding for the top job. The Packer front office assured me I would be seriously considered for the position.

Football coaching was steadily undergoing changes. Back when the Packers were born in 1919, they had signed up the local high school coach to direct the team without pay. Subsequently the team's co-founder and ace passer, Earl Lambeau, took over the coaching duties while continuing to play. It was nine years before he left the lineup to devote all his attention to coaching. (And a year later the Packers captured their first NFL championship!)

When I began coaching in the mid-thirties at Missouri under Don Faurot, father of the split-T, and through the forties with Clark Shaughnessy, who introduced the man-in-motion-T to Stanford, it was standard for a coach to have two assistants. When I joined former Santa Clara College coach Buck Shaw at the beginning of San Francisco's 1951 campaign, he desig-

5

nated me his line coach. His only other assistant was responsible for the backfield.

The game was simpler in those days. College stars were proud of their ability to play sixty-minute football, and coaches like Shaw refused to let the game get complicated by specialists and grab-bags of trick plays. The old-style coaches preferred to work closely with a few assistants and avoid the administrative problems of big staffs.

But the growth of professional ball dictated changes. With no "school spirit" or "alumni loyalty" to insure stadiums full of fans, the pros had to offer a faster game with more long-yardage plays, more scoring, and more thrills. That meant perfection and specialization, which meant more players and more coaches. By the mid-fifties I was a coach of the defense, and Frankie Albert had surrounded himself with four assistants. Today it's common to have five or six, because the tasks divide up naturally into defensive line, defensive secondary, offensive line, receivers, and backs.

Could I handle the increasingly complex role of shaping and guiding an entire football operation? I thought so, and I waited anxiously while Green Bay's directors considered the several candidates. Sportswriters in Wisconsin, Minnesota, San Francisco, Chicago, and New York devoted column after column to speculation and wrong guesses. (January used to be a quiet sports month, and there was plenty of white space to fill.) One of the criticisms directed at me in some quarters was particularly stinging: I was labeled a "born assistant," a phrase that was to echo briefly in 1968. It was of only small consolation that the same millstone was being hung around the neck of another candidate for the position, an assistant coach for the New York Giants by the name of Vince Lombardi.

"Lombardi won't get it; he's too hot-tempered," argued one camp. "Bengtson won't get it; he's not hot-tempered enough," went the opposite line. In the end, of course, the Packers wound up with a coaching staff that ran the gamut of temperament . . . men for all seasons.

Soon after I read in the paper that Lombardi had been

handed the job, I went to the phone and placed a call to him in New York.

"I'm sorry," came the reply at the other end. "Mr. Lombardi is not in. May I take a message?"

I told the operator to cancel the call without leaving a name or a message. He knows I'm available, I reasoned. If he wants me, he'll get in touch.

A phone call like that never comes quite when you expect it. I was puttering in the garage, and when my wife Kathryn told me "Long distance!" I was momentarily irked about having to interrupt my do-it-yourself project. I snapped to my senses when I heard the abrupt salutation in an unmistakable New York accent: "How-*ah*-yuh, Phil? This is Vince Lombb-*bah*-di."

He was frank and to the point: "I'm putting together a complete new staff, and I need somebody with experience to handle the defense. We're going to start from the bottom up and build a *winning* team here. If you're interested, why don't you come out to Green Bay for an interview?" I told him I could be there within a day.

Kathryn's reaction was one of ebullient practicality: "Oh, good! Now we have something to look up in our new encyclopedia." We were happy to find that Green Bay was not as small as sportscasters would have you think (over sixty thousand people then), nor as arctic (it's at the same latitude as Minneapolis and St. Paul). And it is predominantly Catholic, so we would have no trouble getting the kids into parochial school. "If you get the job," Kathryn instructed me, "go directly to a realtor. I'll start sorting and packing."

So now, an hour from Green Bay, my thoughts turned back to the Packers I had watched in San Francisco's Kezar Stadium just a month ago. I thought they had a lot better material than their sorry record indicated. As a lower division team, they had been dealt some high draft choices in recent years, and they were successful in signing their top picks. They had Notre Dame's Golden Boy, second-year man Paul Hornung, although they apparently couldn't decide if he should be a quarterback or a running back. They had the powerful rookie fullback, Jim Taylor, from Louisiana State. When they unleashed him for the first time in that next-to-last game against us, he gained over a hundred yards, and he did the same thing the next week against Los Angeles. There was plenty of talent in veterans like Max McGee and Forrest Gregg, but they just never seemed to get together to play consistent football.

It was true that a few old NFL veterans retired rather than accept their trades to "Siberia," but few rookies were turning down the opportunity to play for the Packers. Some "small-town boys" actually preferred the idea of making their home in Green Bay rather than playing and living in a big city.

Green Bay had the material. What it needed was a new outlook, new drive, and new dedication. In one hour I would be convincing Vince Lombardi that I was the man to help him do the job.

## 2 · THE NEW BROOM

THE SECOND Sunday in February I walked out of my home in Menlo Park, California for the last time and moved to my new job in Green Bay, Wisconsin. I told Kathryn to have the movers pack the framed team pictures from each of my years with the 49ers, but those were virtually the only mementoes I saved.

Monday morning I was sitting at a Green Bay Packer desk, thinking and acting Green Bay Packers. It was a clean break. Although I still considered many of the 49ers close friends, I immediately set about analyzing how we could take advantage of my intimate knowledge of the San Francisco coaches, players, and attack. They were among our first 1959 exhibition opponents, and a victory would bolster our confidence. (My planning was to pay off: We beat them in their own stadium, 24–17, and they were not destined to slip by us until their narrow 22–21 victory late in 1961. In nine years, they beat us only three times, twice by the margin of a single point.)

A new coaching assignment always cancels loyalties. In the 1960s, when Green Bay assistants began leaving to take NFL head coaching jobs, they made good use of what they knew about us. You could see their familiarity with us in the way they attacked, both on offense and on defense. Fortunately we usually had enough power and sufficient counterintelligence to frustrate our erstwhile comrades.

Soon after reporting in, I walked across the hall at Packer headquarters and talked to Red Cochran, the only other Lombardi assistant who had arrived. Red had tasted the success of

NFL championships twice, as a player for the Chicago Cardinals in 1947 and assistant coach for the Detroit Lions in 1957. He was as enthusiastic as I, but he tempered his optimism. "It's in good hands," he smiled. "I'd say we have a reasonable chance of being successful."

Lombardi himself had been careful not to promise too much. "Our number one problem here is to defeat defeatism," he announced at his first news conference. Pressed all that winter for predictions of overnight success, he uttered more than once the now-famous line: "I'm no miracle man."

There was nothing really revolutionary about what they called the Miracle at Green Bay. It was mostly a matter of setting up an orderly administration, starting with the front office. Lombardi had convinced the Packer directors that a winning team could not be put together by a committee of Monday morning quarterbacks. Power and leadership had to be vested in one man, and that man had to be Vince Lombardi, coach, general manager, and spiritual leader—not necessarily in that order.

He demanded and was granted absolute authority to hire, fire, budget, barter, and deal with the press. He decided how many stripes of what width and color he wanted on the jersies. He told the janitor where to move the water cooler, and gave instructions to make the nameplate on his door read "Mr. Lombardi," not "Coach Lombardi." To the first veteran who came asking to be traded to a winning team, he retorted, *"This* is going to be a winning team." If it smacked of dictatorship, that was what was needed.

Lombardi didn't waste that first Monday squiring Red and me around to meet bigwigs and learn the route to the men's room. He took us into the conference room and showed us movies for nearly five hours—reel after reel until we knew each and every Packer veteran and his abilities almost as well as if we had already been coaching him for a year. At the end of the session, he loosed a volley of questions. The answers could come only after days and weeks of necessary homework.

There were no pep talks. Even after the full complement of five assistants was gathered together, there were no ringing pronouncements about getting tough, conducting a revolution, or sweeping clean. But it was obvious from his brusque, positive personality that he was going to run a taut ship, tightly organized and well disciplined. He's always been that way: not outspoken, but always loud, firm, and decisive. He didn't necessarily demand more from his assistants than other coaches do, but he made it clear that he wouldn't settle for any less. He expected top performance. We were assigned our jobs, and we were expected to do them. The discipline he brought to bear that Monday morning was the taproot of a mighty oak: the same discipline that is built into the team today. It is the dominant characteristic of the entire Packer organization, on or off the football field. It's not a burden; it's a habit.

One by one the other coaches arrived in Green Bay to join the rebuilding: Bill Austin, the offensive line coach, left his assistant coaching at Wichita University to work at the side of his former mentor. Austin, an Oregon State star, had played first-string tackle for the New York Giants at the tender age of twenty. That was in 1949, when Lombardi was in his first year as an assistant at West Point. Austin played in the Pro Bowl in 1954, was an All-Pro in 1955, and helped the Giants win the 1956 championship. Called into the service at the height of his career, he was assigned to his first coaching job at the unlikely hotbed of football enthusiasm, Camp Drake in Japan. Once again he tasted the glory of championship: his squad won the Far East crown in Tokyo.

Norb Hecker left a player-coach job in Canada to handle our secondary, joining me on the defensive side of the table. A Little All-American in 1950 at Baldwin-Wallace, he ran up a phenomenal string of eighty-six consecutive games played in the NFL. He was in the lineup when the Los Angeles Rams had their finest year in 1951, winning the NFL title.

The sixth member of the staff took a "trial run" at coaching before leaping into the fray. Tom Fears, another Los Angeles Rams star who once caught a fantastic total of eighteen passes in one game (against the Packers!) as a 1950 teammate of Hecker, joined us at the beginning of the training season to help with the receiving ends. There was no better man for the job. His four hundred career receptions, most of them from Bob Waterfield and Norm Van Brocklin, had been calculated by the statisticians at more than a mile of yards gained. If anybody could tell a neophyte end like our rookie Boyd Dowler how to succeed in the business of receiving sixty-yard bombs, it had to be Tom Fears.

After the first few weeks of camp, Tom left to return to his restaurant business on the West Coast. He was having second thoughts about coaching as a career. As our exhibition season drew to a close, however, and it appeared that we had a potentially successful team, Lombardi knew he had to be equally strong in every phase of the game, and that meant he needed a coach for the receivers. "This is a winning team, and it starts winning next Sunday," he roared into the phone loudly enough so that some of the restaurant patrons in Los Angeles must surely have heard. Then softer, the Italian papa surfacing: "Whatayasay, Tommy? Call me back after you check with the airlines, right?" Tom Fears promised to be on the sidelines for our opening kickoff.

So it was a young staff: The average age was thirty-eight, with thirty-year-old Austin and thirty-three-year-old Hecker helping most to lower the figure. Each of us had been on a championship team in college or as a pro. We knew the good feeling you get playing early in January when everybody else in your league has hung up his shoes for the year. It was a feeling we all wanted to know again.

The key to getting that happy feeling was a thorough shuffling of personnel. Vince put it to me this way when I approached him about shoring up our pass defense: "Look, we're not just going to start with a clean slate; we're going to throw the old slate away. If you look at the roster of returning veterans and don't see what you must have to do the job, tell me what you need. You want to move a man from corner to safety, do it. You want to take five of my offensive men and put them in the defense, give me a list of the names. You want to buy the entire Chicago Bears line, I'll call Halas and see what I can do. That's the way we've gotta go at this. We can't do it with patch jobs and prayers."

And he wasn't kidding. The Packer telephone bill kept mounting. The charges for the month of March equaled the team's entire phone budget for the previous year. When the father of our top draft choice ran interference for his son and said we couldn't talk to the boy until after examinations, Vince ordered his secretary to cancel his standing twice-a-day phone calls to the boy and to call the airport for plane tickets instead.

Vince took three-time losers like Fred "Fuzzy" Thurston, who had drifted from the Bears to the Eagles to the Colts. ("I was such a lost sheep I thought sure the Rams would get me next," quipped the irrepressible Fuzzy when he realized he had finally found a home.) Moved into the starting lineup at left guard, he quickly became a team leader, resident wit, official song-leader . . . and an All-Pro selection.

Vince took unknown quantities, like safety Willie Wood, who was signed as a free agent after nobody else wanted him and he had written to the Packers asking for a tryout. Although he had starred as a quarterback and defensive halfback at the University of Southern California, he was considered too small for pro ball at five-feet-ten and 185 pounds. He turned out to be the surest tackler on the squad and one of the NFL's leading punt returners. He led the league in interceptions one year and has made an annual affair of playing in the Pro Bowl.

And, true to his vow, Vince bought a chunk out of an entire team, the then-mighty Cleveland Browns. Giving up a few of our middle-round draft choices for the following year, plus a veteran offensive end who was destined to be replaced by a rookie, we got tackle Henry Jordan, defensive end Bill Quinlan, plus halfback Lew Carpenter, and later, end Willie Davis. It was a wonder deal of the same magnitude as the famed Anderson-Grabowski acquisitions, for it brought us the keystone of a defense that would hold for many NFL championships to come.

Lombardi's trades strengthened the Packers at almost every position. The notable exception was at quarterback, the most important of all. "We've got a hell of a problem," Vince sighed after hours of movie watching. "We've got to find somebody who can move this club." He had no way of knowing that the eventual solution to the problem would be an unobtrusive third-string player from Alabama already languishing on our bench. So the word went out that the Packers were looking for a field general. Babe Parilli was gone, leaving two modest backup quarterbacks in Bart Starr and Joe Francis, a converted halfback.

I'll admit I was one of Bart Starr's detractors in 1959. Vince showed me a long reel of film clips showing the quarterbacks at work and then asked my evaluation of Starr from the defenders' point of view. "Well," I told him, "he's adequate as a backup man, but other than that I can't say too much for him. I certainly can't see him as a quarterback on a championship team." Lombardi nodded and agreed. "I'll give him a fair look," he said. "But he's no Bobby Lane, no Dutch Van Brocklin."

As is usually the case in the NFL, we expected to find a man worthy of number one by looking around the league at the teams with the greatest quarterbacks and looking at the men working in their shadows. Prime on our list was George Shaw, the stand-in for Johnny Unitas of the then-champion Baltimore Colts.

"He's the man who can get the job done for us," Vince told me the day I arrived in Green Bay. "I'm going to give this deal top priority." When I asked how he hoped to interest the Baltimore management, I expected the answer would be another typical NFL solution: offering our top draft choice for the following year. I was shocked when I heard that Vince was willing to trade them our veteran end Billy Howton, who was runner-up in every pass-reception category to Green Bay's all-time greatest receiver, Don Hutson, and who to this day holds the team records for most yards gained receiving in one game and in one season.

"Sure, Howton led the Packers in receiving last year, but he didn't play regularly because he's slowing up," Lombardi reasoned. "Sure, he's got a following, and he's a Packer from way back. But there's no room for sentiment. My job is to build the best team I can. I'll trade *anybody* on the team anytime I think it will help us. And when training camp starts, it's not thirty veterans secure in their jobs, with fifty rookies trying for a half-dozen vacancies. It's eighty men working their butts off for thirty-six jobs, and plane tickets for eighty more to come in if we can't get what we want."

But the Shaw-Howton deal fell through, as did some other tries at acquiring a top-caliber number-two man. There was always Hornung, but Vince had promised him "You're my halfback," and the new offense he was about to install would keep him true to his word. To make matters worse, our top draft choice, a quarterback, failed to sign with us. Finally we managed to strike a deal with the St. Louis Cardinals which brought us Lamar McHan.

Nobody was ecstatic over the trade. As one sportscaster soon complained, "After saying 'It's from McHan to McGee' half the afternoon, it starts coming out 'Began the Beguine,' and that's when you wish Starr was in there." Starr and Francis were deeply disappointed, of course, but the truth was they just didn't have the experience to handle the team. McHan had played as a regular starting quarterback, and in that position more than any other you've got to have a man with experience.

Because our quarterbacking was still a question mark, and because Lombardi had a system of his own to teach them, he called McHan, Starr, and Francis into camp early in June—practically a month before the normal start of training camp. For their benefit, as well as that of his assistants, he convened a most extraordinary school: the Vince Lombardi Course in Basic Football. The first day of classes made even "Old Dad" sit up and begin taking notes.

"We're going to take a giant step backward, gentlemen," Vince began. I'm sure there was no pun intended, although the philosophy he was about to outline was one he had been developing in his years of directing the Giant offense. Football was meant to be a running game, he reminded us. The forward pass was developed as an alternative . . . a variation that enabled a team to show the opponent a more varied attack. The idea was to have the pass a *threat* that worried the defense and set things up for your bread-and-butter running plays. Through the 1950s in the National Football League, it was the other way around. Which was all well and good when you had a Unitas or a Van Brocklin, *and* he was hot, *and* he had the great receivers working with him, *and* you could keep him healthy for an entire season. It also looked pretty good on that one day each year when the last-place team put it all together and dropped the bombs in a big upset over the eventual national champion.

Yes, passing was fine, and it pleased the crowds, but Lombardi believed the running game could be even finer when practiced to perfection. The hometown faithful were sure to approve if it lifted their team to the top of the standings. So we would return to the basic ground game—classical preaviation warfare. It was to be ball control, with the relentless rolling of the offense denying the foe possession of the ball, robbing him of precious minutes. It was to be a philosophy of dealing from strength rather than weakness, displaying constancy rather than flashiness. It was to be a vocabulary rife with expressions such as "spartanism" and "total dedication," to the virtual exclusion of "heroism," "surprise plays," and the like.

It would mean endless drilling in the fundamental skills of the game. "Some people try to find things in this game or put things into it which don't exist," Vince lectured again and again. "Football is two things: it's blocking and tackling. You block and tackle better than the team you're playing, and you win." As one of Fordham's Seven Blocks of Granite, Vince came to know firsthand the spine-jarring, sweat-drenching drudge labors of the offensive linemen. A former guard, he knew well who it is who opens holes, clears aside would-be tacklers, holds back surging linebackers to protect the passer, "pulls" suddenly from his usual position to complete special assignments on special plays . . . and who it is who is showered, dressed, and on the bus before the newsmen are finished urging the halfback to describe once more the winning scamper through "that gap that just seemed to open up at the right moment." As a former tackle, I could appreciate what Vince was saying.

Lombardi made the offensive lineman's job both easier and harder at the same time with his innovation of "option blocking." Instead of squaring off with the opposite man and locking horns with him like two bull moose, the option blocker was expected to contact his opponent, ascertain the thrust of his drive, and assist him firmly in that direction. Thus deflected, the defender left a momentary hole through which the ball carrier—making the split-second choice that Lombardi called the "delayed option"—could run to daylight. Option blocking. Delayed option running. Run to daylight. Three new terms in the lexicon of football that were summed up in one magnificent play: the Packer power sweep. Within two seasons there would be hardly a player in the league or a regular fan of the televised games who didn't know the particulars: Play number forty-nine in the Packer book . . . Jim Taylor and Paul Hornung alternating as ball carrier . . . one blocking when the other carries . . . Taylor plowing through the secondary and lunging for three extra yards with two tacklers hanging from his iron frame and two more straining against his massive shoulders . . . Hornung suddenly bursting past astonished linebackers and stiff-arming the last defensive back out of his way.

Vince had developed the power sweep before coming to Green Bay, but for the first time the conditions were perfect for developing it as the principal attack. It was suited perfectly to a halfback like Hornung, who wasn't particularly fast but had good balance and control, who could do well at the pass option, and who had the poise and confidence to make the quick decisions necessary if the delayed option feature was to work.

"Theoretically," Vince explained to us, "the play is designed to go around end. But I don't expect it will have to go that far if our linemen do their job properly and our backs learn to watch for that daylight. The opening should develop back inside someplace, sometimes considerably inside. It's going to look to some people like a different play every time we use it. But pretty soon they'll be able to recognize it . . . by watching the official for the first-down signal."

In order for the power sweep to become established as the cornerstone of the ground game, each of the offensive coaches had to study the techniques and prepare to help veterans as well as rookies learn much of their trade over again. As defensive coach, I was charged with anticipating the reaction of our opponents and advising Vince on adjustments and further innovations.

"We may not know any more about football than most of the other coaches in the league," Vince suggested after a particularly exhausting day-long planning session with play charts and the overhead projector. "But if we can put everything we know together so it makes good basic sense and then drill-drill-drill it into *them* . . ." He began straightening the piles of charts, and it appeared he had no intention of completing the thought, when suddenly he jerked his head up to unleash that characteristic grinding smile punctuated at the right corner with a glimmer of gold. ". . . That kind of coaching, gentlemen, can make winners out of losers."

# 3 · A BRAND-NEW BALL GAME

As I PACKED a duffel bag, gathered up my toilet articles, and prepared to report in for the first day of training camp in 1959, it occurred to me that it was my silver anniversary as a football coach. Twenty-five years earlier I had arrived at Columbia, Missouri to help Don Faurot salvage something out of a team that had not won a game in three years. A few seasons later we would be on our way to the Orange Bowl.

Was it to be another success story now . . . or something less?

As grade schoolers in St. Paul, my buddies and I were already playing football at every opportunity on corner lots. None of that touch stuff, but plenty of slam-bang running, hitting, and tackling. We imitated the college teams we saw in the newsreels, which meant running straight at each other full force and frequently knocking ourselves silly. When my closest friend Dave MacMillan and I heard that University High School in Minneapolis was holding early practice for entering freshmen, we showed up for the twice-a-day drills. We made the team, and since I was pretty good sized, they made a tackle out of me.

My high school coach was a fundamentalist named Lloyd Peterson, a tough old son-of-a-gun who believed in making you furiously mad so you'd play your hardest. As I sat in the locker room in a state of euphoria over the idea of playing in my first real football game, I got one of the rudest shocks of my entire life. Coach Peterson burst through the door shouting, "All right, are you *men* ready to go out there and fight?

Are you ready to win? Well, *are* you?" Whereupon he started down the row of benches grabbing two boys at a time by the tops of their heads, great thatches of hair sprouting from between his calloused knuckles, and pulled until the tears came.

"Win, win?" Then on to the next two lads. "Fight? Huh? Are you going to fight?" And when every head had been subjected to the humiliation, he shouted, "Okay, let me *hear* it, boys" and positioned himself next to the passageway, where he could give each of us a good hard kick in the butt as we went whooping and yelling out under the stands and onto the field. We were hurt, we were mad, we were furious, and we wanted to punish the first man who crossed our path. Which, of course, was the opponent. And which was one of the main reasons Coach Peterson's teams were usually undefeated and unscored upon.

Although it is not my personal philosophy that a player has to be scalped and kicked to arouse his deeper passions, I came to realize under my first coach that players have to be aggressive to win, and it is the coach's job to cultivate that aggressiveness. That's why I was one of the few who were not very alarmed when Vince strode into the room full of eighty grown men that sultry July morning and lowered the now-famous boom . . .

"Gentlemen," he began—and they were soon to develop a Pavlovian response to that salutation, part tightening of the spine, part tingling of nerve endings—"Gentlemen, I have never been on a losing team, and I have no intention of changing now. You're here to play football, and I'm here to see that you do your very best. I want *total dedication* on the part of every man in this room: total dedication to himself, total dedication to the Green Bay Packers, and total dedication to *winning*. Your first task is to make yourself physically fit, able to do your very best and to make the most of your God-given abilities. Your second task is to sharpen your mental alertness, to learn your assignment on every play, to learn the techniques and develop the ability to know where you are every second of the ball game. And your third task is to develop the winning habit.

Winning isn't everything, it's the *only* thing. If you can accept losing, you can't win. The harder a man works, the harder it is to surrender, and that's why you're going to work like you've never worked before in these next days, weeks, and months. That's why I'm going to push you until I know you're doing your best. If you can't take it, get out. And I'm not going to worry about what anybody says about me or about the Packers; just as long as I win. That's what I get paid for. We move this club from now on with *execution*. We run a play again and again and again until everybody knows it and everybody does his part to make it work. You have to be able to play your best for sixty minutes, Sunday after Sunday, and you have to be able to execute. This is a violent sport. To play in this league you have to be tough. Physically tough. Mentally tough. And you've got to have pride. Pride is what makes a winning performance. If two teams are the same in physical ability and mental ability, it's the team with pride that wins. And I want to *win*, gentlemen."

Vince went on to enumerate his rules, making it clear that he intended to enforce them. Those who violated the official Green Bay Packers Rules and Regulations (page one of the play book) or Lombardi's Corollaries ("put them on page one in your mind") would be fined, tongue-lashed, or both. Repeated offenders, or those who griped, would no longer be Packers.

"Curfew is 11 P.M.," he decreed. "That means in your room, on your bed, with the lights out. The fine for breaking curfew is fifty dollars." The second night of training camp two young third-year men tested the rule, and the players' committee fund was richer by one hundred dollars. A few nights later when a veteran of many years—a first-string player and team leader—returned to camp just five minutes late, Vince was at the door: "That will cost you fifty dollars." There was no argument. There were no more missed curfews.

"All players will ride the buses to and from practice. There will be no private cars to and from practice. Practice time is not the time the buses leave, it is the time when all players are on the practice field and doing calisthenics. The fine for being late to practice is twenty-five dollars." That was the beginning of Lombardi Time, with assistants, trainers, and players alike setting their minute hands forward a quarter hour for the duration of the football season.

"Meals are served at seven-thirty, noon, and six o'clock. You are expected to eat a balanced meal of training table food, without skipping and without supplementing. If you persist in being overweight, an assistant coach will be assigned to monitor you at the table. He will make certain that you chew all food until it can be swallowed like liquid. The fine for skipping meals is ten dollars, and the fine for being overweight is ten dollars a day." Every day for a week I sat across the table from two of my defensive charges and implored them to chew-chew-chew until it was paste, and if I saw a lump go down, I chew-chew-chewed until they got the idea. "Finely chewed food fills you up faster; don't you understand?" I explained to a rookie whose eyes were on the verge of spilling the huge tears welled up in the corners. He nodded, and in doing so, he dislodged the two droplets.

"Injured men will run in practice. They will go through all drills not affecting their injuries. They will report to the trainer for special exercises. All injuries will be reported to and treated by the trainer. If you break every bone in your body, your first assignment is to start preparing yourself mentally to return to action. I want aggressive players; I want them aggressive even when it hurts."

It's standard on any football team to start practice sessions with calisthenics to loosen the players up, and in the early days of camp the usual set of "burpees" and "jumping jacks" is augmented with conditioning exercises. But Vince felt that what was "standard" would not be enough. He introduced the grass drills and the wind sprints. The former drew their name from the urging of the assistant coach who was selected to shout out Vince's script for the day: "Lift those legs off of the grass . . . now down, down, face in the grass . . . now up, up, and run on the grass; run, run, run, or you'll walk out of here for the last time . . . now look at the grass; *look* at it; put your face in it and push, up-down-up-down . . . now quit killing the grass; up-up-up and lift those feet." When the ground crew appeared early to move the sprinklers back on the field after practice, one departing player chided them between gasps: "I don't know why you worry about the damn stuff; Coach won't let us put our feet all the way down on it."

The wind sprints—mad dashes two or three times the length of the field—were at first the curse of the entire team, even for the ends and defensive backs who were used to spurts of thirty and forty yards on pass plays. The entire pack of eighty grown men charged from one goal post to the other and back, shouting encouragement to those who were on the verge of collapse. No one was permitted to dog it, and soon almost all were able to survive. Nobody vomited after the first couple of days.

The hated wind sprints were perhaps the most vital of all Vince's training regimens, because they made the players able to do what they had not been able to do before: to stay in a game and be strong until the final gun. It was to be the hallmark of the Green Bay Packers. We became known as the team that ground relentlessly through the second half, wearing down the opponent and waiting to capitalize on mistakes. We learned to exploit weaknesses, so we could push the ball over on those crucial fourth-quarter drives that decide so many games.

"Look, Coach," linebacker Tom Bettis grinned to me as he headed for the locker room after our intrasquad game in the second month of training, "I'm not even breathing hard. How about playing another quarter's worth?" Bettis and the rest of my defensive squad lost an average of twelve pounds per man in the first six weeks, and Dave "Hawg" Hanner shed over twenty. Their uniforms had to be altered to compensate for their new, slimmer builds.

But the real payoff, as in so many of the things we did differently that summer, was the psychological uplift. Any athlete whose coaches force him to be stronger and tougher is bound to be more confident of himself. When he knows his teammates have been through the same thing, he has more confidence in the ability of the team to win. And the humiliation of July's grass drills has changed by September to a pride in having triumphed and a spirit of "Now we can conquer anything." By the end of the initial phase of training camp, just prior to our first exhibition game, the players would begin to sense that pride and that spirit.

There were minor crises almost daily. Midway through the second week, Vince got upset (more upset than usual, that is, which means that he brooded on it as well as loosing a torrent of words) over reports that some of the older, single players frequented two of the seamier bars in Green Bay on weekends. In addition to the poor public relations for the Packer organization, there was the chance that the players might find themselves inadvertently in contact with the bettors and underworld characters who inhabit such places.

At the end of the Sunday night meeting, before the defensive and offensive teams split up to watch the previous week's films, Vince laid down his amendments to the team's rules for gentlemanly conduct. Bars and taverns were off limits, and he singled out by name those establishments that he expressly forbade Packers to enter. When in supper clubs or dining rooms serving drinks, no team member was to drink standing at the bar. "Do I make myself clear?" he asked at the end of his remarks, and every head nodded. He reiterated the rules at the beginning of every season thereafter. Perhaps the most heralded infraction was the night he walked into a restaurant and found his superstar Paul Hornung standing at a bar with a glass. He levied the promised $500 fine on the spot. When Hornung left, Vince verified what he already knew; the glass contained nothing stronger than ginger ale. But the rule had been broken.

Halfway through the third week of training, Vince came to early mass so hoarse he could barely speak. The role of task master and drill sergeant had taken its toll. At breakfast he drained a second glass of orange juice in silence, tilting his head back to let the last drops rinse his parched throat. On the field, his first command was never completed: "All right, let's get out there and hit . . ." In a paroxysm of rasping and coughing, he lost the use of his voice.

But the next few days were no less demanding ones. He stomped when the running wasn't fast enough. He jabbed his finger in every direction to indicate that the execution wasn't crisp enough. And he slammed a fist into the palm of his hand when tackles weren't letter perfect. A rookie who fumbled haplessly after colliding with his own interference got up to find Vince standing arms akimbo and glaring with menace. The message was silent but clear.

The intense training and rebuilding gradually shifted from drilling on basic skills to focusing on their application to the power sweep. Austin's linemen churned away at the swinging dummy, throwing up great clods of earth and coating the canvas with layer upon layer of their sweat. As Bill swung the bag to one side or another, the blocker learned to subtley exercise his option and guide it firmly in the desired direction. The backs, meanwhile, drilled endlessly until it became second nature for them to run in tandem. The ball carriers developed the feel, even the "smell" of that chink in the line where they would find the daylight. Offensive linemen and backs alike took well to the system, and their new-found confidence was an inspiration to the defense. Movies of the first scrimmage showed a new determination on both sides, and for the first time I had the feeling that perhaps we were going to make a better than just respectable showing in the coming season.

As the pace picked up and we began to film all scrimmages and two-minute drills, the coaching staff spent almost every evening running the reels over and over again, looking for minor flaws in execution that would have to be corrected in the remaining days before our first exhibition game. In the later afternoons, following the squad meetings, the quarterbacks looked at last year's films on our first opponents, the Chicago Bears. Since I would depend on the same films for defensive information, I sat in on several of their sessions. McHan, the senior man, ran the projector, and young Francis and Starr made comments, asked questions, and took notes.

## PACKER DYNASTY

Perhaps the most important assignment of the quarterback, both on the field and in his many hours of homework, is to recognize the different defenses he will encounter—the half dozen standard ones plus the several variations practiced by various teams. He must have a mental picture of where each man is positioned on each of those defenses, what his assignment is, and where he will move as this or that play develops. Of particular importance is knowing precisely how the defensive secondary men—the bouncing, shifting, free-wheeling men behind the line—will react to your deployment of your backs and ends. For example, if the quarterback sends his fullback out of the backfield, how do the linebackers cover him, what options are open to them, where will they be thin if they move one way or the other to compensate? The answers to these dozens of questions-within-questions must be part of a quarterback's instant recall, for the degree to which he can recognize defensive maneuvers and take advantage of them will determine his success.

No quarterback I have ever seen worked as hard to master those vital lessons than did the twenty-four-year-old Bart Starr. He was as conscientious and thorough as any player I have ever seen at any position. He studied, studied, studied, and at times both McHan and Francis grew impatient with his requests to run a play over "one more time" so he could memorize the most minute details. He never made a snap judgment, never saw something and said "This is it." Even the most obvious things he insisted on reviewing a dozen times, much as a child insists on rehearsing a poem from the very beginning in order to brush up on a single difficult line. He listened to the conclusions of the others, then worked out his own conclusion, even if it turned out to be the same. And then he started all over to see if he could come up with something he thought was sounder. He refused to oversimplify anything.

Long after McHan and Francis had finished and left to wash up for supper, Bart would be at the projector. I came back one afternoon to find him working with films I didn't even recall seeing before. "Do you think this is a zone defense or just a rotated man-to-man?" he asked. Before answering I looked at the can on the table. It was obvious that he was going back through the library, replaying every game since he first broke in under Tobin Rote two years earlier. I sat down and watched him piece together, move by move, an analysis of the Los Angeles Ram defense—information he would put to good use a few months later. I was beginning to respect the quiet Alabaman.

The next day in scrimmage, however, Starr panicked when his protective pocket failed to hold up. He tossed a wobbly pass that was picked off by a defensive man. "One more like that," Lombardi shouted, "and you're on your way."

## 4 · WHAT THIS TEAM NEEDS NOW . . .

IN MID-AUGUST, when baseball pennants are up for grabs and one out of three Americans still hasn't suffered his annual sunburn, professional football begins its six-week schedule of exhibition games. Today those contests are waged in NFL home stadiums before crowds of up to eighty thousand people paying as much as $7.50 a head—much of it for charity. But a decade ago, before television and the fans had developed their insatiable appetite for pro football, the Packers were still warming up for the season in such far-flung locales as Portland, Oregon, Bangor, Maine, and Winston-Salem, North Carolina, on successive weekends. The preseason tour has always been considered an extension of training, a period of trying new personnel and making the necessary adjustments in attack and defense.

But Vince let us know weeks before the first game that he didn't look upon the exhibitions as a time for endless experiments and extended player tryouts. "What this team needs now is a couple of wins under its belt," he admonished us. "And God knows, the fans could use an injection of hope." He began more than a week before the first preseason game to drill against the opponent's offenses and to talk in the evening sessions about going all-out for a win in the first game and each succeeding one. To this day that has been the Packer philosophy: Play *every* game to win.

The preseason opener in Milwaukee could not have brought

a more fitting foe: George Halas and his Bears. The teams had been facing one another since the beginning of the National Football League, and, in fact, the fame of their intense rivalry had helped the league through some of its more desperate middle years. The rivalry was fed by the Chicagoans' resentment of the small-town team from the north, with its roster of "local yokels" and the trainloads of fanatical partisans in bright mackinaw jackets, wool caps, and lumberjack boots who tumbled into the Chicago Loop once each autumn and trooped to Wrigley Field to rant and chant and create general pandemonium. As the years went by, the automatic appellation invoked by Green Bay sportswriters became "the hated Bears," for Halas and Crew to this day are the only team in the NFL with an edge over the Packers in wins and losses. During the past decade, the teams have met three times a year, first in Milwaukee at the geographical halfway point for the Shrine exhibition, then in Green Bay for the game that is considered *the* social event of the year, and finally in Chicago. The team on the short end of the best two out of three "series" comes away with a ready-made emotional edge for the following year's opener.

Vince never said it, but we all knew he wanted to beat the Bears almost as much as he wanted anything. The one exception would be a victory over his former team, the New York Giants. We led off both the exhibition slate and the regular season with Chicago, and we were to meet New York at the halfway mark of both schedules.

The exhibition season went well when you consider we won on all but two of our six outings. But unfortunately the two we lost were to Chicago and New York. And against the Giants we were so lethargic and had so many miscues that we failed to score. Players who could not bring themselves to confess to Lombardi told their assistant coaches: "We beat ourselves. Instead of playing to win, we played *not to lose* so we wouldn't disappoint the coach. Next time we'll play to win."

The day the Lombardi Era officially began was a misty, murky September 27 when a then-capacity crowd of 32,150 filled a stadium that would not have an empty seat for a Packer game in the entire golden decade to follow. It was a scene my Kathryn recalled for me later as the most awe-inspiring in her lifetime as a coach's wife. There were people who had held their tickets through the bad years, people who had purchased one share apiece in the team so the town would not lose the franchise. They weren't like a typical sports crowd, just out for a good time. They were more like the people of a small nation gathered for a coronation: All of them personally involved and intensely interested, straining to see and to hear. When the team appeared, they rose as one, and the welling up of their single joyous voice brought tears to those who were watching the Packers for the first time and to those who were watching them for the hundredth or two-hundredth time.

The struggle on the mist-shrouded field that afternoon was a classic grudge match. The Bears rushed at a nearly impregnable Packer line; the Packers slashed at a mighty Chicago forward wall. The average rushing yardage was a meager three for both teams. At halftime the Bears led 3-0 on a forty-six-yard-field goal.

It was time for Vince Lombardi's first halftime pep talk as head coach of the Green Bay Packers. Some coaches feel it is their duty to fire the boys up with a rousing give-'em-hell tirade calculated to get the adrenalin flowing. Others find the task uncomfortably unnatural. Minnesota's great Bernie Bierman used to deliver a strictly technical briefing, then turn the psychological chores over to one of the fiery orators among the old-timers who frequented his locker room. Lombardi would prove adroitly flexible: he could be a Knute Rockne if he felt the situation called for it, or he could be a parish priest. He could issue a get-off-your-butts ultimatum or fall to his knees alongside blood-spattered players and join them in prayer. In the long seasons to come, he would make each "pep talk" an appropriate one. Today he was gentle but firm combat lieutenant: "Men: . . . Gregg . . . Carpenter . . . Kramer . . . McGee . . . Hornung . . . Taylor . . . Thurston . . . You have marched, and you have held. Now it's time to score, and to win. What you do in the next thirty minutes will indicate what you can do next time and all the times to come. If you want it, go get it."

*Go get it.*

Victory was there to be had, but each yard was more difficult than the next. Halas had obviously given his men the same decree, and throughout the scoreless third period it began to look as if the Bears' 3-0 might hold up. (In the past decade, twelve games between the two rivals have been settled by the margin of a touchdown or less—seven of them by field goals.)

But in the fourth period, the Packer attack gelled. Spotting the Bears another field goal from near midfield, the Pack produced that one big play that can break a game open: a McHan-to-McGee bomb for sixty-seven yards. Taylor scored the tying touchdown on a plunge of five yards, and Hornung added the point after. Two more valuable points were added by Dave Hanner's safety late in the game. As the clock ticked away the final minute, the elated Packer Backers were on their feet and counting. Then the gun . . . and the first of Lombardi's many rides off the field.

Wildly exuberant Lew Carpenter, standing next to Vince, began to hoist him single-handedly and was immediately joined by as many of his teammates as could get a hand on the coach's rumpled tan raincoat. Everybody involved was so inexperienced at it that Lombardi almost tumbled backward before grabbing Carpenter's helmet for support. But it wouldn't be long before the Packers were past masters at the art of coach lofting.

The pandemonious celebrating in Green Bay continued for the remainder of that afternoon and night, and the defeat of the Bears was the sole topic on the streets and in the shops on Monday. Sportswriters and television newsmen hailed the victory deliriously as a new day for Packer football. "Lombardi for mayor" crowed a hastily whitewashed sign in one shop on downtown North Washington Street, a modest proposal in light of the "Lombardi for governor" and "Lombardi for President" signs of later years.

When the coaches sat down to diagnose the game films on Monday, there were many reasons to be encouraged: We had outrushed the Bears by one hundred yards and had produced sixteen first downs to their ten. Taylor alone had churned out almost a hundred yards by bits and pieces, and Hornung showed he could make the halfback option work, tossing a twenty-yard pass to Gary Knafelc that caught the Bears by surprise.

At the same time, there was little encouragement in the quarterback department. Other than his timely bomb, McHan completed only two passes. Starr had to scramble the one time he was sent in to pass, and he lost eight yards. It would have to be better, especially with aerialists like Y. A. Tittle and Johnny Unitas looming on the horizon.

The second week the mercurial McHan pulled himself together and fired four touchdown passes to three different receivers and led us to a decisive 28–10 win over Detroit. Although the Lions thwarted our running attack and held us to ten first downs, they turned the ball over twice on interceptions and twice on fumbles. In the end, it was a pair of long McHan-to-McGee passes that beat them.

The third week, despite the temporary absence of Taylor, our power sweep lived up to its awesome potential for the first time, and we penetrated the San Francisco line for 284 yards on the ground. Hornung posted an amazing 138 yards, and even McHan found half a dozen holes that netted him 45 yards. Our passing was adequate, with McHan delivering two long touchdown throws, and we managed to outlast Y. A. Tittle and the 49ers by a squeaky margin of 21–20 for our third straight home victory. I was particularly happy not only because we beat my old team, but because the defense had held the opponent scoreless in the critical fourth quarter for the second straight week. When the defense can do that consistently, you have the makings of a championship team.

My elation was premature. The following week we played our worst defensive game of the year, yielding over 450 yards to the potent Los Angeles Rams. They scored in every quarter and went on a twenty-four-point binge in the last period. Our offense had managed only to set up two Hornung field goals in the second period, and we bowed 45–6. On the following Sundays we had our moments, but foundered and lost to the Colts, the Giants, and the Bears in three weeks on the road. Suddenly what had been a joyous inaugural season appeared to be slowing down to a brave but losing effort.

Vince was particularly crushed when we lost in Yankee Stadium the first day in November at the hands of his old Giant teammates. He felt that his players knew how much he wanted to win that day, and he was certain that they would give them their best. But again the pressure and the emotions were to backfire on a team which had not yet fully developed the pride and the poise necessary to rise to the occasion of key games. Perhaps because the power sweep was Vince's own baby, conceived in New York and matured in Green Bay, his former compatriots stopped it cold, holding Hornung to thirty-six yards and Taylor to fifteen. When we turned to the pass, McHan completed only two in eight attempts, and lost yardage on one broken pattern. Vince was furious. "You know you can do better than that," he yelled, pounding his fists together until the list of plays he carried was crumpled. "Why? Why?" he implored from the sidelines as McHan stared after a fallen bullet.

Finally Vince turned to his reserve quarterbacks and snapped, "Dammit, what is it going to take to get this team moving?" He looked first at Joe Francis, then at Bart Starr, and back at Francis. "Next time you go," he informed Francis peremptorily, then turned to see his halfback hit the line where there was no longer daylight and lose the ball to the Giants. Given his chance, Francis completed fewer than a third of his eighteen passes, and as a result we found ourselves punting as many times in one game as we had in the previous two. Our scoring was limited to a second-period Hornung field goal. A dejected Vince Lombardi walked away from his old home with a 20–3 loss.

When we found ourselves a losing team instead of the fast-starting winners of October, Vince served notice that there would have to be a shakeup. "It isn't good enough to say we're *rebuilding*," he lectured us at the halfway mark. "I get sick of people who apologize and rationalize. It isn't good enough to say last year we got only one win, this year three, next year maybe five, and that's supposed to be improvement. *Winning* is what counts, and we've got the people here to win. The thing is to get those people working." He served notice on the team that training camp conditions would prevail: No man's position was secure. Each player would have to work each week to earn the confidence of his coaches. Lombardi began to scan the bench for talent that could be promoted out of the development stage and into the lineup.

One of the areas for improvement was the pass-receiving department. Rookie Boyd Dowler had been one of the bright spots in the gloomy loss to the Rams, snatching his first professional pass for an eleven-yard gain. He caught two in the next game, one for his first pro score. As Lombardi went over his roster looking for ways to inject some much-needed adrenalin, Tom Fears advised him that Dowler was ready as a starter. The tall University of Colorado hero had great speed—9.9 seconds for the hundred—and was proving adept at snaring passes from between the outstretched arms of shorter defenders.

Early in November Vince told his offensive assistants to let him take a look at the Starr-Dowler pass combination in practice. It was a gray, misty morning when the duo came under the master's special scrutiny. Dowler ran a sharp turnout as Starr stepped back and cocked. The spiraling ball was delivered at the precise moment when Dowler arrived on station and lifted his hands. When it was firmly in his grasp, he crossed out of bounds as the play dictated. With the whistle at his lips, Lombardi froze in horror: His neophyte end was about to crash into a huge steel cylinder used to store tarpaulins. He watched, anticipating a serious injury, and saw the artful Dowler leap the obstruction like a hurdle and tumble unhurt on the other side. Lombardi led the entire squad in a wild cheer as Dowler came up grinning and tossed the ball casually back to the center. "Good grief, watch yourself, Dowler," the coach admonished gently as the young player rejoined the pass receivers in their huddle. Then he turned to me with a half smile and said, "Be glad he belongs to us. It won't be long before every other defensive coach in the league has to worry about him."

Our rematch with Chicago was a rocking, socking, running affair, typical of the rubber game each year with the Bears—both teams trying to break loose after virtual standoffs in the two early meetings. We received an injection of hope late in the game when Bill Butler, activated after the start of the season, ran back a punt sixty-one yards for a touchdown. But by then the Bears had scored four touchdowns to our two, and neither Starr nor McHan could get a pass attack mounted. After a Bear quarterback by the name of Edmund Raymond "Zeke" Bratkowski had completed a first-down pass in the third period, Vince glared at Starr and told him: "Now *that's* how you drill a buttonhook in there." The final score was 28–17.

Our rematch with Baltimore, although another losing effort—the fifth in a row—indicated to us that we had turned the corner. Unitas was hot, hitting his favorite receiver, Raymond Berry, for two short touchdowns. But Starr was beginning to click, too, hitting Taylor for a twenty-yard touchdown pass. Taylor ran for two more. After having made a habit of losing two fumbles in each of the preceding five games, we managed not to turn the ball over a single time by errors. We were penalized only five yards. And Dowler "arrived" in a burst of glory, receiving eight passes for a total of 147 yards, to the complete chagrin of the Colt defense.

But Baltimore, always a tough opponent for us, emerged on the winning end of the 28–24 score. It's the kind of score that sends you back to the projection room to study over and over again your very first drive when you sputtered inside the thirty and "settled" for a field goal—opting not to go for the four points that turned out to be the margin of defeat. Fortunately the thing that remained in our minds after watching those films was the way our attack was beginning to balance out: similar, effective yardage for Hornung and Taylor, mixed with at least moderately successful passing on Starr's part. We totaled 460 yards, equally divided between rushing and passing. With that kind of offense, we could win. Except, of course, that Unitas and his teammates that day turned out a typically explosive performance: over 500 yards, including 324 in the air.

Things had fallen in place with our defense, too. My four linebackers, Ray Nitschke, Dan Currie, Tom Bettis, and Bill Forester, were beginning to show the precision and the alertness that was to make ours the most impregnable secondary in the league in years to come. In fact, Green Bay sportswriters dubbed them the "Fearsome Foursome" before the season was over, predating the Rams of that name by at least six years. In the first eight games, the defense had intercepted only four passes. In the final four, they intercepted nine, including three against the Rams, who had earlier humiliated them so badly. Not once, in those final four games, did the defense permit an opponent to score in the fourth period. Which is one big reason why we ended the season in the same fashion we began.

The Eastern Conference's Washington Redskins had the misfortune to meet us at the moment we came of age, and the result was a 21–0 shutout before a relieved and happy crowd of Green Bay fans in the final home game of the season. Starr had his first big day, and his first outing with better than .500 in the passing department. He completed eleven of nineteen, compared with McHan's one of four. Later that week, in our then-annual Thanksgiving Day game with Detroit, Starr hit on ten of fifteen for 169 yards. That, plus the solid defense and the ability of Hornung and Taylor to make crucial yardage and second-effort touchdowns, lifted us to a 24–17 win despite the fact that Detroit beat us nearly two to one in yardage and first downs. Lombardi's admonition that consistent execution wins ball games was beginning to prove true.

I should have been able to breathe a sigh of relief about then and start pasting up my scrapbook for the year. But those last two weeks of November 1959 were among the most convulsive in the history of professional football, in ways that had nothing to do with the play on the field. And quite without expecting it, I found myself momentarily at the focal point.

The infant American Football League was heading for a number of showdowns with the NFL in an attempt to get the second circuit operating the following year. After the death of NFL commissioner Bert Bell in October, George Halas made some strategic moves that would lead to expansion of our league into cities rumored as the likeliest sites for AFL teams. The American League founders, including Lamar Hunt and Harry Wismer, decided to meet the competition head-on, and they announced plans to go ahead with their first player selections. The site for the November 22–23 draft and a subsequent organizational meeting was to be Minneapolis.

Meanwhile a group of Minnesota businessmen was holding a somewhat tenuous option on an NFL franchise for the Twin Cities while continuing to play both sides of the street by negotiating with the AFL founders. It was big business intrigue at its best, and slightly out of my league. Even Vince, who would later become one of the power brokers in NFL-AFL dealings, was too busy to be much concerned with the goings-on.

It was midweek, shortly after a practice session, when I got a phone call from the Minnesota combine. They wanted to interview me at once for the head coach position with their AFL franchise. They assured me that, as a former University of Minnesota All-American and a onetime candidate for the athletic directorship at Minnesota, I was a natural for the job. Having followed their plans in the Twin Cities press, I knew they were looking at two or three other coaches, too, but I realized that I probably had an inside track on the job.

I asked them to wait until our season was over in just a few short weeks, but they were adamant: getting the AFL franchise depended on their having an organization ready to go, and they wanted the attendant publicity value of having a coach under contract. They insisted that we meet before the week was over, which meant sometime before the Sunday game. It was finally agreed that they would fly over in a private plane, pick me up, and fly me to the Twin Cities and back for one day of talks.

I took Kathryn along so she could help me make my decision. Aboard the small plane, beside the pilot, were Twin Cities promoter Max Winter, insurance man H. P. Skoglund, and car dealer E. William Boyer. Skoglund was the one committed, along with Oluf Haugsrud of Duluth, to an NFL franchise.

When we were in the air, they talked a great deal about "the Minnesota franchise" and arrangements being made to use the new Metropolitan Stadium in suburban Bloomington. They discussed the availability of player talent, and how there was every chance for a second league's success. Not much was said about AFL versus NFL; in fact, I got the opinion we could have been talking about either league. And they didn't seem to be pumping me for information on what kind of approach I'd take in coaching a team. It was a strange interview, I thought, and Kathryn's glances indicated that she, too, found it a bit odd.

When we put down in the Twin Cities, a man came out on the loading area before we could even debark and called to Skoglund, who got out of the plane. Soon the pilot joined them outside the craft, and a heated argument took place. Again Kathryn and I exchanged glances. Finally the pilot and Skoglund climbed back into the plane, and Skoglund said to me, "I hope you don't mind, but we'll have to continue the interview in the air for a while. Senator Humphrey wants us to pick him up in Madison." So we turned about and headed for the Wisconsin capital, where we picked up Hubert Humphrey and Minnesota governor Karl Rolvaag.

For the next thirty minutes I was Hubert Humphreyed nearly to the breaking point. In a virtual monologue, he told me what a great opportunity it would be to coach the new team, that Minnesotans were ready to rally to football and support it, that the leadership of the new team would be crucial, that the business interests behind the franchise would see to it that the club had the best material, and so on until we arrived again in the Twin Cities. I was not unimpressed. As Humphrey walked away, I was as close to signing a contract as I would ever be.

But back in Green Bay the next day, I made a decision that I would never regret. Walking back into Packer headquarters and sitting down with Vince Lombardi to go over final

## PACKER DYNASTY

plans for our game the next day, I realized that what I had here was the finest opportunity of my life. The Packers were destined for greatness. I knew it that day, and in my heart I could *feel* that we would be winning the NFL championship before much time had passed. Returning to Minnesota as head coach would be an honor and a challenge. But with the job would go a myriad of uncertainties, and perhaps considerable disappointment if the new league's creators failed in their venture and the circuit collapsed. If the position offered were head coach of an NFL franchise, I would have taken it, but as it was, I felt I could do better by staying and growing with Green Bay. I discussed my decision with Kathryn after mass and before leaving for the stadium the next day. Later I called Minneapolis and removed my name from consideration. I would stay with the Green Bay Packers as long as they needed me and wanted me.

Subsequently, near chaos broke out in Minneapolis. The AFL group went ahead with their draft. (Interestingly, a top pick for Minnesota was also one of our first choices, Wisconsin quarterback Dale Hackbart, who turned down both offers to play baseball and eventually wound up first with us, then with the NFL's Minnesota Vikings.) After the selections, the league's framers and some of the franchise holders fell to squabbling, and in the middle of it all, word came that the NFL had assured Minnesota an expansion club. The news hit the AFL people during their Minneapolis meetings, and I was certainly happy to be saved the embarrassment of being on the scene as their window dressing.

When they formally received their NFL franchise in January, the Minnesota group first hired a general manager, Bert Rose, who had no interest in me anyway. Rose felt that the club needed someone like colorful Norm Van Brocklin, then nearing the end of his playing career. Rose had worked with Van Brocklin in the Rams' organization and thought him just the kind of hard-charger needed to start a new club. Van Brocklin, for his part, wanted to end his career in Philadelphia by picking up the coaching reins of my old boss, Buck Shaw, who was about to retire. But Shaw didn't recommend Van Brocklin for

## PACKER DYNASTY

the job, which left the Dutchman available for Minnesota in 1961.

Wheels within wheels within wheels . . . the same names coming up in new and different places. It made me even happier and more secure to be in Green Bay, Wisconsin.

The final two victories of the year were in many ways the sweetest. First came our revenge against the Rams, 38-20 in their own stadium. Dowler grabbed two touchdown passes. Starr passed for 161 yards. Hornung was two for two on the halfback option, tossing for the twenty-six- and thirty-yard Dowler scores. That weapon left the Rams in a state of shock.

In San Francisco on the final Sunday of the regular season, we completed our three-game sweep of my old colleagues. After spotting the 49ers a pair of first-quarter touchdowns, we held them scoreless for the remainder of the afternoon. Hornung had his finest day of the season, running for three touchdowns, and Starr made the grade once and for all as a quarterback, clicking on twenty of twenty-five to six different receivers for 249 yards. It was our finest offensive day, with twenty-seven first downs and nearly five hundred yards gained. The score was 36-14, our widest victory margin of the year.

The spectacular finish to the 7-5 winning season brought joy to the fans, and honors to the team: Coach of the Year for Vince Lombardi; Rookie of the Year for Boyd Dowler; and, best of all, national recognition as Cinderella Team of the Year for all the Packers. It did indeed seem like a magical transformation. If, that is, you were not around to see the toil and labors of July that made possible the glass slipper of December.

# 5 · PRETENDERS TO THE CROWN

WE BEGAN our second season with a contagious confidence. The first year's strong finish convinced us that we could consider ourselves contenders in 1960. "Pretenders to the crown," one sportswriter put it, and we were not about to dispute him. We charged through our exhibition season with six wins and no losses, giving the team invaluable momentum. We were tougher, surer, and more aggressive with each opponent we faced.

There was little turnover, with just one veteran retiring and three going to Dallas in the expansion draft. Only a few rookies made the team, since a number of our top selections went to the Browns and the Cardinals in payment for earlier trades, while the Canadian league and the AFL picked off a few more of our top choices. The players we did add were real plus factors: Vanderbilt's star halfback Tom Moore, for example, and free agent Willie Wood on the defensive side.

Our young veterans were beginning to develop the *esprit de corps* we needed to be a team in every sense of the word. Perhaps the greatest contribution to morale was made by the group centered around Hornung, McGee, and Fuzzy Thurston. They were the devil-may-care fun-lovers who kept spirits high in the locker room and on the bus or plane. When morale was low, they would shatter the gloom with an impromptu song or charade. After a lackluster practice, they might emerge dripping wet from the showers and grab a few of equipment manager Dad Braisher's mops and pails to improvise "There Is Nothing Like a Game" in falsetto. At the next practice session, they would lead the wind sprints, then make it their business to assure a more productive outing than the previous one. A team of forty men all like those three would be impossible to control. A team without a small band of irrepressibles wouldn't have the ability to laugh at itself and triumph over adversity.

Men fighting individual battles set examples for the entire team: Bart Starr, after four seasons of uncertainty and lack of confidence, came into camp for the first time with the notion that there was an important job to do, and he was capable of doing it. Ray Nitschke, after two years as the fourth of three linebackers, set his sight on the post held by great middle linebacker Tom Bettis. It was Bettis who had taught him much of what he knew about a position that was strange to him, and now Nitschke announced his determination to outdo his teacher. Jim Taylor set increasingly tougher physical goals for himself, buttressing his already heavily muscled body for the beating it would take in the brutal second-effort plunges demanded of a fullback who runs for daylight where not much of it shines through. And Willie Wood strived to prove that the smallest man on the squad could make one of the biggest contributions.

In all the major professional sports, there's practically a standard format for a new coach's remarks to the press before the start of the season. The first year he's supposed to say: "I know this club has better material than its record shows. We're going to win some games this year." The second year of his tenure, the script reads: "We made some real improvement last year, and I expect we'll be right up there with the contenders if we get a few breaks." Since Vince Lombardi is a man of action rather than a man of fancy words—nobody ever called him a press agent's dream—he fell back on the standard phrases when the reporters showed up for their annual material.

In practice and planning sessions, he read from the well-worn Lombardi catechism: Know your assignments. Mistakes lose ball games. Winning football is eleven men executing perfectly. Teamwork! Pride! Work, work, work. We can beat anybody, as long as we don't beat ourselves.

## PACKER DYNASTY

With preseason victories over the Bears and the Giants behind us, we felt invincible on the first Sunday of the season as we opened at home. And invincible we were for three quarters, with Hornung and Taylor each piling up short yardage on the sweep and over the middle for a touchdown apiece. Then Chicago erupted for a seventeen-point final period, and the score was 17–14 when time ran out. Our despondency that afternoon would have been considerably relieved if we had been able to gaze in a crystal ball: The Packers were destined to start without a win in four of their six championship years under Lombardi.

In retrospect, perhaps it was part of our character building. A team which can put a defeat behind it and come back with the determination and confidence to start a new winning streak is the kind of team that ends with the best record in a season when the teams in its division are evenly matched. Such was the case in 1960. With the exception of the Dallas expansion club, the teams in the NFL's Western Conference were in a six-horse race right down to the wire. We came back from the opener to post four straight wins, including a 35–21 victory over the defending champion Colts. Then the race toughened up. It was win one week, lose the next until the final weeks of November when two losses in a row seemingly put us out of contention.

As we entered the home stretch and prepared for our third game with the Bears after an exhibition and a regular-season win, the Packer organization lost personnel director Jack Vainisi, who died the Sunday after Thanksgiving. He was the man who had signed many of our players to Packer contracts, and was perhaps the best-liked member of the Green Bay front office. Chicago was his hometown, and he liked nothing better than to arrive a day or two before the team to visit his old friends and warn them, "My Packers are coming. Get ready for a rout." This game would be in Vainisi's honor.

After a scoreless tussle through the first period, the Packers went to work, chalking up a touchdown and two field goals. But the Bears, who also had an eye on the conference title,

PACKER DYNASTY

came back and used the two-minute rule to advantage, crossing our goal line in the final minute and sending us to the dressing room at halftime with only a narrow lead. Before the game, our dressing room had been abnormally quiet. Nobody needed to be reminded who we were playing for. At halftime, Lombardi announced simply: "This is a moment of decision for the Green Bay Packers. Have we passed our peak, or are we going all the way?" That's as close as any good coach dares come to saying the entire season is on the line, because it's a device that becomes "cry wolf" if you use it the second or third time.

Within minutes we were on a one-way street to the championship. The second-half kickoff went to rookie Tom Moore, five yards deep in the end zone. Charging straight up the middle, he ran unobstructed for better than twenty yards, then began to veer to the right as the opposition loomed in front of him. At the thirty he picked up his blockers along the sidelines and continued to the forty, to midfield, past the anguished Bear benchwarmers. He got four-fifths of the way down the field before being hauled down from behind. On the next play Taylor bucked for four yards, and then Starr tossed a short pass to Hornung, who faked and dodged three defenders to reach the goal. That lighted our fires. Even the defense scored in the ensuing 41–13 romp when Willie Davis blocked a punt and recovered it in the Chicago end zone for six points. As we ran down the passageway to the dressing room, we learned from the equipment custodian that the Lions had upset the Colts in Baltimore. With two games to go, we were in first place.

The following week in San Francisco we faced another of the pretenders to the crown and their much-discussed "shotgun" offense—a dropped-back quarterback firing at a whole flock of receivers. What ensued was perhaps our toughest ground game of the year. It proved once and for all that the combination of a solid defense and the relentlessly regular running yardage of the power sweep was a winning format in the late-season games between title contenders. Pounding out 251 yards in the mud of rain-soaked Kezar Stadium, we made the 49ers play our

## PACKER DYNASTY

game. At halftime it was 3-0 on a thirty-eight-yard Hornung field goal. At the end of three periods, that was still the margin. The shotgun had been jammed.

In the climactic fourth-quarter drive, the daylight glimmered through. Hornung ground out the necessary yardage behind the blocking of linemen Jerry Kramer, Fuzzy Thurston, and Forrest Gregg. And at the twenty-eight-yard line, the vital block was provided by fullback Taylor, springing Hornung loose for a six-pointer that put the game out of reach. All of our points were credited to Hornung in the 13-0 shutout, but it was a day when every man—both on offense and defense—performed his job to perfection.

That game was played on a Saturday, and the next morning we hurried down to Los Angeles to watch the Rams, who would be our last opponent. We saw not only an explosive team, whose quarterback, Bill Wade, could unleash a last-minute scoring barrage, but a stadium full of some of the angriest fans in the league. Disappointed that their Rams had been mathematically eliminated from the running, the crowd of fifty-four thousand demanded that their Coliseum live up to the reputation of its Roman namesake: They wanted blood.

But we were not about to succumb to emotions; our task was to find weaknesses to exploit when our turn came the following week. On the defensive side, we paid particular attention to the Ram punter, and after checking our personal observations against game films, we decided we could get to him. I made a mental note to plan the maneuver for halfway through the game, after he had punted successfully a few times and would be a little more relaxed than on the first attempt. Knowledge of a chink in the armor and a careful plan to exploit it at the right moment can give a defensive squad a lot of emotional fuel, much as a special play can fire the offense.

In the Los Angeles Coliseum, on the afternoon of December 18, 1960, both sides were at peaks. Our overanxiousness was responsible for spotting the Rams a 7-0 lead on a forty-yard scoring pass. But we sobered quickly, and when their defense slowed our ground game with alert blocking, we turned loose

## PACKER DYNASTY

our own pass game. Starr hit McGee on a fifty-seven-yard pass play to tie with seconds left in the first quarter. Then he unleashed a bomb to Dowler for a ninety-one-yard touchdown to begin the second-period scoring. The spectators leaped to their feet, yelling and tossing wadded-up programs, but we were on our way.

As it became apparent that we were holding the Rams in their first set of downs after our second touchdown, my defensive charges urged me to let them spring their punt block attempt. After the second down went for little gain at the Ram ten-yard line, they gave me the sign. I responded by touching the brim of my hat: "No." I had told the ends and backs that we would make the attempt when they held somewhere near the twenty-five or thirty. A blocked punt usually rolls back that many yards. If you block a punt and it rolls back through and out of the end zone, you get two points for a safety. If a defensive player can recover it in the end zone, it's six points. I wanted the full count.

After holding again at the ten and bringing about a fourth down, the excited defensive players signaled once more. They were so enthusiastic that I feared we'd give ourselves away, so I returned an affirmative signal. The punter stood in his own end zone. As he stepped forward and began to swing his toe in an arc toward the ball hanging in the air before him, Packers began to round the corners and converge. The usual thud of toe against leather was instead a quick thump-*thwump* double sound that sickened the fifty-four thousand Angelinos who were already halfway out of their seats. Packer Paul Winslow was closest to the ricocheting ball, and he fell on it before it could bounce out of the end zone. Our big defensive play had worked.

The offense came right back with its surprise for the day: Hornung connected with McGee on an option for a forty-yard touchdown. In the space of a few minutes, we had toted up twenty-one points, for a 28–7 halftime lead. The final score was 35–21, in a wild scoring match that saw a combined total of only thirteen first downs for both teams, as everybody went

## PACKER DYNASTY

for broke. Wade threw thirty-three passes, two-thirds of them successful and three for touchdowns. But a cool Bart Starr stressed quality over quantity, connecting on nine of eleven—and the two incompletions didn't come until the fourth period after victory was assured. The two squads chewed up 721 yards of field, giving every spectator in the stadium as much action as he could expect in any two games. It was a fitting coronation ceremony for a team that was wearing the Western Conference crown for the first time since 1944.

Lombardi broke into a half-moon smile as the gun went off and his players swept him off his feet. This time there was no faltering; they could have carried him all the way to Philadelphia for the NFL championship game.

On a dreary day after Christmas, the young upstart Packers met the veteran Eagles in the mud at Philadelphia's Franklin Field. The Eagles had dominated the Eastern Conference with a lightning pass attack and came into the game with a strong 10–2 record. It would be the last game for Norm Van Brocklin as a quarterback and for Buck Shaw as head coach of the Eagles. As defensive coach I knew what a psychological boost the finale would provide my former 49er boss. We had great respect for all of the Eagles. Their squad was an honorable assemblage of veterans, many of whom had played on other clubs around the league. They had a great star in Tom Brookshier, and one of the last of the two-way men in Chuck Bednarik, who played the entire game.

We thought we could win; a coach has no right to bring a team into a game that he doesn't think they can win. We acknowledged the poise of the opponents, and we planned to offset it with youthful vigor and prideful determination. A Philadelphia sportswriter pointed out that Green Bay brought "a roster with few standout names" to town that day. But a glance back over our lineup is like looking at the All-Pro team of the decade: Hornung . . . Taylor . . . Starr . . . Hanner . . . Forester . . . Tunnell . . . Skoronski . . . Kramer . . . Gregg . . . Dowler . . . Davis . . . Jordan . . . Nitschke. They were all starting in the first of many championship clashes. Most of them were destined to play in the first Super Bowl six years later.

We led 6–0 early in the game on two Hornung field goals, and we led late in the game 13–10 after a Starr pass to McGee. We came out on the winning end in almost every statistic, gaining four hundred yards to their two hundred. We ran half again as many plays, and made half again as much yardage on each play as they did. We gave up the ball only once on a fumble, while they turned it over to us three times. We had twenty-two first downs to their thirteen, and we punted farther by an average of six yards.

But we lost, 17–13. Lost a game, and lost a chance to be the world champions. But we gained some valuable experience and learned some mighty important lessons.

We learned that you have to make good when the so-called "breaks" come your way. On the first Eagle series of plays, defensive end Bill Quinlin recovered a Van Brocklin fumble. We marched it down to their goal line and weren't able to score. We chose to run the ball on fourth down rather than try a field goal, and it boomeranged. Our idea was to get off to a seven-point lead for the psychological value, and we were sure that with our strength we could make the short plunge. The Packers of later years would know that it is important to get a score out of every drive, and in our type of grinding game the field goals that come on approximately a third of those drives are as important in aggregate as a touchdown play may seem to be at any particular time. On our next drive, after another turnover, we settled for a three-pointer.

We learned that you have to expect the unexpected and be prepared to execute assignments consistently. A big gain for Philadelphia came when Van Brocklin uncorked his shovel pass behind the line of scrimmage, half pitchout and half sidearm fling. He threw it right through the middle of our onrushing pass defenders, which was one of the wily old quarterback's specialties. One of our less experienced defenders, momentarily surprised by the maneuver, missed a key tackle after the completion. It emphasized to us that in order to face the tension of a

## PACKER DYNASTY

big game and avoid panic situations, your preparations have to be the best so that you know for certain that no player will blow it on poor execution or a missed assignment. If you have a weakness—like a young defender who hasn't seen it all—the opponent will exploit it. That's true in any game, of course, but it's especially acute in a championship game where two teams of top caliber come together to see which makes fewer mistakes in sixty minutes of play.

Sometimes it's hard to get the importance of perfect execution across to the players because the reason you're in the championship game is that not many of the players blew assignments during the regular season. Then all of a sudden, there it is: You give up a score in a crucial game—maybe the winning touchdown—because a good player missed a tackle that should have been like a hundred of them that went before. That was probably our biggest lesson of the day.

Too often we didn't make the third-down play. The Eagles, however, had the poise to make vital first downs toward the end of each half.

The big drive that wiped out our 13–10 lead in the final period came after the Eagles returned our poor kickoff for nearly sixty yards. Eight plays later the same player who had shocked us with the runback darted through our defense from the five to score the winning touchdown. It emphasized to us the need for faultless kick coverage, and for a good kicking game as a whole. We had failed to score because we had failed to kick, and we had given them the winning goal because we had failed to kick well. A championship team is above average in all departments: running, passing, kicking, and defense. To be just average in one department is to lose the big stakes.

We came back valiantly, forging to the Philadelphia twenty-three. With time for only one play, Starr found Taylor open to his left and connected. Jimmy lowered his head and charged. But at the nine, tireless old pro Chuck Bednarik hit him with a standing bear-hug tackle—two titans slamming together on the muddy field and wrestling until they fell. And there it ended.

Coming so close and not making it gave us new character.

After our first attempt at climbing Olympus, it was clear to us how closely matched the final contestants are, how little difference there is between winning and losing efforts, and how important it is to expend *all* your effort in *every* game.

From that day in Philadelphia on, we were an all-the-way club.

## 6 · TITLETOWN, U.S.A.!

PACKER FANS remember 1961 and 1962 as "twin" years: back-to-back NFL championship victories over the New York Giants, following runaway seasons with 11–3 and 13–1 records. Certainly we were at our mightiest in those years, with our superstars at their prime. Our approach to football was by now appreciated and understood by opponents, but not yet seriously checked by more flexible defenses. We enjoyed the heady feeling that our reputation preceded us, without yet having to worry that every team in the league was "pointing" for us the way they would be in later years.

There was a big difference between those "runaway" years, however: The 1961 season was about ten times as hard on the coaches. First, we had to teach and train so that the players could proceed to new heights from the plateau of the previous campaign. Sometimes it can be awfully hard to pick up in July where you left off the preceding December. Second, we had to reshuffle our lineups constantly throughout the 1961 season because of injuries and the military obligations of players. First-stringers Hornung, Dowler, and Nitschke were marching down the field for us one week and for the U. S. Army the next. We assistant coaches spent part of nearly every week teaching somebody an entirely new position, and part of every week on the phone to Fort Riley, Kansas, or Fort Lewis, Washington, trying to find out if our top players would be peeling off yards or potato skins. Vince, meanwhile, managed to keep a semblance of cohesion as we went out to do battle every Sunday.

We lost our opener—again. By less than a touchdown—again.

## PACKER DYNASTY

But then we posted six straight victories. One was a 45-7 rout of the still-strong Baltimore Colts, with Paul Hornung scoring thirty-three points on four touchdowns, six extra points, and a field goal—getting himself off to a fast start toward his third straight individual scoring title. A week later, in what Coach Lombardi referred to as a "perfect" ball game on our part, it was Jim Taylor's turn. He gained 158 yards, scored four touchdowns, and almost singlehandedly knocked the Cleveland Browns out of first place in their conference. We were now in first place ourselves, and ecstatically looking forward to providing football lessons to the new Minnesota Vikings on two successive weekends.

Jerry Kramer fractured his ankle in the second Viking game and was sidelined for the season. The following week Baltimore took revenge on us for its earlier loss, 45-21. Next we outlasted the Bears in a rematch, 31-28. Then came the word from Fort Riley: Hornung wouldn't be able to get a weekend pass to play in the Los Angeles contest, our final home game. We brought in forty-two-year-old Ben Agajanian to take over Paul's placekicking duties, and he made five conversions after two runs by Taylor, two catches by McGee, and a reception by weekend warrior Boyd Dowler, who had his pass from Fort Lewis. We won 35-17, thanks to Bart Starr's passing.

We met the second-place Detroit Lions on Thanksgiving Day, with a good chance to insure ourselves of the Western crown. On the Monday before the game, Vince and I got together to compare the lengths of our injury lists, and he wound up giving me rookie halfback Herb Adderley, our top draft choice after he was Michigan State's All-Big Ten back. I spent three days giving him an intensive course in playing defensive halfback. As a member of our kickoff return squad, he already had the speed and moves to play in the secondary. I had to break him in on how to cover deep receivers and deny the opponent a long gain. Herb was a fine pupil. Detroit didn't score a touchdown all day, settling for three field goals in their 17-9 losing effort. The key defensive play of the day was Adderley's interception that turned the game around and started us on our game-winning drive. (In subsequent years, he would average five interceptions a season and set the league career record for touchdown runbacks of interceptions.)

In the twelfth week of the season we faced the Giants, and the word went out in football circles: "This is the preview of the title game." All week long we watched the films, drilled, talked it up, said our special prayers, and put more into this game than any we had ever played. Lombardi yelled himself hoarse, imploring the offensive line to "work together, work together; sometimes you look to me like the keys on a typewriter." I showed films of leading Giant rusher Alex Webster and receiver Del Shofner to the defense, and we recited out loud what could happen if they got away from us. Cornerback Jesse Whittenton had roomed with Shofner when they were Rams, and he wanted especially to help contain Y. A. Tittle's favorite receiver. I'm always glad when there's a personal rivalry in a key game, because I know my defender will be playing his best that day.

When Vince was on the phone to Hornung making arrangements to get him from Kansas to Milwaukee, Paul inquired if my mother would be at the game. She had become something of a talisman, since we had never lost a game with her in the stands nervously saying her rosary. "She's *got* to come, Phil," Hornung insisted when I took the phone. "This one's too big to do without her." So plans were laid for his plane to pick her up in a quick stopover at St. Paul. With that, we had done everything we could.

It was a tough game. Jim Taylor had a great first half rushing, getting a touchdown and moving us into range for two Hornung field goals. But New York, matching us drive for drive, scored two touchdowns and one field goal to lead 17–13 at halftime. The second half settled down to a defensive struggle worthy of the two conference leaders, and it appeared that the halftime score might hold up. The big play came late in the game when psyched-up Jesse Whittenton took the calculated risk of making a grab for the ball instead of tackling Webster. He came up with it, and the shift in momentum culminated in Taylor's three-yard plunge for the victory score. Winning 20–17, we clinched our second Western Conference championship in a row.

"The kids did it; they were tremendous," Vince shouted happily at the television commentator in the locker room. "What odds they faced . . . but they were great." Two weeks later our season officially ended, and we just barely made it. Down to two healthy running backs in sophomore Tom Moore and rookie Elijah Pitts, we had to count almost entirely on them to make us look respectable in the finale against the Rams in Los Angeles. They rose to the occasion and scored three touchdowns between them. Agajanian made a field goal and three conversions. Our entire point output in the 24–17 victory was produced by three "replacements" who weren't even in the lineup when the season began.

The signs read "Titletown, U.S.A.," but a few Giant fans who "took the stagecoach" to Green Bay for the game on New Year's Eve day gleefully altered the slogan to read "Tittle Town, U.S.A." in anticipation of what their quarterback might do. It was their last chuckle of the day.

Jim Taylor had to wear a special corset to protect his sore back, but he was healthy enough to give us a three-pronged rushing attack, along with Hornung and Moore. All our servicemen were there on special holiday leave, and it wasn't just holiday spirit that ran high. "Bring on Roosevelt Grier; bring on your Sam Huff" crowed the offensive linemen as they dressed, and the defense yelled back: "They'll have to, 'cause we're going to fix it so we don't have to work much today." Sitting in our little coaches' room down the hall, we could overhear the banter, and Vince smiled, "I guess there's hardly any need for a pep talk today."

On the field, the breast-beating was made good. As the Giants took the kickoff and tried to mount a drive, I watched my defensive platoon carefully for signs of unsureness. On the first play, Henry Jordan slammed into the runner and held him to one yard. The second play was a repeat. Moments later, after Dan Currie choked off a pass play for only a short gain, Giant punter Don Chandler went to work. It would be an easy afternoon for him: We were destined to get the ball free five times on fumbles and interceptions. On the next Giant drive I watched as Hanner and Quinlan provided the bulwark of a defensive line that was almost impervious. Jordan and Davis rushed at Tittle to force hurried passes or stabbed at rushing backs to force fumbles. The linebacking corps knotted up short receivers, the deep secondary matched strides with deep receivers, and Tittle was cut down still searching in vain. It was soon established that the defense would hold. It looked like the beginning of one of those delightful afternoon rides when we can leave the driving to Bart.

Four seconds into the second quarter, Paul Hornung capped an eighty-yard march with a six-yard run for our first score. Four minutes later, after Nitschke intercepted a Tittle pass tipped up by Jordan in Giant territory, Starr hit Dowler for our second touchdown. Soon after, it was Hank Gremminger's turn to pick off a Tittle pass. Taylor and Hornung moved us by easy four- and five-yard stages down to the Giant fourteen, where Bart connected with Ron Kramer, who bowled over one Giant defender per yard in his last three yards of plunging to the goal. Trailing 21–0, the Giants drove the length of the field to our six-yard line, where they sputtered on an incomplete fourth-down pass into the end zone.

Seconds remaining in the half, Starr moved us quickly to the Giant five with no-huddle pass plays, and Hornung kicked a field goal to make it 24–0 as the gun went off. In the second half we turned a fumble and a Jesse Whittenton "repeat performance" interception into a pair of field goals. A final touchdown came on another Starr-to-Kramer pass.

By then the outcome was in no doubt, and the fans got their delight from sensational hijinks on the part of their romping Packers. Starr pulled a masterful bootleg that sucked in the entire Giant line and linebacking contingent. As they converged on him, the New Yorkers realized that Starr was empty-handed, and only then did most of the spectators—and the Giants—

notice Jim Taylor literally sneaking thirty-three yards downfield. The defensive trick of the day was turned in by Herb Adderley with seconds remaining in the game. Tittle launched a desperation pass, hoping to spring a deep receiver and get a face-saving score, but Adderley loped into the target area to prevent the reception. Although he was falling and facing the wrong way for an interception, he twisted, flung his arm out wildly, and clasped the ball firmly as he landed on his back. He managed to retain possession, and since he had not been touched by a Giant, he sprang up and galloped fourteen yards before he was hauled down.

One play later, the NFL championship flag took up residence in Green Bay, Wisconsin, and this time it was the turn of Dan Currie and Dave Hanner to hike Vince Lombardi on their shoulders and carry him onto the field. His yellow woolen cap bobbed high above the heads of a swirling group of us: Coaches, trainers, players, and water boys jumping up and down like kids, slapping each other on the back, and yelling, "We're the champs; we did it!" to everyone and to ourselves.

In the locker room, Vince climbed up on a bench and raised his arms for attention. Dozens of newsmen mixed with the players and coaches, but Vince spoke warmly and emotionally to his men as if they were alone to share their joy: "You're the greatest team in the National Football League today. And I *mean* it."

The newsmen clamored for his attention. "They played a hell of a ball game," he told them. Why the improvement over last year? "We had a little poise today which we didn't have a year ago." What about Paul Hornung, who set a playoff record of nineteen points and won a sports car as most valuable player? "The bigger the game, the better he plays."

Then, seeing Giant president Jack Mara, he smiled and exchanged New Year's wishes. Lighting a cigarette, he pondered the next question: Was it his biggest personal thrill in football? He paused, as he always does when asked that kind of question. Finally he grinned and answered, "I would say so . . . yes."

## PACKER DYNASTY

Meanwhile, down at the Green Bay *Press-Gazette,* they were putting the final touches—color picture and all—on an extra. And right under the main stories was the matter-of-fact headline announcing: *Pack Duels All-Stars Next.* We were exhausted, but the fans were ready to start all over again.

It was one of those days when nobody wants to go home yet, even though the icy winds that whipped through the stadium all day had turned even colder. Wrote New York *Herald Tribune* columnist Red Smith: "The poisonous polish of the Packers was equaled only by the fortitude of the natives, who turtled down into their mackinaws and buffalo robes and parkas, and stayed on into the bitter dusk, yelping and bawling for blood."

The chant rose, died, and rose again and again: "Titletown, Titletown, U. . . . S. . . . A. . . . Titletown, U. . . . S. . . . A.!" Even Packer board members beamed with approval as whooping fans methodically swayed back and forth on the crossbars until the uprights of the goalposts bent, sagged, and tore off ten feet above the ground. It was a two-thousand-dollar expenditure that would become an annual budget item.

Those particular goalposts became a tangible symbol of the town's pride in the revived Packers. For several hours after the game, a huge section of one post—the crossbar with two pieces of upright—was paraded around the stadium parking lot, then dragged behind a station wagon to the downtown area where exuberant fans took turns riding up and down the main street of town on it while a caravan of hundreds of horn-tooting cars circled the impromptu ceremonial grounds.

Finally the goalposts were carted off to a nearby foundry and neatly cut with a torch into foot-long sections which were apportioned to the faithful. Visitors to the lunch counter of Holzer Drugs at Washington and Pine can view and touch a section of the yellow pole, and John Holzer will gladly list several dozen recreation rooms within a few miles where the remaining lengths can be found on mantelpieces. By 1965 the Green Bay fans would have goalpost distribution down to a science: the uprights from that year's championship were neatly sliced into one-inch pieces and mounted on polished wooden plaques with a brass-plated legend carrying the score and date.

The following season both the Packers and the Giants were improved teams as they aimed for a rematch. In six exhibition games and fourteen league games, we had only one loss. Our over-all score was 415–148, with matching 49–0 victories over the Bears and the Eagles. The latter came in our return visit to the City of Brotherly Love, to show that we had learned the lessons of 1960.

Many ardent Green Bay fans considered the 1962 team the finest of the decade, not only because of the winning record, but because so many players were at their peaks, and so many of the special qualities ascribed to Lombardi teams came to be recognized and appreciated. Herb Adderley and Willie Wood set career records of seven and nine interceptions respectively for the season, and Ray Nitschke was voted Most Valuable Player of the championship game, an honor usually accorded to an offensive player. Bart Starr had his best passing year, with 62.5 percent completions, and set an all-time team record for most yards gained on passes in a season, 2438. Jim Taylor, meanwhile, was matching that with the record for most yards gained rushing in one season, 1474, and most touchdowns in a season, nineteen.

More important than any statistics, however, was the fact that the Packers now had the winning habit. The attitude, as verbalized by CBS telecaster Ray Scott, was "Here we are; try to stop us." By striving to become the epitome of fundamental football, we had finally arrived as the most awesome power in the sport. Most important of all, we had developed the "big-game mentality" so important to going all the way. The Packers had learned through hard work and devotion how to minimize their own mistakes and to make the most of miscues by the opponents. When the writers and commentators began making it the main topic of their stories and pregame shows, it became almost a psychological weapon. ("When are you going

## PACKER DYNASTY

to drop it, now or later?" Nitschke yelled across the lines to the Giant backfield in the finale. When it was over, Ray had picked up two fumbles and tipped a Tittle pass into the hands of Dan Currie for three costly turnovers, while our offense never gave up the ball on a turnover.)

The only team to give us trouble was the second-place Lions. We sneaked by them, 9–7, on three Hornung field goals in an early-season game, and they never forgot it. In a year when every team in the league was gunning for us, the Lions carefully planned a Thanksgiving Day party that nobody in Detroit has ever forgotten. Most television fans recall it as "that Thanksgiving Day game a few years back when . . ."

For us, it was a matter of the safety valve finally blowing. We came to Detroit with the pressure of ten straight league victories—sixteen wins in all since training camp. The last, just five days earlier, had been a grinding, brutal struggle with Baltimore in which we trailed during most of the second half and finally won, 17–13. We were tired, strained, and in need of rest. Some of our players were ten or fifteen pounds under playing weight.

In the first half the mighty Detroit line, led by vengeful Alex Karras, got to Bart Starr for one big loss after another as he tried vainly to find receivers. In the second period he was tackled in the end zone for a safety. The Lions led 23–0 at halftime, and made it 26–0 in the third. As the struggle continued, one Packer after another was hurt—not injured, but hit, knocked down, dazed, bloodied. The *little hurts* Vince says you have to play with if you want the championship badly enough. Little hurts that add up.

Huddling late in the game, the battered Starr asked one receiver after another for a word of encouragement, but each reported he was hurting or too well covered. Finally Max McGee suggested, "Why don't you throw an incomplete pass and *nobody* will get hurt."

The pandemonious laughter that erupted from the eleven bent and broken forms in shredded Packer uniforms was completely perplexing to the fifty-eight thousand Detroit fans, not to men-

## PACKER DYNASTY

tion the bench. Karras stopped pawing the ground and looked over at Vince as if to say, "You call this a football team?"

But on the sidelines, we were already beginning to realize that in that moment the team had turned the corner. We had stopped our decline after just three quarters of play. Scoring fourteen points in the final period while holding Detroit scoreless, we showed that the Lions had merely twisted our tail. The momentary lapse, while embarrassing, was another step in our character-building.

Forty-mile-an-hour gusts of dust and sixty-five thousand wind-whipped New Yorkers chanting "Beat Green Bay! Beat Green Bay!" in unison threatened to sweep us out of Yankee Stadium before the December 30 championship game could begin. The Packers scored in every quarter and never trailed, but it was a much closer game than the previous year's. Jerry Kramer, who handled our placekicking through the second half of the season after Hornung was injured at San Francisco, attempted five field goals and connected on three to provide the winning margin, 16–7.

I don't recall another game in which football players tried harder. Jim Taylor, who had to be hauled down at times by half the Giant line and all three linebackers, required stitches. He bit his tongue so badly he bled through most of the game. Willie Wood was so hyped up that after an interference call he waved his arms wildly and accidently punched an official, sending him reeling.

And Y. A. Tittle, who passed for two hundred yards despite the wind and the cold, was valiant in his efforts. At the final gun, he sagged to his knees on the cold, powdery ground, bent his noble head forward, and pounded the earth with his numb hands. Taking the title again from a true champion and an old friend made it a bittersweet moment.

But the sweet is what you remember. The 1962 season went into the record books as the finest year in the history of the Green Bay Packers. All-time marks included most first downs, most touchdowns, and most total points.

## PACKER DYNASTY

There remained, however, a juicy plum we wanted to pick: the first NFL triple crown. The Packers had won three championships in a row back in 1929-30-31, but nobody had pulled it off in the modern history of the league. Without invoking the "no-hitter jinx" of talking about it, we all began thinking ahead.

Unfortunately, the jinx was already on the third crown; a few shocks awaited the Green Bay Packers.

# 7 · BEING NUMBER TWO IS NO FUN

"**D**EFEAT MUST be admitted before it is a reality," is an old West Point motto that Vince Lombardi recalled for the Packers during the "middle years" of his reign, and by that standard we were not defeated until after the final seconds of the 1963 and 1964 seasons. When you consider that the fall from the top of the heap is always the longest (Philadelphia and New York both plunged to last place after their title years), perhaps in retrospect we should not lament the seasons when the Packers had to settle for second best. But Vince had given us that other motto, too—"Winning is a habit"—and it was tough breaking it.

Shock number one came after the 1962 season when Paul Hornung was suspended for gambling. For two years NFL commissioner Pete Rozelle had been working especially hard to track down rumors concerning betting by professional players, and speculation had centered on wagers made in Chicago and Detroit. We felt certain that the combination of Lombardi's discipline, the remoteness of Green Bay, the postseason earnings, and most of all our team spirit, were all factors that insured us against the likelihood of our players getting involved.

Lombardi called those of us who were in Packer headquarters into his office and closed the door. His face was flushed, and he looked through and past us as he spoke:

"Paul is out for one year. Rozelle has suspended him for betting . . ." He turned, picked up a pad from next to the phone, and read from his scrawled notes: ". . . for his pat-

## PACKER DYNASTY

tern of betting and transmission of specific information concerning NFL games for betting purposes; that's what the report will say." Then he threw down the pad and turned away. "God, Paul Hornung, I can't believe it."

"A full year's suspension?" I asked. "Isn't that pretty severe?"

Lombardi hunched his shoulders. "Rozelle said the bets were mostly on college games, and none on our games. But he did it . . . Paul admitted it. I can see the commissioner's point." Later, after a long silence, he shook his head and said: "A year. That's bad enough for Paul, but what will it do to us?"

Lombardi advised Hornung to lead an exemplary life for his year out of action and to keep himself in good physical shape. Without condoning Paul's actions, he let him know that we had confidence in him and we would count on him to play again. We could expect Tom Moore to fill in for him at halfback, and Jerry Kramer would handle the placekicking. But our backfield depth was hurt, our pride was wounded, and we would miss the inspiration and leadership that made Paul Hornung valuable beyond what his record showed.

Shock number two came on an August evening at Chicago's Soldier Field. We had an exhibition winning streak of nineteen straight victories stretching back to 1959, and we would go on to win all the rest of our preseason games this year. But that night we lost to the College All-Star team 20–17 in the third of our trilogy of character-building losses.

We took the game seriously, despite what some second-guessers said afterward, and we prepared to play our best. The previous year we had beaten the All-Star squad by 42–20, but it took a fourth-quarter splurge of twenty-one points to insure a victory. This year Otto Graham would be coaching perhaps the finest All-Star team to date, with Ron VanderKelen, Pat Richter, Bobby Bell, John Mackey, and two of our top rookies, linebackers Lee Roy Caffey and Dave Robinson. VanderKelen was a Green Bay native, which made for a special rivalry.

We lost that game because the things we don't usually let happen *did* happen. We fumbled in their territory more than once, and we settled for field goals on two occasions, giving the collegians great inspirational lift.

A Starr pass was picked off at midfield late in the first period and returned to our twenty-seven. VanderKelen passed to the six, and moments later we were down, 10–0. We tied the score before halftime, capitalizing on their fumble. Trailing 13–10 in the final period, we committed our big sin: On a pass play from deep in All-Star territory, our corner back guessed wrong and missed his tackle on receiver Pat Richter, who tightroped the sideline for the remainder of the seventy-four yards to the end zone. A slight error in our pursuit and the assumption that we had forced the receiver out of bounds had led to our downfall.

We really didn't think for a minute during the whole game that the All-Stars would beat us, and we were working hard right down to the final minute when we got our second touchdown. But suddenly there it was: We had lost to the rookies, and it was humiliating. We didn't let the memories die throughout the entire season. "You didn't play like a professional championship team should," Vince told them after watching the films. "You *should* be humiliated, and you must channel that humiliation into hard work so that you will deserve to be champions again."

Vince never forgot the loss, and when we appeared in the All-Star games of later years, he demanded as much effort as he did in any championship game. In our next two meetings with the neophytes, the scoreboard would read 38–0 and 27–0. Even four years after, at the beginning of the 1967 season, Vince would demand that we all hark back to the 1963 loss. "You may be labeled champions when you start a season," he lectured, "but you're in no better position than the weakest team as far as what you have to do in order to become champions again. You can't trade very heavily on reputation in football because the game has probably the biggest upset reputation of any sport. That's what makes it exciting. That's what makes rivalries so important in football."

Fired up by the defeat, we began a campaign that was successful in almost every respect. We tried our darnedest to make it all the way, but the third and final shock of the year was that we missed by only half a game. Our twin nemeses were the Bears and the Lions. We were 11–2–1 at the end of the season. The two losses came at the hands of the Bears, and the tie was another unappreciated Thanksgiving Day gift from the Lions, who also threw in a broken arm for Ray Nitschke. The Bears finished with an 11–1–2 record, just half a game ahead of us, to win the Western Conference title.

That second tie by the Bears which kept us from identical records came in their rematch with Minnesota. They set up their touchdown with a forward pass to the fullback that should have been covered easily, but the Viking defender executed poorly and the Bears scored. After the season ended, and before we went to the second-place Playoff Bowl to beat the Browns 40–23, I got a print of the Bear-Viking game and ran it several times. I watched the sloppy defense on that one play, and it stuck in my mind as much as any of our plays that year because it always seemed to me to be the play that ultimately kept us from winning the conference title. But then how frequently you feel that way in years when two or three teams of equal ability come down to the wire and only one can wear the crown.

The second of our also-ran, almost-made-it seasons, in 1964, was a year of considerable misfortune. We won our opener against the Bears, 23–12, on two Starr touchdown passes and three Hornung field goals. Just like the old days. . . . But then adversity crept in. Suddenly the effects of Hornung's layoff began to be reflected in his kicking. We lost two of our first four games by one point when Hornung missed conversions. We lost two games to Baltimore, the eventual conference champion, by a total of four points, both times when place-kicking faltered. In the 24–21 rematch game with Baltimore, Hornung missed five field goal attempts. A different outcome in those two games would have given us a record equal to theirs, and our big-game mentality would have carried us the rest of the way.

## PACKER DYNASTY

We should have been able to bring Kramer in to handle the kicking, but he was taken ill after our first game and spent the entire season in and out of the hospital for a long series of abdominal operations. Kramer had suffered numerous injuries and ailments, but he was always back in the lineup sooner than the doctor's most optimistic predictions. This time, however, he could not get on the road to recovery, and Vince made repeated trips to the hospital to cheer him up and assure him that he would be back before long. The mysterious "intestinal ailment" turned out to be three wooden splinters—one over six inches long—that he had carried since he was a youth, apparently as a result of a freak accident when he was struck by a flying board.

Bart Starr was the league's leading passer; four defensive players were All-Pro selections; our defense was the league's toughest, allowing an average of only 257 yards a game; Jim Taylor gained over a thousand yards rushing; we scored more touchdowns and more total points than in the three championship years that followed.

But in 1964, that was not good enough. We didn't make the big play at the big moment. We didn't score on twenty-two occasions when we were inside the thirty-five-yard line, sometimes going two or three drives without scoring a point. The final blow came when we lost in the Playoff Bowl to St. Louis, 24–17 . . . by the margin of the one elusive touchdown we had not been able to make all season.

# 8 · SUDDEN DEATH, SUDDEN LIFE

I AM ONE of those persons who falls sound asleep two minutes after he hits the pillow—and I don't make that claim merely because I happen to endorse a certain bedding firm's products. You can't be a football coach for thirty-five years if you toss and turn before a big game. And if you've lost, you need all the rest you can get, because you'll be studying films at eight o'clock the next morning.

But 1965 was no ordinary year. According to my wife, I sat bolt upright in bed at 2:14 A.M. on December 26 and said, "Who's the quarterback? Who's the quarterback?" Not *where's* the quarterback or who's *covering* the quarterback, which would be normal worries for the defensive coach, but *who's* the quarterback. During the frantic 1965 season we had to tangle with Baltimore three times in order to win the conference championship. It took twelve quarters of the roughest play professional football has ever seen, plus thirteen minutes and thirty-nine seconds of heart-stopping sudden-death overtime play, to decide who would wear the Western crown.

It was a season in which we spent half our time playing peerless football and half glancing nervously at slide rules, stopwatches, the tops of goalposts and other instruments of hair's-breadth measurement. It was a season of seconds and inches; a season to end them all.

Immediately after the 1964 finish, Vince took action to get us out of our second-place rut. In mid-January he traded away a future draft choice to the Giants in return for thirty-year-old Don Chandler. Placekicking had suddenly become our nemesis, and Chandler, who was the league's leading scorer in 1963, was also a highly rated punter. In a sense, Vince exchanged positions with the Giants' Allie Sherman. Now we allowed ourselves the luxury of a kicking specialist, while Sherman, faced with rebuilding his club, opted for some draft choices and trade material—men who could kick and also play a position.

We took a risk on Chandler, because he had told us frankly that he wasn't sure he'd sign a contract. He preferred to play for Dallas, closer to his home in Tulsa, and the previous year he had badgered Sherman with requests to commute weekly from Oklahoma to wherever the Giants were playing. He had even threatened to retire when Sherman turned his request down. The day Vince got his signature on our contract was a quietly joyous one in the coaches' offices. The joy would have been even greater if we could know that his kicking would provide the victory margin in the two critical postseason games that lay ahead.

Another acquisition before the season began was that of Carroll Dale, obtained in a trade with the Rams. I was disappointed to lose linebacker Dan Currie, but Vince felt that the depth of our linebacking corps had to give a little in order to insure the same depth in the critical area of pass receivers. "Besides," Vince reminded me as he looked over the memorandum he was preparing for the Rams and the league office, "it looks like Bill Curry, our rookie from Georgia Tech, may make the team, and he plays linebacker as well as center. You wouldn't want two guys with the same name in the defense, would you?" I pointed out that he had had two Kramers in the offense until he traded Ron Kramer to Detroit for a first-round draft choice, but he just smiled and signed the memo. He knew what he was doing, of course. My defense was more than adequate, scoring five touchdowns and making twenty-seven interceptions that year. Dale would turn out to be our second-leading pass receiver after Dowler, and his key receptions in the Western Conference playoff would set up the touchdown that kept us in the game.

## PACKER DYNASTY

Lombardi's shrewd trading in the winter and spring of 1965 was a prime factor in our drive for championships in the coming three seasons.

At halftime of our first game, against Pittsburgh, we trailed, 9–7, and the lone touchdown had been scored by the defense when Herb Adderley returned an interception twenty-nine yards. Pittsburgh's points had come on three field goals. Lombardi was upset at the slow start by the offensive squad, and he purposely insulted them in the locker room: "So far this season the defense is doing a fine job—they've even scored six of our seven points. It's about time the offense returned the favor." The insult worked. The offense scored thirty-four points in the second half, while the defense held the Steelers scoreless.

In the second week we faced the Colts, who showed every intention of maintaining possession of their NFL championship. Unitas was at his peak—again—and each time a Packer went into a drugstore to buy a pack of gum, there was Johnny's face on a row of magazine covers spreading the width of the rack. It all helps to build up the defensemen's "hate," as Bart Starr would find out the following year when his picture was on the covers of the sports publications.

Since Baltimore, the strongest team on our schedule, was strategically placed in the second and the second-from-last games of the season, it was obvious that our performances against them could be both the starting block and the tape in the race. We wanted this win badly for the emotional value—it could carry us a long way or hand us a bad setback.

Psychology was the order of the day in both camps, and too much of it was negative at game time. It was too cold and chilly for an early-season game, and the usual spinal tingles were magnified. We stretched our pregame calisthenics by a few minutes in an attempt to loosen everybody up. "Just let 'em lie there a minute and feel the ground," I suggested gently to the captain of the drills. "Let a little of the excess electricity drain into the turf or somebody's going to fly right out of here."

When the game got under way, the two teams came at each other the way wise old wrestlers do: straight ahead with great

## PACKER DYNASTY

assurance and untempered strength, but holding in abeyance certain moves that will be more useful after the opponent is explored and tested. There was one score in the first period, a field goal by the Colts' Lou Michaels when they had pushed to our twenty-six and we had held.

In the second period, Herb Adderley whirled at midfield to grab the first of his two Unitas interceptions and returned it for a touchdown. It was one of a dozen turnovers that day; Adderley also picked up a fumble, as did Nitschke, Wood, and Brown. And three times we handed the ball back on bobbles. Some fans thought it was the weather, but cold hands had nothing to do with it. When two teams are high from a previous year's rivalry and both consider themselves contenders, there are apt to be more mistakes than when less talented teams meet. The coaches expected a few turnovers from the pressure and the excitement.

What we hoped against were injuries to key players, since our offense was already hindered by the absence of Jim Taylor, whose ankle was unsure. That's why Vince gave out an audible moan as Hornung got up slowly from a run in the second quarter and came to the sidelines. He had reinjured his neck—an old malady that would eventually spell an early end to his glorious career. This day it meant we were missing our two top backs, and the foe knew that we'd have to rely more on our pass receivers, thus making his defensive task a bit easier.

At halftime the score was knotted at 10–10. Again our offense had not caught fire; but nobody hoped for a repeat of the previous week's late explosion. It would be a close one to the end, and everyone knew it. The third quarter was a scoreless struggle that gave you that sinking feeling: "We're absolute equals. This is one of those dead heats when one call, one error, one decision in the fourth quarter will spell sudden success . . . or failure."

Vince bellowed, I lighted cigarettes that were never smoked, the reserve quarterback clenched the phones to the pressbox until his white knuckles made cracking noises, and still the deadlock continued. We controlled the ball for seven full min-

## PACKER DYNASTY

utes, running fifteen plays, including a nineteen-yard run by Starr when he couldn't find a receiver and defenders threatened to swamp him. There was a twenty-seven-yard toss to Dowler, too, but in between came losses, then gains, then penalties, then delays, and in the end we had advanced only thirty-three yards in what amounted to an eighth of the game's playing time. We were forced to punt.

Minutes later we had the ball again. This time we would have to get a march going. But, desperate again because he had to rely on pass receivers—and they were all more than adequately bottled up—Starr started to look for room to run. Powerful, quick Ordell Braase burst through, grabbing him in his huge arms and twisting him to the turf. When the defender stood and walked away, Bart was left crumpled on the ground, his leg turned under him. He pushed slowly on his hands but didn't get up.

"What's the matter?" Vince asked. Not to Bart, who was too far away, nor to anyone nearby. His words had the pathetic anxiety of a coach who senses an ill wind moments before it reaches him—the intuitive reaction that bids us turn to call a man from the bench before we even get the sign.

"Zeke, Zeke," called Lombardi. And he acknowledged the official's signal that we would be charged for a time out. Starr limped painfully to the sideline supported by two of his teammates. The trainer motioned to his assistant to bring ice as coach and quarterback exchanged a few spare words and glances that spelled "out for the rest of the game." That made four key injuries. Boyd Dowler was also shaken up, and we had to use him sparingly, taking him out after every few plays and alternating McGee at end.

Four key injuries: first-string fullback, halfback, quarterback, and end. By rights that should have spelled failure. But for the Packers, after three long, hard quarters of stalemate with an opponent like the Colts, it need not be so. The desire is still there; the linemen and the defense are still there. If the coaches instill in the men the feeling that victory is still there, it can be had. It meant now that men who had already given 100 percent would have to give a little more. We were willing to try.

With a fourth-down-and-one-inch situation, Lombardi made a change in his usual conservative style.

"One inch," I said out loud as the official held up two fingers.

"Jeez," Vince whistled, "one stupid inch. Is that what it comes down to?" He looked at the spot on the field where the ball lay near the heel of a dusty boot belonging to a mammoth Colt defender. "We'll go for it." He sent in a running back to carry his decision to the huddle. "Hell, we've practiced it a hundred times—just a regular short yardage play. I don't know." Then he stopped musing and yelled lustily through cupped, gloved hands as the players moved up to the line: "Get in there. Go!"

Three seconds later the cadence rose in a steamy vapor as the quarterback leaned over to scan right and left. Then the uptempo last digit of the key number . . . the sudden pulse of pounding feet and excited yells as lines clashed and defensive backs read the developing play. Then the whoop of the forty-eight thousand fans as they saw the gateway between a Baltimore guard and tackle swing wide for a precious instant, and the green-and-gold flash pass through. A moment later, nineteen yards downfield, half a dozen behemoths converged, and the play was whistled dead. We had gained eighteen yards and thirty-five inches more than we had needed.

"It wasn't a very smart decision," Vince said toward the field and no one in particular. "But it worked. McGee! Get in there, McGee." One instant, one decision. Then on with the game.

Another key call a short while later gave us the go-ahead touchdown. With a first down in Colt territory, we opted for the surprise play and sent McGee deep. He threaded his way through the secondary, then suddenly broke free at the ten and went into the end zone standing up with the Bratkowski pass.

With moments remaining, we led, 20–17. But the Colts were threatening to score. That's when we made our final and deciding break. Nearing our twenty, runner Tom Matte was tackled by our linebackers and the ball squirted loose. Herb Adderley, well on his way to being one of the big heroes of the season, alertly snatched it up. It gave Matte a reason for revenge in a game nobody yet knew would be necessary at the season's end. But more important for the moment, it prevented a Colt win. Crippled and bruised, we limped back to the dressing room with a hard-fought victory and precious early-season momentum.

We went on from there to beat the Bears and the 49ers at Green Bay. Then it was on to Detroit, where the fans were talking about Thanksgiving 1962 as if it were yesterday. We must have spent too much time listening to them at first, because we were down, 21–3, at the half. Lombardi took Bart Starr aside and talked to him briefly and kindly, but firmly, about how this was *not* going to be another turkey for Detroit's platter. Bart went out and threw three third-period touchdown passes—for sixty-two, thirty-one, and seventy-seven yards—to three different receivers and ran a fourth touchdown in himself while the defense held the Lions scoreless. We stood 5–0 for the season and would have been feeling quite comfortable . . . except for the fact that the Colts were right behind us at 4–1.

The sixth week the surging Cowboys, no longer a weak expansion club, came to Milwaukee. This was one of the games I personally had been pointing toward, because the Dallas club had handed us our only preseason defeat, in the Cotton Bowl. It was not particularly the defensive squad's fault—the offense had failed to cross the Dallas goal line and had scored all twelve of our points by field goals. But the Cowboys had scored twenty-one points on our defense that day in September. If we had held on a couple of key plays, we might have won 12–10 instead.

We've had a preseason game with the Cowboys every year since they were formed in 1960, and all but the first were played at the Cotton Bowl. Unlike teams which look for easy competition during the exhibition season to build up confidence— and perhaps regular-season ticket sales—we schedule the toughest opponents we can find, including potential championship material. In addition to building a lucrative preseason gate, it gives our players additional experience against tough foes. When we lose, as against Dallas in 1965, it also gives us special incentive to come back for a win in a regular-season rematch.

That was the case now, and I found my defensive charges eager to do their homework. In the exhibition loss, for example, one of the Cowboys' touchdowns came when cornerback Herb Adderley was beaten by Cowboy deep receiver Buddy Dial. The forty-six-yard bomb from Don Meredith came in the second half when we were trying desperately to make our cluster of field goals hold up. Adderley started planning to prevent a recurrence of the big gain as soon as he got on the plane for home. He made a few notes, and when the films came in, he viewed them over and over again. Using slow motion, he ran Dial's scoring play until he got the rhythm of it: jog, jog, jog for about twelve yards, then Go! "I let him get a little too far behind me," Adderley said to me during his session with the projector. He worked his legs in time to Dial's running on the screen. "It won't happen next time. He's not really fast, but he's got good moves. But this time I'll be moving right along with him."

And he did. The Cowboys tried hitting Dial again—you always come back with a play that worked before—but this time Adderley denied him the big gain. And so it was up and down the line and throughout the defensive backfield. Each man had prepared himself in much the same way as Adderley had, improving on his performance in the previous outing against the Cowboys' opposite number.

Now it was Dallas that could not score a touchdown. Trying desperately to set up a scoring situation on a punt return, two Cowboy backs collided, the ball carrier fumbled, and rookie Bill Curry seized the ball, setting up a score for us. Only that morning Curry had stood in the locker room and studied one of Vince's slogans freshly posted on the wall: "Covering kicks is football's biggest test of courage." Courage and faultless play were our defense's forte that day, as they intercepted twice and picked up three fumbles. Our offensive squad, meanwhile, maintained tight control, and when the bitter contest was over, we had won, 13–3.

Now we were 6–0 on the season, a fantastic start. But there was Baltimore right behind us, at 5–1. And there were the Bears, our next opponent, pressing hard in third place, and smarting from two defeats already at our hands. It is a rare year in the fierce Bear-Packer rivalry when one team can win all three games, for such a sweep adds up to a disastrous season for the loser as far as the fans are concerned. We had to beat the Bears—but we had a fatalistic premonition.

Another disturbing development as we neared the halfway mark of what promised to be an illustrious season was the persistent rumor that Vince would leave at the end of the season to coach the new Atlanta expansion club. Rumors about the coach's career at midseason are always damaging to team morale, but especially so when a team like the Packers is in the middle of a fight to regain the title. Vince tried to hush the talk, but it's the kind of situation where a denial only seems to add fuel to the flames.

In 1961, when rampant rumors had him returning as head coach of the Giants, Vince had stopped the talk by announcing that his contract had been extended at Green Bay, even though it still had three years to run. In 1964, when the rumors started up again, the contract was set aside in favor of one running through 1968. Thanks to the finality of my decisions at the time of the Minnesota expansion, I was no longer plagued by rumors. Although other members of the Packer coaching staff were being tapped for head-coach positions throughout the league, Vince and I both believed that our future lay with the Packers, and we felt the morale of the club depended on the finality of the decision.

Coming into Chicago, Vince told me that he had renegotiated his contract once more and would announce the news after the game. We agreed that it was a strange situation, because he hardly needed to pressure the management, especially at midseason, to give him more assurance than he already had. As for myself, I had come to such a fine understanding with Vince

## PACKER DYNASTY

that I didn't even have a written contract—just a verbal agreement between the two of us that I was his assistant as long as he needed me.

Adversity finally caught up with us at Wrigley Field. A jarring tackle by Roosevelt Taylor knocked Starr almost senseless, and when Bart was sent back in later, he didn't have his usual poise and timing. In the second period the Bears went wild with seventeen points, and in the second half they added fourteen more while holding us at the ten we had scored in the first half. Somehow the shakeup of our field general seemed to affect every player on the team, and we made mistakes. We missed tackles and finally did something the Packers rarely do —played their game instead of making them play ours. "Maybe I shouldn't have put Starr back in there," Vince said when the 31–10 upset was over. "He said he was okay, but I think he just didn't want to let us down. We don't need to panic."

Later, announcing that his contract had been extended through 1973, Vince told the press: "I'm very happy to stay in Green Bay. This is our home. This is where our friends are and this is where my job is." It was the end, once and for all, we hoped, of the popular tale that he longed for New York and considered Green Bay a hick town.

The announcement boosted morale immeasurably, and we hoped to snap back to do something about the 6–1 record we now shared with Baltimore. Our next opponent was Detroit, however, and the Lions were mean, angry, and unwilling to give us any help in our title quest. In fact, a win against us would lift them to third place, and that's all the incentive they needed.

The catalog of our mistakes that day in Green Bay went on for pages. The Lion pass rush against our overeager line was ferocious. They seemed to have a price on Starr's head— an uncommonly fierce desire to capture and punish him for past encroachments on their territory. As a result, they held us to negative pass yardage, which led Alex Karras to crow: "We did a better job on the Packers than we even did on them Thanksgiving Day of 1962." Thanksgiving Day 1962. How long will that fuel the Lions, I wondered?

Other things went wrong, and the fourth quarter was a nightmare. We came down to the closing stanza deadlocked in a 7–7 tie. Karras taunted when the Lions were on defense, and Nitschke returned in kind when we faced their offense. It was another one of those make-a-mistake-and-pay games. This time we made the mistakes. Hornung tried a halfback option pass on the run to Marv Fleming, who was wide open. The Detroit rushers swerved and closed in on Paul, and he heaved with all his might. The ball went far—too far—and the Lions intercepted. The play had been designed to move us down into position to try a tie-breaking field goal, but now Detroit was moving into our territory. Moments later they made it 10–7.

The Lions kicked off. There was time for us to come back and at least gain a tie. The ball sailed long . . . deep in the end zone. Elijah Pitts looked upfield, pondered momentarily the value of getting good field position for the final drive, and elected to run it out. He hoped for a break—a block that would open it up so he could run us into position. But the break didn't come, and he was tackled at the six. Deep in our own territory, we faltered. The Lions trapped Starr behind the goal line, and the game ended with the score at 12–7. We now trailed Baltimore by a full game and led Detroit and Minnesota by only one. What had happened to the ethereal feeling of sitting at 6–0 on the top of the heap? A season that had promised to be short and sweet was now becoming a week-to-week struggle.

"Everybody's pressing real hard—too hard," Lombardi told the anxious fans after the Detroit loss. "We're in a pressure cooker because of the race. We've got to learn to relax. Bart Starr is trying to force things. Everybody is. It's a question of the players relaxing themselves. Nobody else can do it for them. Before it's been everything to lose and nothing to gain. Maybe it's the other way now. We can still make plenty out of this season. Always it's been one man breaking down on a play. We've got to go back and stress maximum efficiency and perfect execution. That's what we always have to come back to when the winning stops and the worrying begins. It's going to get better."

## PACKER DYNASTY

With the offense in a stall, it was incumbent on us to make the defense peerless. Accordingly, our next game was the defensive struggle of the decade.

Although the Rams were not impressive in the win-loss column, that was only because the Western Conference race was exceptionally tight. We didn't take the Rams for granted, and we planned our usual early-game approach of running at their strength. The game plan was to start with a halfback running alternately off tackle to the right and left. The first time Tom Moore gained one yard to the right. The second play was a three-yarder to the left. On his third run at the line, Moore fumbled. The Rams took over in our territory and scored a three-pointer from the thirty-five. Later in the first period we scored a field goal from their twenty-two to tie it up.

Then it settled down to a game fought between the twenty-yard-line stripes, with turnovers, penalties, and third-down losses denying both teams scoring opportunities. It was the kind of day when everybody feels as if he's working twice as hard as usual because there's no reward—no points being chalked up periodically to give incentive and spur you on. At halftime Vince talked to the quarterbacks and decided to go with Zeke Bratkowski in the second half.

The change wasn't dramatic. The entire half was scoreless down to the final minute, although our offense was able to grind out some yardage over the positions they had softened up in the early part of the game. With the clock ticking away the last minute, we moved down to within a few yards of the Ram goal. Then to within inches. But just as they had done all day long, the Los Angeles linemen held when it was most crucial. With a fourth down on the six-inch line and thirty-seven seconds to go, we brought Don Chandler in. His seven-yard field goal—at the same distance as for a conversion attempt—gave us a grudgingly gained 6–3 lead. With a half-minute remaining, Ram quarterback Bill Munson threw a wild pass, Doug Hart intercepted, and we ran the clock out in the same manner as we had begun the game: Jim Taylor running straight at their line four times.

Narrow as the victory was, it kept us alive. The local press and fans were happy, but other journalistic snipers zeroed in on both Starr and Lombardi. In the first half Bart had appeared confused on occasions, but we knew in most cases that the fault was not his. Once Jim Taylor had slipped and missed a handoff, leaving Starr standing with a ball that he had no plans for. Soon after, Bart's mixing of plays was disrupted when a couple of foolish offsides on our part nullified gains. When Vince put Zeke in, the sportscasters and Monday-morning quarterbacks rallied suddenly to Starr's defense. A few columnists picked up Vince's remark in the dressing room after the game that he had put Bratkowski in "to give us a lift because the other boy hadn't been able to get us moving." The phrasing rankled some writers and fans, and Vince was upset when the criticism didn't subside. His wording wasn't meant to cast aspersions on Starr; the remarks just came out as he was thinking them in the postgame unwinding. One of the reasons Lombardi shied from the press and so often was upset at columnists is that he is by nature honest and straightforward, but ill-at-ease with questioners. A quote out of context three days after a game often sounds all wrong, and it has the potential of destroying team morale.

So, during preparation for our next game, Vince took pains to make it clear to the press that Bart was still his starting quarterback. "There was nothing unusual about the fact we changed at halftime in the Rams game," he explained carefully to the wire service reporter looking for hints of a rift or breakdown in the Packer organization. "I've done it before lots of times, and I'll do it again if the situation demands." In a twenty-game schedule (including exhibitions), a team's leader could not possibly expect to be at maximum efficiency week after week, a fact of life that Bart, Zeke, and every other quarterback in the game well knows.

The following Sunday, Bart was right back in there, tossing three touchdown passes in a 38–13 romp over Minnesota. That put an end to the rumors. A week later in Los Angeles we met the Rams again, and they apparently had been seething for two weeks over the 6–3 loss. They punished us, 21–10. Bratkowski set up our only touchdown with an eighty-yard pass play to Pitts in the waning minutes, and the rumors started up again. The following week, we continued the seesaw schedule by beating the Vikings once more, 24–19, this time using both Bart and Zeke and scoring once in every quarter.

At least we had a choice of quarterbacks. The Colts had lost Johnny Unitas in a 13–0 defeat by the Bears the week before and were depending on Gary Cuozzo. It didn't seem to hold them up too badly—subbing for Unitas a few weeks earlier, he had unleashed a flurry of bombs in a runaway victory over Minnesota. At the end of twelve games, the Colts stood 9–2–1, the Packers, 9–3, and the Bears, 8–4. The Colts faced us in game number thirteen, then we both had trips west: we ended with San Francisco and they finished at Los Angeles. The Bears, meanwhile, faced the 49ers and the Vikings. There were possibilities of two different two-way ties for the conference crown, as well as a chance for either of the top two to win it outright. The columnists were delirious writing about quarterbacks one day and mathematics the next.

So we faced Baltimore with a "must-win" situation; a loss would give them the championship outright. The tension was unbelievable—greater than anything we had faced before. Not even the 1959 opener against the Bears or our early championship games could match it for drama, and Vince realized that we had to do something extraordinary to keep the team on course in the thick of the fiercest battle the NFL had ever seen.

Immediately after the Minnesota game and the Colts' loss to the Bears, Vince decided that we would have to revert to training camp routine in order to maintain the discipline and spirit he felt we needed for the final push. After a day's rest, we left our families, boarded a plane for Washington, and "went back to camp" in a motel outside of the nation's capital. In addition to giving us four days of practice in warm weather —winter weather had already lowered on Wisconsin—it kept the team together, their minds occupied with nothing but football and winning. Vince installed a 10:30 curfew and let it be known that he expected everybody to stay at the motel preparing and resting for the entire week.

At game time, Baltimore's Memorial Stadium was downright eerie—almost lost in the dense fog that rolled in from the sea on a typical cool seaboard November afternoon. But we knew where we were, even without being able to see past the tenth row. Baltimore fans are the loudest in the league, and their stadium is one huge concrete amplifier. As we came out of the runway for warmup, I was glad we had the extra sleep and psychological preparation. Every little thing would count today.

And every little thing did count, as we played our best game of the year. We did lose two fumbles, and the Colts turned them into ten points. They scored the opening three points of the game when they intercepted a wild pass. But that was all we gave away, and we offset those scores with three interceptions, two of which were turned into touchdowns.

The big story of the day was Paul Hornung. He equaled the club record with five touchdowns in one game—a thirty-point effort that came on fifteen rushes for sixty-one yards and three scores, plus two pass receptions for 115 yards and two scores. In addition, he threw three key blocks for Taylor, who racked up sixty-six yards. The most beautiful play of the game was the second touchdown, with Hornung feinting his classic block for Taylor while Starr masterfully faked the handoff, bootlegged, and then lofted the ball to Paul in the clear. Hornung loped fifty carefree yards to put us ahead 14–3 as the first quarter ended.

The Colts ran off seventy-two plays to our fifty-two—not surprising considering that we were forever kicking off to them. But our defense was supreme, and they could not move through much of the game. Four times our rushers got to their quarterback, and when they had jolted him to the ground early in the second half, Cuozzo had to be taken to the dressing room to be taped for a shoulder bruise. Before he came back, we got a crack at Tom Matte, halfback-turned-quarterback, for a series of downs. We also got through to him. So strong was our line

## PACKER DYNASTY

that day, with Fuzzy Thurston and Forrest Gregg having one of their finest outings, that only once did the Colts get through to Starr. The line play had been one of our main concerns for the previous month, and the sight of it blocking as in days of old gave us a sign that the team was back in form, fit to go all the way.

We came out of it not only rejuvenated and victorious, but half a game ahead in the race, with only a week to go. Again the mathematicians published their tables: If we won the finale against San Francisco, the conference was ours. If we lost while the Rams beat the Colts, that would yield the same results. If we lost, however, and the Colts won, they would wear the crown. One more possibility was added almost as an afterthought: *If* the Packers came from San Francisco with a tie while the Colts beat the Rams, it would leave the two leaders in a 10–3–1 deadlock, and, under the NFL rules at that time, a special playoff game would be necessary.

Our partisans could think of three good reasons why it was inevitable that we would triumph: 1. Cuozzo was now ailing from his injured shoulder, and halfback Matte would have to be counted on to run the Colt offense; 2. in our earlier game against the 49ers, we had run easily against them and had scored in every period for one of our more impressive wins of the season; 3. finally, we had finished the previous season on the West Coast with a 24–24 tie—the law of averages was doubtlessly heavily loaded against the prospect of tieing there two years in a row.

But we weren't taking any chances. In the locker room after the Colt game, the newsmen interviewed Hornung, who attributed his fantastic performance to "a week of clean living." When they asked Lombardi how he intended to plan for the 49ers, he replied: "Another week of clean living." Instead of returning to Green Bay and letting the players rest up for a day with their families, we boarded our charter plane and headed directly for another home-away-from-home training camp in the San Francisco Bay area. Vince was determined to win, and there was no disputing it from any quarter. He had long since evoked a faithfulness from his players that transcended personal considerations in times when championships were at stake.

From the very beginning the game was no runaway. Scoring in the first half was limited to a field goal for the 49ers and a touchdown for us on a Starr-to-Dowler pass play of forty-three yards. As the second half wore on, 49er quarterback John Brodie struck for two touchdowns by air, but we matched them with an interception runback by Adderley—giving him three touchdowns in one season—and a five-yard run by Jim Taylor. We were ahead 21–17 in the fourth quarter, with just minutes left.

From Los Angeles to the pressbox and then over our phones came the word on the Colts: Tom Matte, wearing a special bracelet inscribed with the Baltimore plays, was holding his own. We couldn't count on a Colt loss; we had to win on our own.

Trailing by only four points, Brodie unleashed a pass from deep in his own territory toward midfield. Roving over from his deep position toward the sideline, nimble Willie Wood leaped and intercepted the ball to halt the threat. A minute later, Chandler kicked a thirty-one-yard field goal that raised the margin to 24–17.

Seven points. Vince and I looked at each other, and his face seemed to read: "They wouldn't score seven points, would they?" I'm sure mine read: "We couldn't wind up in a tie, could we?" I implored the kick coverage team to be especially alert and to force the runback to the inside. We had to keep the 49ers in their own territory until the clock ran out.

We covered well—too well. Stopping the runner at the twenty-five, the Packers rushed at him with such force that one defender's hand flew up and twined about Kermit Alexander's face mask for an instant, and the official spotted it. The resulting fifteen-yard personal foul penalty moved them to their forty. One first down and they'd be at midfield.

"They wouldn't score seven. . . . We couldn't tie. . . ."

Brodie struck Dave Parks with a thirteen-yard pass over the middle. Into our territory. They wouldn't. . . . We couldn't.

## PACKER DYNASTY

. . . A six-yard running play, another pass to Parks for a first down on our twenty-seven. Now they were in field goal range, but the regular season was one minute from being over. A field goal wouldn't win the game. A loss would leave San Francisco at 6–7–1, a losing season. Would they. . . . Could we . . . ?

From up in the pressbox, Y. A. Tittle sent a fateful word down to the 49er bench. Into the game came a player by the name of Vern Burke, who had been inactive until a few games before—an unknown quantity. He lined up at tight end in place of Monty Stickles, whom we had contained most of the afternoon. His clean uniform stuck out with almost ridiculous obviousness—was he just a messenger, a relief man for a tired regular? Or was he a secret weapon? In the seconds it took to count the cadence, the possibilities ran through the mind of every defensive player.

The snap. Brodie dropped back and looked to one side and then the other. Burke ran a fast but standard route to the end zone, leaped up behind strong side safety Tom Brown, and stretched his hands up toward the spot where Brodie had delivered the ball. The two players fell to the ground and the official's hands went up in the air. Seconds later the kick went through the uprights, and it was 24–24.

They did . . . and as we headed dejectedly to the dressing room, we got the score from Los Angeles: Colts 20, Rams 17. It meant a playoff the day after Christmas in Green Bay. Vince took a weary look at the press corps and snapped: "We threw the game; is that what you want to hear?" He was angry with himself, and so was every man on the team.

In the week of anxious preparations for a third and decisive clash between the two Western giants, interest centered on the Baltimore quarterback situation and the problems facing young Tom Matte. Rightfully so, but what not too many fans realize is that an oddball situation that forces one team's offense to improvise also gives the other team's defense much the same headache.

Going into this game we had a record of seven wins in the last ten games with Baltimore, owing in large part to our pass defense. In past years, Adderley, Wood, and Jesse Whittenton had all run punts or interceptions back for scores against the Colts, and our defenders had worked especially hard and well against the Baltimore bomb threat. Our linebackers, too, worked doubly hard on the pass rush, getting a special thrill out of penetrating the tough Colt line and trapping Unitas in his pocket of security.

Suddenly everything was different with the Baltimore we had known and understood. Matte had been a rollout quarterback in his Ohio State days, and he preferred to use his speed and running strength to run around in back of the line until he found his man or his opening for a run. That gave us a completely different defensive situation. There's a pretty common theory among the college coaches with whom we visit, including Matte's former mentor, Woody Hayes, that you can't stop an attack that features a rollout or bootlegging quarterback with the standard 4–3 defense that the pros use against a heavy pass attack. The consensus of the coaches who meet the scramblers week after week is that the defense must put its ends wider in order to contain them. Then, if the quarterback goes wide, you have to have three men (instead of two) in between to fill up the gaps, which means that you have to present a five-man line with only two linebackers. In order to maintain flexibility, one end has the option of dropping back instead of crossing the line of scrimmage, in effect giving you the 4–3 if a pass develops quickly.

We rarely came up against the running quarterback, Fran Tarkenton, then with the Vikings, being the only scrambler regularly on our schedule. But much of his scrambling is of a desperation type, not a planned rollout attack, so we had always stayed with the 4–3 for Minnesota and hoped to counter the imponderables with heads-up play and a crackerjack middle linebacker.

I decided to stay with our regular formation for Baltimore and make adjustments during the game if it didn't work. They, of course, had to ponder whether we would change for them or stay the same. When we lined up for their first set of offensive plays, it turned out that they had expected us in the 4–3, and we had figured out their alignment pretty closely. In a way it was a tribute to both sides. We were both saying: Here's what you expected; what are you going to do about it? We genuinely had the feeling that we would come out the better in the head-on clash, and they decided to play as if they felt the same way about themselves.

Three games, three quarterbacks . . . and three wins? We felt we couldn't be denied. In fact, in later years tie finishes would be automatically resolved in favor of the team that had dominated in regular season play between the two winners. But this time we had to fight one more battle for the right to meet the Cleveland Browns a week later in the championship game.

What happened next is classic football history.

We won the toss and took the opening kickoff. On the first play from scrimmage, Starr faked to his fullback, then passed to the tight end near the sidelines—a bread-and-butter ten-yard play that had all the earmarks of a quick first down and the beginnings of a drive. But a crisp tackle after the reception caused a fumble in the air. The Colts' Don Shinnick caught the ball on the run at our twenty-five and headed down the sideline for our goal. It's a situation that leaves the quarterback as the last man between the onrushing defensive man and six points, so Starr flung himself forward in an attempt to make the saving tackle. He was blocked by a huge Colt lineman, and as Shinnick galloped in for the touchdown, Starr was knocked to the ground with badly bruised ribs. He was out for the game. It was as if fate had decided to equalize the situation by making us play with a different quarterback than the one we had planned on. I had never heard 50,861 fans moan in agony before, but they did when the team doctors helped Bart first to the bench and then to the dressing room.

At the half we were down 10–0, after Lou Michaels had added a field goal from the fifteen. So many things that "couldn't happen" had indeed happened this year. The thought would not go away that the same strange forces at work in San Francisco were haunting us again. Lombardi raised genuine hell in his halftime talk: "If you go down today after coming so close . . . how hard do you think it will be to climb this high again?" He stopped in the middle to switch from what was beginning to sound like a threat to a rhetorical question; he knew well the danger of threats, promises, or overstatements when the possibility of a still greater plateau lay ahead. It was better to leave it a question—that way each man could scrutinize himself during the moment of quiet and prayer before we went back out on the field. Perhaps each could come up with an individual answer that would help him do better. We went out knowing we were going to win.

In the third period, Bratkowski, who had had two interceptions but was passing well in Starr's stead, let loose a bomb in the direction of Carroll Dale, who was streaking across trying to make his goal-line rendezvous with the ball after being slowed up for a moment. His defender was literally on his back when Dale made his wild, leaping effort and snared the ball at the one-yard line. Hornung ran it in from there, and we trailed by only the margin of a field goal.

We held the Colts scoreless in the second half, but it looked as if they were also about to bottle us up, which would leave it at 10–7. We had to have a touchdown, and Bratkowski's passes together with Taylor's short runs into the line moved us slowly but surely downfield in the last few minutes. As the two-minute warning was given, we were at their twenty-two and could go no farther. In a regular-season game, we might have gone for a win with either short passes to the sideline or one pass to the corner of the end zone. But this was a special case. In playoff games, says the rulebook, when the score is tied at the end of regulation play, there shall be a sudden death overtime. It had happened only once before: in 1959, when these same Baltimore Colts went into Yankee Stadium against the Giants and pulled out a victory on a snowy afternoon.

Could history repeat itself? It had for us the previous week. But Vince felt we had a better chance of winning in sudden death than we did of making a fourth-down desperation play in the tense final two minutes. So Don Chandler came in to kick a field goal.

It was probably the most famous—or infamous—field goal in football history. He kicked from the twenty-five. The ball went up and drifted to the right. It curved upward, outward, and over the right-hand upright. Chandler shook his head in desperation, wishing he had brought it more to the left and fearing it might be no good. The fans, already on their feet, gasped. One excited sportscaster in the booth was already yelling, "No good, no good. The field goal is . . ." But the official beneath the uprights raised his arms without hesitation. The score was 10–10 with 1:58 remaining in the game.

Was it really good? Each picture showed a slightly different angle, and each fan in the stands or watching on television had his own recollection of what it looked like. The Baltimore "season highlights" promotion film for the year used stop-action photography and a superimposed dotted line extending from the top of the goalpost to demonstrate that the kick was wide. But that film, which has been shown many times on nationwide television, is a Colt production prepared for use on their banquet circuit, and not proof positive. So the narration and conclusions are understandably biased.

The man standing at the bottom of the pole is the only person—or lens—in the stadium with an accurate bead on the fair zone. There was no indecision on the official's mind, and it was a good thing that he threw his hands in the air without hesitating. It settled the matter once and for all as far as coaches, owners, and league officials were concerned. There was no exchange between teams or with the league on the matter, so the subsequent whines and cries have to be discharged as understandable chagrin on the part of Colt fans and sportswriters. There are always disputes over field goals in every season, and there are questionable calls in every game—all teams have been on both the lucky and unlucky end of such decisions. But when it comes at such a dramatic moment, it's understandable that people will talk about it for years to come.

Baltimore tried desperately to get in scoring position during the remaining time, but the gun went off and there we were, destined for sudden-death overtime. All at once those ridiculous little stories tacked onto the end of the main piece—"Here's What Happens if Pack and Colts Wind Up in Tie"—are reality, and a coach's mind runs madly through the special plays that might apply: onside kick . . . free kick . . . halfback option pass . . . shotgun pass pattern. The mind boggles at the thought of how a miscue could be magnified out of proportion. A fumble . . . an interception . . . a kickoff runback . . . a safety. A silly little two-point safety could lose you the championship in an eyeblink.

We lost the toss. The Colts received. They marched into our forties before we held. Lou Michaels came in to try the field goal. It would be from the forty-seven. The record was fifty-two yards. During the previous year Michaels had beaten us with a forty-yarder. All the statistics rushed through our minds. Lombardi, fists clenched, stared at the spot almost directly in front of us where Michaels stood driving his toe into the ground for feel and balance. I yelled with all my might at the linebackers to rush, although I knew that they could not hear me over the crowd's roar. Whatever they did, it would be too late for me to help. The snap, the kick, the ball in the air . . . and halfway through the arc we could see that it wouldn't make it. Lombardi was already turning and barking to the offense to get ready.

It seemed like an instant; it seemed like an eternity. We played nearly a full fifth quarter near midfield, and finally, after thirteen minutes, thirty-nine seconds, of sudden death . . . slow agony . . . hard work . . . we came to rest inside the Colt twenty-five. This had to be it; there would not likely be another chance. Chandler came in, looked briefly at the precise spot from which he had kicked the tying field goal, then stepped back and waited. The snap. The kick. It was all over. It took nearly thirteen quarters of football, but we had finally convinced the Colts—and ourselves—that we wanted to resume our journey down the championship road.

Did we deserve to win? With twenty-three first downs to nine

## PACKER DYNASTY

and 362 total yards to 175, we considered it as clear a win as if the score had been 30–10.

The week of December 27, 1965 was when we first learned that the Green Bay Packers were *old*. "Tired . . . over the hill . . . past their prime . . . not up to the challenge," said the columnists, toting up the number of players over thirty years old on our roster. They pointed to the "rested, poised, and *young*" Cleveland Browns, picking them to repeat as NFL champions. Jimmy Brown was hailed as the "smooth, strong, sophisticated superstar of the time," compared with "weary, hurting Jim Taylor, who has seen his better days." In short, the sportswriters did their part to ensure a Green Bay victory by giving us a shot of the very tonic that would spur many a Packer to play his best ball well past the age when many athletes are looking into Chicken Delight franchises.

True, we were patched and limping. Bart Starr winced after every contact in practice, trying bravely to forget the bruised ribs dealt to him by the Colts. Boyd Dowler had suffered two damaged ribs and was also nursing a bad ankle. In addition to "Packer ribs," Hornung had a twisted knee and a sprained wrist. Taylor's malady was a severely pulled groin muscle.

But we were not dead. While the trainer kept the whirlpools swishing and laid in an extra store of tape for the final push, equipment manager Dad Braisher distributed to each player mock pay envelopes containing checks for ten thousand dollars championship money signed by Nathan L. Leg. "I lisp," Dad explained to newsmen. "Nathan L. Leg is supposed to sound like me saying National League."

Coming out to drill on a frozen field during the week between Christmas and New Year's Day, we looked back to the hot July day when training camp opened on the same spot. It seemed impossible that we were still going, still running a two-minute drill to keep our no-huddle plays sharp, still brushing up on fundamentals. My defense had put together one of its finest seasons, yet we were working, adjusting, and drilling just as if we were all new at the game. Constant practice and preparation were what had brought us where we were, and only rigorous attention to small details would carry us the rest of the way.

As the week of practice drew to a close, Ray Nitschke and I conferred in the conference room adjoining the dressing area and worked on a revised list of defensive play numbers and on an updated signal system. It wouldn't be good enough just to rely on experience and past reputation. We knew from watching the Browns' films that they could do severe damage to us on their sweeps if Jimmy Brown made a cut into an "alley" created when our linemen were all drawn to the strong side and our cornerback was over too far. The key to preventing these sweeps was having our end and left linebacker turn Brown in so that the middle linebacker could nail him. The finger wigwags and hat-brim touches that I made in Nitschke's direction would alert him to minor adjustments against their double wing that could make the difference in stopping Brown before he swung out and away.

The morning of January 2 saw five inches of fresh snow on top of the tons of hay protecting our field. By the time the ground had been cleared, the thermal inversion had created a moor-like effect, and the thawed turf was slippery and muddy. "Packer Weather!" the fans exulted, not minding the marrow-creaking dampness or the extremely limited visibility. In later years, local historians would label it the "Fog Bowl," to differentiate it from the "Freeze Bowl" and other famous afternoons in Packer lore.

The first half was a standoff. Each team scored a touchdown through the air and a pair of field goals. A missed conversion by the usually faultless Lou Groza gave us the edge, 13–12. During the minutes of rest between halves, our locker room was quiet as each player scraped off caked layers of mud, poked at mucky cleats, and pondered whether we were just "as good as" the Browns—we knew we were—or better than our foe. Trainer Bud Jorgenson checked tape jobs, added binding to strengthen rib protection on two or three men, and then made a point of saying a few words of encouragement to each of the wounded and weary he had patched for the last time that year.

In the second half, we answered all questions about where we stood. Our offensive line began to establish its superiority, pushing the white jersies back, opening holes for Hornung and Taylor. Nitschke and crew, keying relentlessly on Brown, held him to nine yards and denied him any points. They got to quarterback Frank Ryan four times and forced him to swallow the ball. When he did get it away, receivers Gary Collins and Paul Warfield were too bottled up downfield to make the long gain. Paul Hornung came back to the huddle after being sprung loose for a first-down run, slapped two linemen on the rumps, and laughed, "Hey, this is 1962 all over again."

That gave his teammates the final charge. Taylor gained eight yards, then ten, and after a fake to him, Starr handed the ball to Hornung, who carried it to the Cleveland fifteen. A minute later, Paul rambled thirteen yards for the score. Chandler converted, and we led, 20–12. We ran thirty-five plays to only sixteen for Cleveland in that downhill second half, and in the waning minutes Chandler added an insurance field goal for a 23–12 triumph.

"Tired, aging, hurting" backs Taylor and Hornung had gained a hundred yards apiece, and it was they who hoisted Coach Lombardi to their shoulders this time for the victory ride.

"Hey," Vince laughed, his battered rainhat tossing wildly above the sea of green jersies, his tan coat smeared with mud from the uniforms that formed his perch, "I guess there's a little left in you old fellows yet."

# 9 · AN APPOINTMENT IN DALLAS

There are only two people in the National Football League who are not superstitious: myself and Vince Lombardi. And I'm not 100 percent sure about Lombardi.

When you are on top, you try to stay there by doing everything exactly the way you did it the previous time. If you put your left shoe on first before the big clincher over the Bears, you remember to put your left shoe on first the next time you play the Bears. If your neighbors had you over for shish kebab the afternoon before the shellacking of the Colts, you remind them of it again before the next Baltimore game. If your youngest son lost a tooth the morning you left for two weeks on the Coast last year at the start of the big winning streak . . . well, you might just be tempted to box the little fella around a bit and see if you could loosen up another one before driving out to the airport for this year's trip. Once, before an important game with the Rams, Willie Davis shaved his sideburns a half inch higher. "I want everything to be exactly like it was last year," he explained.

We had put it all together again in 1965, and we were determined to start 1966 where we left off. We had all the old players back plus a million-dollar list of potential superstars headed by Donny Anderson and Jim Grabowski, the "Golddust Twins" who would be groomed to fill the shoes of Hornung and Taylor.

Of course, wanting to win and having the horses to win are

not the whole story. There is some kind of chemistry that takes place when some sixty or seventy veterans and rookies open training in July. A man you expected to be a stalwart shows up overweight, doesn't quite seem to have the hustle and quickness he had at the end of the previous season, and makes the team with the reservation of coaches who sign him up again on the basis of what he should and can do if he regains the proper mental attitude. Another man, perhaps your sixth back or an extra offensive lineman who rode the taxi squad most of the previous year and is back for a second try, comes to camp under a full head of steam, runs in practice as if it were midseason, and works his head off until he beats out a backup man or even a regular for the starting position. If you find yourself mostly with pleasant surprises, as in the case of the second man, you should be on your way to an improved record.

The chemistry was all there this time. Although we took eight rookies, a high number for us, our personnel situation worked out well enough that we could enjoy the luxury of letting Anderson and Grabowski "understudy" their great predecessors. (The leading scorer among our backs, in fact, would be a fifth fine runner, Elijah Pitts.) A couple of writers for national sports magazines who came into camp in August expecting to find friction and fireworks in the Packer backfield went away with stories praising the high morale and the spirit of veterans grooming the stars of the future—the whole lot of them looking ahead to sharing a rich Super pot at the end of the combined NFL-AFL rainbow.

If there was one small spot of tarnish, it was Jim Taylor's decision to "play out his option"—to play without a contract through the season, an action which would lead to his departure for the infant New Orleans franchise at the end of the year. But it was a quiet, personal test of will and financial principles between Taylor and Lombardi that never threatened team morale. Most Packers consider themselves well and fairly paid—especially when you consider their frequent championship earnings. They know Vince's policy of not cutting the salary of a player who may have had a bad year, and they also know that

Lombardi won't stand haggling or financial end-arounds. One player who in 1964 got fancy and sent an agent to "negotiate" a contract was told flatly that he had come to the wrong office; Vince simply traded away what he considered to be a disloyal man.

I think Taylor had an inflated idea of what worth was involved. Knowing that his career was coming to an end, he wanted to stretch his earning ability as much as possible. According to the league rules, playing out his option meant that the Packers, who offer their players standard annual contracts, could pay him only 90 percent of his previous year's salary. As a free agent at the end of the year, he could look for a cash bonus and a longer contract from some team eager to get him. He and his wife are from Louisiana, and he had an eye on the new franchise there, but I know he would have gone to Houston, New York, or Timbuktu—if they were where the money was.

There was one small moment of doubt about the team during the training season. For the second year in a row we lost an exhibition game to the Cowboys in Dallas. To make matters worse, this time we scored only a lone field goal against the Doomsday Defense of Tom Landry, losing 21–3. Sportswriters around the country, predicting that the two teams would probably be meeting for the NFL crown in Dallas, started talking about a "Cotton Bowl jinx." It was a wry thought a few years later, when the so-called Packers' "jinx" consisted of four straight wins over the Cowboys on their home ground.

The regular season, however, was smooth sailing almost all the way to a 12–2 record. The only blemishes were a 21–20 loss to San Francisco ("Remember, gentlemen, three converted touchdowns beat two touchdowns and two field goals any day of the week; the system rewards those who go all the way.") The other was a 20–17 loss to the Vikings in Green Bay, the unfortunate harbinger of their little "jinx" over us that has prevailed for three years running. Those so-called jinxes are what makes football a fascinating, sometimes frustrating, game.

Once again the true measure of our success was best reflected in the two meetings with Baltimore, as we extended our winning streak over the erstwhile champions to five games. In the Milwaukee opener, we expected them to be "high" because the papers had carried stories of how they pasted up pictures of *the* field goal for emotional fodder. We were high, too. Willie Davis sat in front of his stall and flexed his massive shoulders trying to loosen up. "You can't fool your stomach," he admitted to a teammate. "This one is a real gut-twister. I was up half the night." All around the room others who had finished suiting up lay on the carpeted floor, heads resting on spare pads or on the edges of dressing stalls, trying hard to play I-am-lying-on-a-cloud-and-can't-feel-a-thing, a variation of I'm-so-relaxed-I-can-take-a-little-nap.

Everybody on both sides was high, but the Packers, as usual, had timed it so that the peak of emotions crested at game time. Not the day before, not in the middle of the fourth quarter, but precisely at the thud of toe leather against pigskin when the clock blinks from 15:00 to 14:59, the crowd leaps up to let loose its first mighty roar, and the adrenalin surges within every green-clad Packer.

In the first period, the Colts massed for a first-down push on our nineteen—opting for a touchdown opportunity instead of a field goal. Our defensive line anticipated the rush at the center, closed ranks, and we held. We took possession.

In the second period, the identical situation occurred on our nineteen again. This time the Colts were happy to take the field goal. It gave them their only points of the game.

Roaring back, we scored two quick touchdowns to lead 14–3 at halftime. The second Packer score came when Bob Jeter, who was once a flanker but had been turned into a defensive back the previous season, pirated a Unitas pass and ran forty-six yards for the score. Laughing, but with tears welling up in his big, dark eyes, he came running back to the bench, clasped my arm, and shouted, "That's the way, huh?" I slapped him on the shoulder and nodded in agreement, remembering back one year to his interception against the same team. That time he had gotten so excited that he slipped and fell right in front of my feet. "Get up, get up; you can run," I had yelled. "Go, go.

## PACKER DYNASTY

Nobody touched you." He tried desperately to get up, but he was so excited he just couldn't get his legs to function, and he ended up crawling eight yards on his hands and knees, the ball clutched frantically in the crook of his arm, before a Colt finally fell on him. But that was last year. Like everybody else, Jeter was better now.

We began the third period with a classic Packer drive, starting with the sweeps, then working end Boyd Dowler for a couple of medium-range passes, followed by a surprise toss to Hornung, a little running by Starr in the pinch, and Taylor through the middle. Unable to find a receiver from the eight, Starr spurted forward and dived in himself. A field goal and peerless defense iced the opener at 24–3.

Twelve games later we came to Baltimore determined to wrap up the conference title against the same second-place Colts who had dogged our footsteps for the entire season. For the second year in a row, the same two iron combatants faced one another in a decisive match. No "backing in" to the conference crown, with somebody half a continent away doing the job for you. It would be here, now, today. Both sides were resolved.

"We've said all along it would probably come down to this game," Lombardi told the players at the first practice of the week. "Before the season people said the Green Bay Packers were too old, but here we are. And it's the old fellows who have brought us here. Believe me, gentlemen, we're going to go all the way."

Once again we left early in the week and set up camp in a motel near Washington. We had three victories in a row, discipline and morale were superb, but Vince would not take any chances. Perfection demanded that we repeat our rigorous preparations of the previous year. Of course, it wasn't all work and no play, because we watched movies in the evenings: movies of the Baltimore Colts.

We didn't expect the rematch to be easy, and it wasn't. It got off to a fine start, with Starr hitting Elijah Pitts for a forty-two-yard pass play that gave us a 7–0 lead. But then the brutal contact led to a series of injuries. Guard Fuzzy Thurston had to be replaced by rookie Gale Gillingham. A jarring tackle on Tom Matte knocked Jeter out of action. Boyd Dowler had to be replaced by Max McGee. Then, worst of all, Bart Starr suffered a muscle spasm in his back and had to sit out the entire second half.

The shuffling of personnel during that almost disastrous second quarter gave Baltimore the opportunity to cap two drives with scores, and we trailed, 10–7, at halftime. When we came out after the half, Memorial Stadium was awash in a steady downpour. Mired in the mud, the two giants labored to move up and down the middle of the field. I had seen games like this one more than once in San Francisco's drizzle-prone Kezar Stadium. Too often the prerain score held up.

But backup man Zeke Bratkowski managed to move us down to the Colt twenty-five in the fourth period, and he prepared to hit Max McGee on a short pass sufficient for the first down. With Baltimore blitzing heavily on the third-down situation, McGee exercised his option to break deep over center instead of running the primary pattern. Bratkowski alertly read the development, calculated the dangerously small area McGee would have between two converging pass defenders, made an allowance for the effect of the downpour on the trajectory of the ball, and let fly. McGee hauled it down in a mighty splash on the four. Two plays later, Pitts carried it over the right guard to give us a 14–10 victory and the Western Conference crown.

Soon after, we had an invitation to spend New Year's Day in Dallas.

In each of our previous three NFL championship victories, we had met our opponent previously that year—either in an exhibition or in a regular game—and had beaten them. These victories had given us the psychological boost of knowing already that we were capable of winning against them. It also worked the other way: It was their turn to win. So always it had been a matter of making our psychology triumph over theirs.

This time we had the memories of that preseason defeat when we had been unable to score a touchdown against Dallas.

## PACKER DYNASTY

For the first time in a championship game we had most of our usual inspirational forces at work plus the classic revenge motive. And, of course, there was the extra incentive of the first Super Bowl jackpot.

We made three basic decisions in our planning for the Battle of the Cotton Bowl:

First, Vince worked the team harder than ever, ignoring our 12–2 record and acting as if we were coming in as ten-point underdogs. No player escaped criticism and upbraiding; each was made to understand that the outcome of the game might well hinge on his ability to eliminate error and mental laxity in his play. Lombardi never let up.

Second, our game plan for the offense centered on the careful, consistent ball control mix of backs running at the line—occasionally sweeping, and occasionally taking short passes—while the ends went for short- and medium-range receptions. There were no plans to throw long unless circumstances dictated it. As it turned out, Starr would have to unload one fifty-one-yard bomb to Carroll Dale early in the second quarter to break a tie. But by and large it would be a day for fifteen-to-twenty-yarders. Bart got first downs twice in third-and-nineteen situations, and touchdowns to three different receivers, with tosses of seventeen, sixteen, and twenty-three yards.

The third decision was perhaps the most important of all. After hours of watching Dallas films, I told Vince that we would not have to alter our defense to allow for the explosive Bob Hayes, the "world's fastest human," with his awesome ability to outrun deep defenders to snare the Meredith bomb. Herb Adderley, Willie Wood, and Bob Jeter were in good physical and mental condition. They, too, studied the films, and they were confident of their ability to contain Hayes. Most other teams had tried in desperation to stop the deep threat, playing two-on-one, trying the zone defense, or coming with the blitz—anything to cut off either Hayes or Meredith. In doing so, they either failed by letting Hayes through one or two fatal times, or they failed even worse by overcompensating so much that other Dallas receivers and rushers had a virtual amnesty that they readily capitalized on.

We felt, too, that shaking up our defense would be a sign of weakness—it would undermine the confidence of our men and let the opponent know that we were worried. We double-covered Hayes on a few patterns, but by and large we demanded that he respect us as much as we respected him. It was a good decision. Our deep defenders played nearly errorless ball, and Hayes made but one reception—for a gain of only one yard.

The game was one of the most exciting sixty minutes in the history of football, but to this day most people remember only the first four minutes and the last four. So perhaps it would be better to say that the two teams played fifty-two minutes of exceptional football sandwiched between four-minute slices of near-fantasy.

Green Bay's first touchdown featured Elijah Pitts. On the first play of the game he sprinted thirty-two yards on a special counterplay Vince had dusted off for openers after studying computer predictions of what we were supposed to do. The drive ended with Pitts taking a Starr pass in the end zone just past the four-minute mark.

Scant seconds later, by the clock, Cowboy Mel Renfro's attempt to return our kickoff was rudely interrupted by onrushing rookies Bob Brown and Gale Gillingham, the latter poking the ball from Renfro's grasp. Another rookie, Jim Grabowski, picked it up and ran eighteen yards for our second score in a period of twelve seconds. It was 14–0 already, and the thirty-five hundred Packer backers squeezed into the Cotton Bowl along with seventy-one thousand Texans exploded with glee. So did millions of television partisans who figured the game was sewed up.

But a "safe" pro football lead has been variously calculated at up to twenty-nine points: four touchdowns and four conversions plus an insurance point. Indeed, four touchdowns and four conversions was the first quarter's output, two for each team. And at halftime it was 21–17 in our favor.

## PACKER DYNASTY

With four minutes left in the game, we had reinstituted our fourteen-point lead at 34–20. It should have been a more comfortable 35–20 lead, but Don Chandler's fifth extra point attempt was blocked, creating a parity between the fifth touchdown and the two Dallas field goals. Who said that extra point attempts are routine? The missed extra point loomed more and more important as Dallas marched up the field twice in the final minutes.

With 4:09 remaining, Meredith found his tight end momentarily free, and lobbed a pass to him for a sixty-eight-yard instant touchdown. Tom Brown, who was covering, had twisted, slipped, and fallen when his man broke to the inside. He came back to the bench dejectedly, realizing that the seven-point margin set up the possibility of a tie at the end of regulation play.

The thought was on every mind: another sudden-death overtime? Two years in a row? Could it happen to us? Could we do it again if we had to? Baltimore had won one championship that way and lost an opportunity for another. Were we destined to succumb to the law of averages?

The aroused Cowboy defense held us by blitzing twice, dropping Starr for a loss on one play and tackling Taylor behind the line of scrimmage on a screen pass. We had to punt. It was beginning to look like sudden death. Chandler's kick was uncharacteristically short and weak, popping out of bounds in *our* territory—at the forty-seven—with 2:19 left in the game. Dallas, down by a touchdown and a conversion, could work the two-minute rule for all it was worth.

A twenty-one-yard pass from Meredith to Frank Clarke put them at our twenty-six. Field goal territory . . . but no worry about that. Vince whirled toward me and yelled: "Phil, shake those linebackers up, can't you?" He was already turning back to look at the field, but he continued: "Watch Reeves. Watch that Norman." Then, over his shoulder to Starr: "If we get it back, just lie on it. Lie on the damn thing."

Fullback Dan Reeves moved it four yards. Second and six on our twenty-two. Two minutes. Meredith was going to pass.

The ball arched high and plummeted toward Clarke. They would rendezvous in the end zone if . . . but the pass fell incomplete as our defender tied Clarke up. . . . Interference! The Dallas crowd, already on its feet, roared its approval as the official signaled pass interference on our defender and placed the ball at the two. With a first down and 1:52 remaining—time, plenty of time; how well we knew that after all the games we had snatched from the jaws of defeat in just such circumstances—Reeves came straight at us and cut the two yards to one.

One yard. Three downs. It meant we were committed to protect the center of the line, but we knew those Dallas probabilities by heart, and we knew that Meredith would go to a receiver in the flat. On the next play he dropped back and passed to Pettis Norman in the end zone, but it fell incomplete.

Dallas fans wailed as the ball bounced harmlessly past the end stripe, but practically every player on the field was turning to look at the flag lying on the grass, thrown there immediately after the snap. Probably each player on the field asked himself: "Me . . . you . . . us . . . them?" The Cowboy left tackle had jumped offside.

"The yards, the yards," Vince yelled and signaled simultaneously, and I waved signals openly to Nitschke and Davis. It was second down—again—but with the threat of a rush greatly reduced. Now it meant that pass defenders in the end zone would have to be doubly alert, and the linebackers could be used to blitz on third down.

Three chances. Meredith had three chances to toss a tying touchdown pass from our six. Nobody was interested in computers now; human computerization, the product of hundreds of hours of drilling, had taken over. But if we had stopped time long enough to feed the data into our computer (Cowboys . . . Meredith . . . one minute and twenty seconds . . . three tries), the feedout would have read: 80 percent probability of Dallas score.

The first try was a swing pass to Reeves in the left flat. He dropped it. The clock was stopped. Still, more than a minute remained. The second try was a pass to Norman as he crossed the line of scrimmage. He caught it, and fell at our two. Fourth down and two. One more chance.

I signaled to the defense: Look for an off-tackle drive by one of the backs. But there was a possibility that Meredith would bootleg after faking to the back and roll out looking for a receiver. It was fifty-fifty. I signaled to be alert for either possibility.

Meredith took the snap and turned. Did he keep it? Would he pass? Linebacker Dave Robinson had filled the off-tackle hole. No chance of driving through there. Madness in the end zone. Receivers and defenders crisscrossing, arms in the air. Meredith began to roll—he had the ball. But Robinson recovered immediately, shoved his way past a blocker, and closed in on Meredith near the ten. He came at the Cowboy quarterback with arms raised.

We had taken our fifty-fifty chance; now Meredith took his. At the last instant before Robinson battered him down, he managed to let the ball fly toward the end zone . . . toward white jerseys, green jerseys, black-and-white striped jerseys. Toward fifteen thousand dollar Super Bowl money, for them, for us, for . . .

For Hayes! The world's fastest human darted out of the melee and out under the spinning ball. But coming across also was Tom Brown, mindful of his earlier slip in the footrace with Clarke. This time he was in the right place at the right moment. The ball settled in his hands, and he pulled it down, down, into the safe cavity formed by his abdomen as he slowly sank to the ground, hugging an NFL championship to his bosom and crying with joy as his teammates lifted him and seized him in a tumultuous group embrace.

# 10 · SUPERCHAMPS!

THE TOUGHEST coaching job we faced in the entire nine years of the Lombardi regime was preparing to meet the Kansas City Chiefs in the first NFL-AFL World Championship game, on January 15, 1967, in the Los Angeles Coliseum.

How do you convince men who have already played twenty games—only two of them easy victories—that they must work their hardest and play their best in order to win the twenty-first?

How do you convince men who have beaten the Colts, the Rams, and the Cowboys over the past three weeks that they'll have to be prepared to make the same supreme effort to top the representative of a young, new league with no reputation and allegedly no strength to match your own?

And how do you prepare tactical adjustments when you have never met your foe, nor any team in his league, nor any team in your league which has played the opponent? We had films on Kansas City, but no frame of reference to help us interpret much of what we saw.

The most difficult problem was the emotional preparation. The so-called Super Bowl, despite all the promotional hullabaloo by both of the television networks that would carry it, was not yet a *great* game. It had no tradition, no heritage. Consequently, the very idea of playing in it did not sufficiently arouse the players the way they would have been aroused and "up" for a game with their old rivals—the Bears and the Giants—or their new ones—the Colts and the Cowboys. There was no geographical factor, such as when we travel to Minnesota and find many of our own followers sprinkled among the Viking fans. Nor the special situation you get when you meet your old teammates, your old coach, or old fans—the extra effort I always called for and got when we met the 49ers in the years after my departure from San Francisco. None of that was here; we might as well have been meeting a baseball team from Japan as far as the emotional buildup was concerned.

The main impetus, of course, came from our desire to represent the NFL well. We *had* to win. If we got complacent and let the Chiefs pull an upset, we'd go down in history on the same page with Goliath and the Spanish Armada.

Our game plan would not be much different from those we'd worked up all year long. When you're winning, you don't alter your basic style of play. The first half would be for probing, testing, spotting weaknesses. In the second half we would turn loose the regular season's leading passer in professional football for as much as we needed to win and enough to prove NFL superiority. The idea of a rout, in the sense of collegiate ball's occasional colossal mismatches, did not cross our minds.

We could see that their defense was conscious of the deep threat whenever they met strong passing quarterbacks, but they were less than adequate on the flanks. That meant Starr could expect to hit Dowler, Dale, and McGee. When you can count on the success of your flankers and spread ends, the first-down outlook is good.

Studying the habits of their personnel, we found a few defensive linemen and a linebacker with problems of ego and eagerness that made them ripe candidates for "setting up" by our offense. By showing them certain basic plays early and giving them ideas on how and where to rush, we felt we could make variations of those same plays click in the second half. That approach is no big secret or innovation, but it works especially well when age meets youth, experience meets ambition. Nothing gives a veteran lineman more hours of warm, contemplative pleasure than the thought of setting up a youngster for the big play in the third period.

We could see indications that blitzing tactics on both sides might make a difference as the game wore on. I advised Vince that I would refrain from calling the blitz in the first half, giving the quarterback a false assurance that we could capitalize on when we needed to later in the game. Kansas City quarterback Len Dawson ran a play action pattern of the type we rarely faced, but we felt it was particularly vulnerable to a surprise blitz. They, on the other hand, would doubtless be coming at Starr, based on the pass attack we had been depending on to win games and the effective blitz they had been depending on to deny their opponents victories. So we drilled our receivers in handling the man-on-man defense.

We made one small adjustment in our thinking. Ordinarily the coaches in any contest hold a frequency chart on the opponent for quick reference regarding "what they'll do in this situation." Usually a strong team goes with its successful attack, knowing that the other side has the set of statistics, but saying, in effect, "Try to stop me." We decided that since the opponents in this game were complete strangers and would be relying much more heavily than usual on frequency charts, we could keep a completely uncharacteristic choice of plays as an ace in the hole to be used in the later stages of the game if we found ourselves in need of a real shot in the arm. Bart had done a page or two of Kansas City's homework and knew what the Chief defense expected from him. Smart Bart, the A student. From ancient history he could recall two inscriptions on the Delphic oracle: "Know thyself" and "Nothing too much."

As always, Vince kept the necessary number of turns on the thumbscrews. Arriving at our special training camp at a Santa Barbara motor inn, he complained as we stepped off the bus: "This is too beautiful a place for a training camp. It should be more barren so everybody thinks about football instead of gazing at the mountains. Let's run all the plays the opposite direction from the mountains." So only the defense looked at the mountains. The offense looked at the blue waters of the Pacific Ocean.

The Chiefs held secret practices, possibly to keep us guessing about their capabilities, more likely to plan a few new forma-

## PACKER DYNASTY

tions they sprung on us in their opening drive. We held closed practices to keep the players' minds on preparing for the game. Every time they walked from their quarters to the dining room they were besieged by flocks of sportswriters asking them the same questions: "How many touchdowns do you think you'll win by?" "Is there a chance they'll spring an upset?" Finally some of the players came up with a sure-fire answer to any and all questions: "Fifteen thousand dollars, man; fifteen thousand dollars."

According to plan, we moved slowly and cautiously on the green floor of the Coliseum. The Packer fans among the sixty-two thousand in the stands and the sixty-five million watching on television recognized the old ball control game, the unwillingness in the early stages to try fancy plays that could result in errors, the attempt to establish superiority on the ground before going to the air. On our second series, after nine minutes of play, Starr hit for a thirty-seven-yard touchdown pass to Max McGee, who had come in when Dowler was injured.

The crowd, surprisingly partisan toward the Chiefs in an NFL stadium, saw Kansas City come back to tie it up with Dawson scrambling, throwing to the talented Mike Garrett, and finally connecting with Curtis McClinton for the score. We came back with a seventy-three-yard march in thirteen plays, capped by a fourteen-yard Packer sweep with Taylor escorted by Thurston and Kramer for the score. It could have been a scene out of a 1962 newsreel.

That second touchdown did more than put us ahead again. It showed the way to victory. Not only did we move steadily on the ground, but a pass to Carroll Dale in the end zone (unfortunately nullified by a penalty) was made possible when we suckered the cornerback into going for the fake to Taylor and letting the receiver slip past. Our homework was paying off. On subsequent plays Starr picked at the defensive backs, hitting his ends for ten- and fifteen-yarders. Our bread-and-butter plays were working. We wouldn't have to get very tricky.

It was 14–10 at halftime, tighter than we wished, but no cause for worry. Lombardi went at it more or less as if we were in the third week of July and a drill had not gone quite as smoothly as we wished. After a short coaches' huddle, we went to the dressing room and talked to each group of players, pointing out where they had been weak, suggesting adjustments for the second half, and giving a verbal kick in the butt to those who had not functioned at 110 percent of capacity.

Then Lombardi made a few general remarks, goading linemen into tackling harder and cleaner, demanding that the defense pressure Dawson harder to deny him the advantages of the rolling pocket he had enjoyed in the first half. He knew our poise would hold us, but he wasn't sure we were mad enough at ourselves and at them to win the way we should. So he gritted his teeth, brandished a clenched fist at all of us, and demanded: "Are you the World Champion Green Bay Packers or aren't you? Get out on that field and answer me."

As the second half began, we lined up just a little differently against the Kansas City attack. Down the line we met them in their spread-out pattern by placing each of our men squarely head-on instead of offset, as in the first half. The linebackers were spread slightly wider to protect better against Dawson's rollout. And there was a change in attitude: "Now we know what they are and what they do, so let's get in there and break it up instead of just containing them."

The new alignment and the new attitude set up the defensive backbreaker of the day. The Chiefs were driving at midfield with a third-and-five situation. Against the Packers, that means pass. One of our decisions at halftime was to take the embargo off the blitz, and I signaled Nitschke that this was the time for it. In the defensive huddle he alerted the corner linebackers to push over the line and shoot for Dawson. Lee Roy Caffey and Dave Robinson flew off the mark at the snap of the ball. Robinson struck out closer to the quarterback and managed to tip the ball so that it wobbled crazily, tumbling toward their tight end, Fred Arbanas. But it was Willie Wood who came up with it, and he ran the interception all the way back to the Chief five before Mike Garrett managed to bring him down.

That, for all purposes, was the end of the game. The Chiefs never got within our forty again. Elijah Pitts ran in the third

## PACKER DYNASTY

Packer touchdown, and he would get still another, as would McGee. For Max, who had hinted at retirement at thirty-four, it would be a day to remember. The aging veteran, a stand-in for Dowler, he caught seven passes for 138 yards and was the hero of the game. It was almost as if we had played a cruel trick on the young AFL hopefuls, threatening them with Taylor, the ailing-but-ready Hornung, and a host of other players in their prime, then sending out an "old man" to humiliate them. As if to make the point stick, McGee even made one of the pass receptions behind his back.

Before the whistle blew on our 35–10 victory, the Packers made a point of righting everything that had been wrong before. A Chief who had bragged before the game that he would lay Packers low with his karate-like "hammer blow" was carried off the field unconscious, the victim of his own abandoned tackle against an onrushing Donny Anderson. A Kansas City lineman who displayed the bad judgment of hurling Taylor to the ground after a play had been blown dead, found the Packers sending their next two plays directly over his spot in the line. The spot was obliterated both times by Taylor's angry teammates. Similarly, a deep defender who had the temerity to intercept an underthrown Starr pass intended for McGee found that on the very next drive Starr came back to hit Dale, then McGee, then Dale again for big gains, all three times directly in the tracks of the uppity Chief.

Late in the game Zeke Bratkowski came in to give Starr a rest . . . and to give Anderson and Grabowski some practice. Before it was over, most of our bench had been used.

Afterward, pressured by newsmen to evaluate the Chiefs, Vince remarked on nationwide television: "It's a good team, but it doesn't compare with teams in the NFL. Dallas is a better team. That's what you want me to say, isn't it? Now I've said it."

It was one of those remarks that looks different when you see it in print, and Lombardi was sorry he ever said it on-camera. He meant it in the same frank, of-the-moment vein as he felt the insistent questioner meant it, not as an example of graceless triumph.

## PACKER DYNASTY

By the very seriousness of our preparation, we felt we had shown that we took the American Football League seriously. They get their players from the same places that we do. They have good coaches. And they have been in operation just as long as our Dallas and Minnesota franchises.

What held the AFL back from the very beginning was that the distribution of their playing talent was so terribly uneven, a result of the business operations among the early owners in the league. In addition, the leading teams—Kansas City among them—worked it so they had relatively easy schedules, and not much competition. That was bad for the entire league. The thing that makes a good football player great is the competition, first of all to make his own team, then to earn a starting position, and finally to beat other strong clubs. The player and the team develop in the face of real competition, so the stronger the opponents the better.

We felt that the NFL competition made the difference between our strongest and weakest teams in any one year much less than that in the AFL. Look at the AFL scores during their first seven years and you'll see too many 45–7 games. As strong as we were in 1966, we had won only four games by a margin of two touchdowns or more, and our only "laugher," or runaway game, was against the New Atlanta expansion club.

But the *top* AFL teams by 1966 were not a great deal different from a typical NFL team. They proved that in the following exhibition season when their stronger teams won a few games against our squads. By 1968, parity was closer than ever.

All that really mattered, however, as we headed to the locker room for the last time that season, was that we were the first true World Champions of football. Center spotlight in our Green Bay Packer Hall of Fame trophy showcase was accorded the magnificent Super Bowl trophy. And in most of the homes of Packer personnel, the center of the mantelpiece is occupied by a large, full-color picture of the white walls of the Coliseum with the scoreboard frozen at the historic moment when the gun sounded and we were Super Champs.

# 11 · SHOOTING FOR THREE

IN 1929–30–31 the Green Bay Packers had won the NFL crown three times in a row. But since the league was split into two divisions in 1933, no team had won the championship more than twice successively. After winning in 1940 and 1941, the Bears were shaded 14–6 by Washington in the playoff. Detroit beat Cleveland for the crown in 1952 and 1953, but in 1954 the Browns denied Detroit its third consecutive victory with a 56–10 rout. Our narrow loss to Philadelphia in 1960 championship, and our mathematical elimination from the tight 1963 race, had bracketed the 1961 and 1962 winning efforts.

Now we had two championships behind us and another shot at the triple crown, but the task seemed even more formidable than the first time around. The Eastern and Western Conferences had each been subdivided into two divisions, and an extra playoff game was set up between the divisional winners to determine the conference champions. Another factor was the improvement of the Colts and the Rams. And of course the biggest question mark of all was: Can the Packers do it without Taylor and Hornung?

The touchdown twins had both left for the New Orleans expansion franchise, but under very different circumstances. Having played out his option, Taylor made his last bid for an increased Packer salary and then waited for the mechanics of the agreement between the teams and the league to be worked out.

Hornung's departure came as a result of the special expansion draft, where New Orleans—under former Green Bay assistant coach Tom Fears—could select players from each team's roster after a certain number were frozen.

Under ordinary circumstances, a star of Hornung's caliber would have been untouchable. But Hornung's recurring neck injury made him something less than indispensable. He had sat out virtually the entire second half of the 1966 season, including the championship games. The team doctor and Lombardi came to the conclusion that he might never play again, certainly never at his same effectiveness.

Vince had a special affection for Paul, almost as father to son. But the Packers were not a family; a forty-man roster did not leave room for sentimental positions of halfback emeritus. After weighing the decision for days, Lombardi decided not to include Hornung on our freeze list. In the back of his mind, I know he hoped and believed that the New Orleans people would be so shocked at the move that they would realize the folly of trying to gamble on Hornung.

When the list went in to the commissioner, Vince called Paul and broke the news to him. Both have admitted unashamedly that there were many tears, many regrets, but a manly resolve and a spirit of undying friendship in the last official exchange between the two as coach and player.

The day the list was given to New Orleans, Fears called Vince to ask about Hornung. Lombardi recounted his reasons for placing Paul on the draft list, and he told Fears bluntly that Hornung, who was scheduled for more operations, would probably never play. Fears decided to gamble. He reasoned that even a slowed-up Paul Hornung would provide valuable leadership and example for his young, new club, as well as creating considerable fan interest. Word went out to the sports world that the Golden Boy from Notre Dame was now a Saint.

In a town where the football team is always the number one topic of conversation, Hornung's departure was a hot enough item to melt the ice on the Fox River. Shortly after, the Taylor move was cemented, and outsiders speculated that the loss to the Packer backfield might be devastating. The greatest static came from a pair of perennial critics—two former Wisconsin

## PACKER DYNASTY

residents now ensconced as a St. Paul columnist and a Viking player—the former crowing: "It could be more damaging than the Packers would like to think. Sure they have some fine young replacements in Anderson and Grabowski, but neither has had much exposure. Now Lombardi will be forced to play them."

The response from Green Bay was sufficient to silence the dissenters. Superfan Howie Blindauer reported that at Martha's Cafe, clearinghouse for Packer prognostications, "Everybody had Hornung on the list and Taylor moving out. It'll be a real asset for Tom Fears, but it won't hurt the Packers as much as some people would like to think." And local sports columnists, always more cool-headed than those in St. Paul, reminded Packer fans of orderly departures during the past years. Trading away All-Pro center Jim Ringo, for example, hadn't hurt the team, despite the dire predictions of a few.

Lombardi told the press in his first news conference of the 1967 season: "I feel we were more than well compensated for Jim Taylor. He is a fine football player, and we will miss him this season. But the draft choice and the veteran player we will get for him from New Orleans will help the Packers in the future. That is the future of the Green Bay Packers. The Packers have been in this business for forty-seven years, so we'll always have to replace the Jim Taylors." Vince was reciting pro football's facts of life for the benefit of those who had forgotten them.

On July 1, 1967, at the opening of the Green Bay Packer Hall of Fame museum in the arena across Oneida Avenue from the stadium and team headquarters, Lombardi made a surprise announcement to the dedication crowd: "We will not have a number five this year, and so far as I am concerned, there will never be another number five in Green Bay." And so Hornung's legendary digit was retired, joining two others from the Packers' glorious history: Don Hutson's 14 and Tony Canadeo's 3. Hornung left behind six personal scoring records, and his influence on a dozen team marks reflects the Golden Boy's contribution to the Golden Decade.

There were other realignments and other rumors as we prepared for our run at the triple crown. A Chicago columnist with a few spare inches to fill suggested that I would be the successor to Norm Van Brocklin at Minnesota and the Dutchman would join Lombardi as his top assistant. It had been a couple of years since I had last been contacted by any team; most everybody knew it would take an extremely attractive offer to lure me away from the Packers. Lombardi squelched the rumor, and I told the press that I intended to stay where I was.

Shortly thereafter, I seemed to have developed an automatic identification in the press: "Lombardi's heir apparent, Phil Bengtson." I did nothing to foster it, Lombardi never once hinted at it, but it would not die. Some columnists and fans managed to convince themselves that Lombardi and I spent most of our spare time up in the throne room discussing lineage, but nothing could be farther from the truth. The simple fact is that Vince Lombardi and I never mixed a great deal socially, rarely talked about high-level posts at any length, and devoted precious little time to speculating on our coaching careers together. The amount of planning, detail work, and concentration a coach's job calls for precludes any playing at politics from June to January. Usually about February 15, before I left for my annual vacation in Arizona, Vince would stick his head in my office and ask some mundane question like, "How many sheets of poster board will you need to set up your depth charts for next year?," and I would say "About six," and we would both smile because something unspoken carried the assurance that we both intended to work together for another year.

My defensive squad was intact—and it would well have to be. Injuries would keep our backfield in a state of flux for the entire season. After the first two games, Starr and Grabowski would be out, and the combination of Bratkowski, Pitts, and Ben Wilson would have to fill in. Starr would come back after missing three games, but in a disastrous game with the Colts at midseason, Pitts would be lost for the rest of the year with a torn Achilles tendon, and Grabowski would sustain a knee injury that would knock him out for most of the remaining games. Starr would miss another game before it was over, and our final game would see an unheard-of backfield of Don Horn, Travis Williams, and Chuck Mercein. Somewhere along the way Donny Anderson and Wilson would also make appearances. In the entire season, we were never to go more than two games with the same backfield intact. Few teams in NFL history have achieved success with that kind of attrition.

Starr sprained the thumb on his throwing hand in an exhibition game, and then suffered a painful rib injury in the Chicago preseason game. He missed exhibitions with Dallas and Cleveland, and when he tried gamely to muster himself for our first two games, he was intercepted nine times—compared with three the entire previous season.

The first of those trying games ended in a discouraging 17–17 tie with Detroit, but in the second we managed a 13–10 squeaker over the Bears on Chandler's forty-six-yard field goal late in the fourth quarter. In the third game Bart was injured early in the contest, and Bratkowski came in to direct a 23–0 win over the Atlanta Falcons.

In a rematch with Detroit in the fourth week of the season, Ray Nitschke broke the game open with a fourth-quarter interception and runback for a touchdown that spurred us to a 27–17 victory. But he, too, was hurting in a year that saw almost every Packer among the "walking wounded." One of his legs was so gimpy that he hobbled into the end zone like a crippled sea captain.

The following week it was Minnesota's turn to intercept late in the game and hand us a 10–7 loss, perpetuating their so-called "home jinx" over us despite the absence of Fran Tarkenton. That's when the latent critics began their annual chirping about the Packers being "old men, over the hill." Before our sixth game, with the Giants in New York, co-captain Bob Skoronski decided to make the pregame talk to the team in the locker room. "I'm tired as hell of being called an old man," he told his teammates, and he suggested that they go out and prove their youth by whipping the young club that held the league offensive lead through the first five weeks.

# PACKER DYNASTY

We trailed 14–10 at halftime, but the return of Bart Starr re-established our rhythm, and two key interceptions re-established our momentum. We went on to post a twenty-eight-point fourth quarter for a 48–21 win over old nemesis Tarkenton and his new crew. The previous year we had struggled for five or six games before we became a good team, and we were doing it again, we felt.

The next week, on Halloween night in St. Louis, we got another boost: a ninety-three-yard lightning strike that gave the world of professional football a new worry, Travis Williams. It was an historic evening, for suddenly the kickoff runback became a "play" in our book and that of other teams around the league, and the popularity of the "squib" kickoff would rise in the weeks to come. Williams did what a Gale Sayers or a Lem Barney can do, but he did it in the most spectacular way. With the score 23–17 in favor of the Cardinals after a Jim Bakken field goal, he took a fourth-quarter kickoff at the St. Louis seven, streaked up the field past twenty-one startled men, and tore ninety-three yards for the touchdown that put us ahead for good. Another touchdown and conversion made it a 31–23 triumph. Early in the year, Travis had fumbled repeatedly in practice, and he began to lose confidence in himself. But Henry Jordan took him aside one day in the locker room and told him, "Travis, here in Green Bay we don't consider that thing a football. It's bread: twenty-five thousand dollars." He didn't fumble it for the remainder of the season.

The next week Baltimore not only chewed up Grabowski and Pitts, they handed us our second loss by scoring thirteen points in the final minutes on two Unitas touchdown passes that wiped out our ten-point lead. The 13–10 final tally gave them great joy, for it was precisely the same score as the sudden-death playoff of 1965 for which they had never forgiven us.

It gave them joy, but it made us furious. The following week we met the Browns in Milwaukee, and we worked up such a passion all week long that we were like uncaged tigers at the beginning of the game. The kickoff went to Travis Williams, and he promptly ran it back eighty-seven yards for a touchdown.

## PACKER DYNASTY

Before the quarter was over, he would do it again from virtually the same spot. The first-quarter score was 35–7 for the Packers, and the game ended in a 55–7 rout that squelched all talk of age slowing the Packer running game. Four of our seven touchdowns came on runs by Anderson and Williams.

Victories over San Francisco, Minnesota, and Chicago sewed up the Central Division title for us. We lost our final two games for a less than spectacular 9–4–1 record, but there was no lessening of pride or desire in those defeats.

Facing a Los Angeles team that was on the way to a brilliant and hard-fought win over the strong Baltimore Colts for their division title, we played not like we were resting on our laurels, but as if we needed and wanted to win. It would have been easy to rationalize coasting through the last two games and saving our strength, but that would have been counter to our teachings. So we threw ourselves at the vaunted Fearsome Foursome with everything we had—remembering that we, too, had carried that name and reputation for many years. At halftime we led 10–7, and with a minute remaining, we led 24–20. A blocked punt and, with thirty-four seconds remaining, a brilliantly executed fake-and-pass play gave the Rams a "must" victory, 27–24. The following week, frankly, we did rest a bit and played our reserves. The Steelers sneaked past us 24–17 while we were looking ahead to a playoff with either the Rams or the Colts, two powers that had already dealt us defeats, each by the narrow margin of three points. As it turned out, it would be a climactic return match with the Rams in Milwaukee.

By the end of the season, it had become standard practice among our opponents not to kick off in the direction of Travis Williams. His performances against the Cardinals and the Browns were the sensations of the day, and opponents who saw the films laid plans to prevent his explosive runbacks. In our December 9 game against the Rams, they had just gently kicked the ball close to the ground the first couple of times— squib kicks that were fallen upon at the thirty or thereabouts. After they had gotten ahead 17–10 in the third quarter, they became a bit cocky and booted a regular, deep kickoff in

## PACKER DYNASTY

Travis's direction. He took it in the end zone and ran it back 104 yards for a touchdown to tie it up. It was the sensational rookie's fourth runback score in seven weeks, all of them blasting straight up the middle.

Consequently, when we met December 23 in the Western Conference playoff, the Rams stuck with the squibs, and as a result we got the ball on the thirty-five or forty. Despite those advantages, we lost the ball three times early in the game on two fumbles and an interception to trail, 7–0. But, as is always the case in the "big" games, we were particularly determined to win. First we blocked a field goal attempt, which reversed the momentum. Then our offensive line began to show that it could neutralize defensive end Deacon Jones by double-teaming him and running plays right at him. That further demoralized the Rams, and our offense caught fire. A thirty-nine-yard punt return by Tom Brown followed immediately by a forty-six-yard touchdown sprint by Williams showed Los Angeles that we were ready to roll. Dale, Mercein, and Williams added three more scores for the 28–7 win and our third straight Western Conference crown.

One reason the Ram scoring punch was negated after the initial quarter was that tough old veteran Henry Jordan pressured Roman Gabriel all day, felling the huge quarterback four times for losses. "Never mind the Fearsome Foursome," Jordan's counterpart, Ron Kostelnik, laughed. "We've got our Fearsome Onesome." By the time the toast had made it once around the locker room, it came out: "Never mind the Fearsome Foursome, we've got the Fearsome Forty." Lombardi summed it up: "A lot of people said we were dead, but we can still rise to the occasion." Indeed, if there was one thing we liked about the new divisional setup, it was the fact that it placed more emphasis on the key games at the end of the season. As everybody knows, the Packers are at home in that kind of situation.

And so, the Cowboys again. Returning to the Cotton Bowl in preseason play, we had beaten them, 20–3. A reminder of the past. A new thorn in their sides. Now we would meet them at Lambeau Field on New Year's Eve . . . for us, a chance to realize the Impossible Dream . . . for them, an opportunity to replace us at the pinnacle.

The sights, sounds, and sensations on that frigid afternoon in Green Bay added a strange new dimension to the usual tenseness and ethereal quality of a championship arena. Coming into the stadium to "warm up" in thirteen-degrees-below-zero weather, it was not the cold we noticed first, but the red halo surrounding the playing field. In September, the coloration of the shirt-sleeve crowd is light and white; in October it turns to the brown of car coats splotched with the autumnal hues of women's hats and scarves. Today the hunting jackets, lap robes, and Peruvian helmet-masks gave a bright blood tinge to the stands. I only had time to notice the crowd for a brief instant as we first emerged from under the stands, but on this day of days, the panorama of red left an unusually vivid imprint on my mind.

On the field, the turf crackled at the first footfall, then turned slippery. Through the practice period and the early minutes of the game, brittle frost-green gave way to glistening moist-green as cleated shoes eventually found and erased every virgin trace.

Over all the familiar sounds—horns, hands on leather, breathless panting, the hawking of wares, and impatient whistles—came the alien rumble of hollow-throated gas heaters blowing furiously into tarpaulin lean-to constructions at the sidelines. Sometimes the collision of hot, fume-laden heated air and cold north winds created a dissonant chord over which men standing a foot apart had to raise their voices to be heard. When they did, their frosty sentences hung visibly above their heads for an instant like the words in a comic strip and then were wafted away to be replaced by others.

In football, weather dictates style, not outcome. Total yardage in this game would be under four hundred all told, less than Dallas alone gained in the previous year's meeting when conditions lent themselves to the bullets and fast getaways that characterize the Cowboys. It looked very much like a Green Bay-approved script for a while. Our initial march began on the eighteen and took sixteen plays—almost evenly divided between short passes and rushing. Early in the second quarter, Starr found himself in his favorite situation: third-and-one, just past midfield. He faked his fullback into the line, stepped back, and sighted his fleet end, Boyd Dowler, outrunning the Dallas safety. The frozen fingertip catch gave us a fourteen-point lead reminiscent of the early margin a year before.

Then the "breaks," which is a handy catch-all label for the other side's defensive moments and our uncharacteristic lapses, all went the other way. Two Dallas ends looped in from either side while the rush was forcing Starr back deep in his own territory; the first man dumped him as he raised his arm, and the other scooped up the fumbled ball for a quick score. A short while later, a punt deep into our territory slipped through the surest hands on our squad—those of Willie Wood—and Dallas recovered. Our ability to hold gave them only three points instead of seven, for a 14–10 halftime score.

Dallas adjustments at halftime were superbly intelligent, ranging from realigned blocking patterns that hampered our defense to the innovation of cutting a small slit in the front of Don Meredith's jersey so he would have a place to warm his passing hand between plays. Realizing that our receivers were taking longer to make their cuts on the icy field, they made their rush take advantage of the extra moments Starr needed to wait, and as a result they got to him more in the third period than most teams get to him in an entire game.

We made some changes, too, of course, but we were just a little less sharp on defense during much of the second half. It happens when you've been playing heads-up ball for two quarters and your mind is about to split from talking to itself constantly for an hour or more. "Move here. . . . I've got to do this if he. . . . When I hear the snap, I. . . . If he cuts, he'll try to. . . . The signal; I should get the signal from. . . . Last year on this play he. . . ." Suddenly you stop talking to your-

## PACKER DYNASTY

self for just an instant, and there it is: a big gain, maybe a critical scoring play. Being just "a little less sharp" against a team like Dallas can be disastrous.

The miscalculation that put us in the hole came on the first play of the fourth quarter, after a scoreless third period that saw the Cowboys succeeding, but not breaking loose, with sweeps to the left by Dan Reeves. Dallas took over near midfield after a short punt. They ran the Meredith-to-Reeves handoff again, but this time they triggered the halfback pass option. Our right cornerback started moving up instead of back for a fatal instant, and that left receiver Lance Rentzel streaking unattended toward the end zone. A well-aimed ball was heading for the same spot. Suddenly it was 17–14, and our defensive backs agonized over their failure to communicate quickly enough to decipher the play and break it. It was particularly maddening because we well knew that Dallas springs the play once every game—often to Bob Hayes—and in almost every previous meeting we had denied them a score on it.

After that, the fourth quarter was much the same scoreless tussle that the third had been; we were thoroughly ineffective on two tries at mounting a drive. With four and a half minutes to go, we got our last chance at the triple crown, the Super Bowl, immortality, and a renewal of our pride and confidence in ourselves.

Earlier in the game, when Bob Skoronski had broken his helmet on a jarring block and had stood helplessly at the sidelines waiting for the equipment manager to find him another that would fit, Lombardi had yelled impatiently, "How can you fall asleep on a day like this?" It was not really a criticism of the blameless individual as much as an expression of Lombardi's insistence that everybody and everything must fall into proper place in order to win a critically tough game. His words, though voiced almost absently and immediately forgotten by him, did not die. They became part of the vapor cloud that hung in the air and spread along the bench area. "How can you fall asleep on a day like this? Fall asleep? A day like this!" The players had learned not to let Lombardi's harsh words hurt them deeply, but they had also grown accustomed to their strange power to provide the necessary catalyst.

"Fall asleep on a day like this?"

Suddenly, on that last drive, we were not asleep. Perception quickly returned. Execution was sharp. Starr showed that characteristic, cool ability to rally the team; his receivers and runners suddenly clicked on every play. Coaches Jerry Burns and Bob Schnelker in the pressbox relayed the information the offense needed to put together a drive. Donny Anderson caught two passes for crucial yardage. After an option pass failed to click, Starr and Anderson teamed up for a twelve-yard surprise looped right over the heads of onrushing linemen. A moment later, again denied his long receiver, Starr safety-valved it again to Anderson, this time for nine yards. Each time Donny managed to move on the ice, and his second run gave us a first down on the Dallas thirty with two minutes to go. "On that drive, you became a man," Lombardi told him.

On the next play, Starr found Chuck Mercein, the fullback acquired from the NFL reject list to compensate for the injuries in our backfield, and he eluded tacklers all the way to the Dallas eleven, where he went out of bounds to stop the clock.

At that point, within striking distance and pressed for time, most football teams—college or pro—would have gone for a sweep, a rollout, or a short pass into the end zone, four times in a row if necessary. The pass attempts, if incomplete, would have stopped the clock, avoiding the necessity of using up valuable time outs.

But this was no average game. We would not run the risk of interception or using an inordinate amount of time running around in the backfield. That ran counter to the entire Packer philosophy. Instead, Starr and Lombardi did what they had done for years in putting together championship victories: They made use of the information they had received during the period of preparation that started months ago and continued right up to the previous play.

With first-and-ten on the eleven, Starr called a play to take advantage of the fact that our young left guard, Gale Gillingham, had been hard pressed to keep All-Pro Bob Lilly at bay. At the snap, Gillingham pulled and headed to his right—indication of a running play to that side. But it was sucker bait—the kind of trick you can put over on a wise veteran only rarely, and then after careful preparation. It also called for a sure block on the defensive end by our left tackle, Bob Skoronski. Starr handed the ball to Mercein, who bolted through the hole vacated by Gillingham and already passed through by Lilly, who had the mistaken notion that he was pursuing a play to the strong side. Pushing, shoving, struggling, writhing, Mercein made his way to the Dallas three. On the next play, Anderson ran at the line. It was first and goal to go on the one.

First and goal to go with half a minute remaining. A script already played out in reverse a year earlier in Dallas. Glued to their television screens, a third of a nation's people could hardly believe what they were seeing. To those of us at the Packer sideline, however, it was a drill becoming reality, a set of statistics turned into twenty-two live, breathing football players massed at one end of the stadium making tomorrow morning's headlines.

No time for fanciness. What was called for now was a halfback plunge over right guard. If it did not work, we would call an immediate time out to stop the clock, and then we would probably run it again. Anderson got the call. On the slippery turf, he would have been expected to dig in his cleats for the necessary traction. Against some teams he might have done that. But not against the alert Cowboy defense; they would have read his intentions. So he merely lined up and waited for Starr to wheel after the snap and put the ball in his belly. It went with precision until Anderson tried to pump his legs. He slipped to the ground for no gain. Time out, and then another try. Again the snap, the ball gathered in, the feet digging for traction and slipping out from under him. Anderson barely managed to hold onto the ball.

Time out with twenty seconds left—our last time out. A field goal would have given us a 17–17 tie and the sudden death playoff again. Two gambles: first that the kick would be good, then that we could win in overtime once more. Fate might not give us the first chance to score, and there might not be a second. Starr walked to the sideline to confer with Lombardi, both men knowing in their own minds that they wanted to go for the touchdown. With the time outs used up, it would have to come on this down.

The play would be straight at their line. On an icy field with time running out, there could be no wavering from the true course. Should it be a dive over the line by the halfback, or a wedge play with the fullback carrying the ball? Guard Jerry Kramer had prepared for such a situation as this by watching an entire reel of Dallas goal-line stand films to study the moves of the man he would face. He noted that the Cowboy left tackle held his head just a bit too high for maximum efficiency at digging in at the goal. Kramer had informed his coaches of the observation before the game, and he reiterated it to his quarterback now. Lombardi gave his assent to calling the wedge.

On the way back to the huddle, Bart continued to percolate the play in his mind. He pondered the treacherous footing that had caused Anderson to slip twice, and he realized that the same fate might befall Mercein, his fullback. But the quarterback, in an erect stance, with a clear view and a split-second head start after the snap, might just lunge into the momentary opening and fall over the top. He deliberated all the way back to the huddle, where he called the wedge. But he didn't tell his teammates of his decision to keep the ball himself. Later speculation about who was responsible for "one of the greatest gambles in the history of professional football" would neglect the simple truth that three men who had worked together for nine years were involved, and none could have made the decision alone. In that moment, the secret of the Green Bay Packers was bared to those who could perceive it.

At the snap, Kramer, aided by center Ken Bowman, hoisted his man aside, and Starr lunged over Jerry's right leg into the momentary gap. Into the end zone. Victory!

At that moment of triumph, the most uncharacteristic behavior erupted. Lombardi, who had been standing stiffly in his overcoat and fur cap, hands plunged into his pockets, suddenly threw his arms up over his head in joyous approval of the same signal from the official who stood over Starr and Kramer. Henry Jordan, standing near me, grinned and winked, "Whatayasay, Phil . . . another day, another dollar, huh?" Boyd Dowler, who had run a short pattern and then cut back to the five, realized what had happened and suddenly sprang like a deer across the expanse of field toward Lombardi, whose hands were back at his side by then. Straight at his coach the ebullient player ran, plunking his ample hands down upon Vince's shoulders and propelling himself high into the air over the man's head. It sounds ridiculous. Any other time it would have been.

## 12 · THE LAST RIDE
## OF VINCE LOMBARDI

AFTER THE emotional peaks of the last two weeks in December—in fact, after the whole mountain range of emotional peaks over the past three years—it was difficult to get the players up for the second Super Bowl, this one in Miami. Gone was the incessant publicity posing the question, "Is the AFL as strong as the NFL?" Gone were the concerns over the perils of old age colliding with youth; the value of experience had been proven against Kansas City. Gone, too, were the taunts of the opposition that could fire a team out of complacency. Where Kansas City had bragged of innovations and itched for a "showdown," Oakland coach Johnny Rauch and his players admitted nothing but respect for the Packers and allowed that they would have to take advantage of every break and be in top form if they were to win.

Followers of the game expressed little doubt over the outcome a week in advance, as we set up temporary training headquarters in Fort Lauderdale. When we came out to practice on the same field used by the New York Yankees for spring training, some of our Green Bay fans were there with a banner reading "Packers 37, Raiders 10." They had the total points right and were off just four points on either end. At about the same time, the New York *Times* was reporting the breakdown on Las Vegas oddsmaker Jimmy (The Greek) Snyder's fourteen-point nod in favor of the Packers. He gave us two points for Starr over Lamonica, two for Nitschke over their middle linebacker, two for our defensive front four, a whopping four points for our defensive backs, plus two for receivers Dowler and Dale. The two extra points were allotted to "intangibles": Coach Lombardi and the Packers' "big game" record. While we don't make any use of the odds, it's always nice to know they're running that heavily in our favor.

What helped us most to prepare was a film of the Oakland-Kansas City game—now we at least had the experience of playing the Chiefs once—and the detailed report by our chief scout, Wally Cruice. Meeting with the coaching staff, Wally went over some general points first. He pointed out that Oakland had a great many Packer and Wisconsin ties that would give them emotional fuel. Their star back, Pete Banaszak, came from Crivitz, Wisconsin, and center Jim Otto was from Wausau. Quarterback Daryle Lamonica was the Packers' twelfth draft choice in 1963. On the defense, end Ben Davidson and back Howie Williams were former Packers—Williams had been with our 1962 NFL championship team and Davidson with our 1961 title winners. And then there was quarterback and kicker George Blanda, whose familiarity with us dated back to his days as the right arm of Papa Bear Halas.

As Wally ticked off the merits of the Oakland offense, a "control" team as we are, with a strong running attack, I took notes so I would know what to watch for in the films:

Daryle Lamonica, quarterback: Likes to work from play action . . . rollouts, bootlegs; can drop back and throw, though.

Hewritt Dixon, fullback: Strong runner, big and powerful. Heavier than press book indicates.

Pete Banaszak, running back: Not impressive in size or moves, but churns out yards. Watch him if he gets an opening.

Fred Biletnikoff, flanker: One of the best in his league. Other ends, Miller and Cannon, are hot, too. All are heavy guys. ("Jeez," Cruice interjected, "the last time they weighed those guys was in high school.")

Gene Upshaw, offensive lineman: A rookie, but he sure doesn't look like it. Treat him like a veteran.

Jim Otto, center: AFL-All Star team. One of the great ones.

Remainder of offensive line: All big, strong men who are good straight-ahead blockers.

With a rundown like that, and additional comments on special abilities and past performances thrown in for good measure, I had no cause to take our defensive task lightly. As I completed my notes, Cruice went on to describe the "Angry Eleven" Oakland defense to Lombardi and his offensive aides. It was a light, fast outfit that stunted, blitzed, and moved around, showing a different defense on every play. They had succeeded all season long in confusing AFL offenses by varying the positioning of their line and linebackers. The defensive backs reacted with lightning speed and had been known to snatch the ball right out of the hands of unwary would-be receivers.

One more scouting note wrapped it up: Blanda was the hottest kicker going at the time. His four-field-goal performance in the AFL championship game made him a serious threat any time they penetrated our side of the field. We walked out of the session knowing that we had to teach and preach as much as ever to ensure that the players had the winning attitude on Super Sunday.

Starting on the Tuesday before the game, our practices were closed to reporters—again, so that we could devote all our attention to preparations without the pressures of national press attention that a bowl game brings. But it turned out that the secrets which tantalized the scribes more than our selection of plays were the private thoughts of Vince Lombardi regarding his career. At every luncheon meeting or chance encounter they pressured him about rumors that he intended to quit coaching while he was on top. Vince was smilingly noncommittal—even cagey—about it at first, but soon it began to wear on him, and he cut off all inquiries. He was still thinking it over: "A long, hard look at Vince Lombardi," he would call it after the game.

## PACKER DYNASTY

But those close to him knew that he was drawing inexorably to the conclusion that he had carried his coaching career to the summit, and now there beckoned an even more challenging career of business management—both in and out of professional football.

In that subtle way he had of phrasing questions about "next year" to me—the careful wording of an otherwise inconsequential reference to a future event—he gave me to understand which direction he was heading. And he knew where I fit in. With his careful sense of timing and his shrewd psychology, he would not upset the delicate pregame balances by making an announcement of any sort.

But as the week wore on, the players began to sense something. It began to look like Packer Old Home Week in Miami, with former players, including Paul Hornung, on hand. And there were former Lombardi assistant coaches, plus expatriates of Green Bay, who were combining a Florida vacation with renewal of old gridiron loyalties. After the last practice session on Friday, Vince called the team together.

"I want to say, first of all, that we all know we can win our second Super Bowl trophy Sunday; but we are all old hands at this game, and we also know we have to work harder than ever without letting up for one minute. I . . ." There was a pause for just a brief second, and a few heads moved slightly to discern if indeed there was a slight catch in the usually strong, husky Lombardi voice. "I . . . want to tell you how very proud I am of . . . of all of you. I have told you before that you are the finest team in professional football. It's been a long season and Sunday . . . may be the last time we are all together. Let's make it a good game, a game we can all be proud of." By now most everyone was looking down, away. They did not have to see his face to know there was a tear in his eye. They knew, because every eye in the room was moist, and every throat was dry.

As it had been the previous year, the first half was an exploratory one, and the score was similar after the first thirty minutes: 16–7, in our favor; it had been 14–10 against Kansas

City. But there were some big differences: We had scored four times to once for Oakland, and Don Chandler had proven as hot on field-goal attempts as his rival, Blanda, was reputed to be, with boots of thirty-nine, twenty, and forty-three yards. Nitschke was magnificent as the defense stopped the first Oakland drive in its tracks, and Starr had calmly moved the offense from our own three to the second field goal. Shortly after, he faked to Williams and hit Dowler for a sixty-two-yard touchdown pass play. The defense then denied Oakland a score the second time they got in our territory, and moments later a fumble of one of Anderson's relatively unfamiliar left-footed punts set up our third field goal.

Despite the favorable omens, we didn't feel a nine-point halftime lead was sufficient—especially if Lamonica and Blanda started connecting with their long-distance calls. In the coaches' room, Lombardi went over our deficiencies so we could take the necessary corrective action. But the decision that really sewed the game up for us was being made at the same time in the players' dressing room. A group of veterans who remembered winner-take-all championship games in Philadelphia, New York, Dallas, and the first Super Bowl as well as three in Green Bay, realized that this might be their last chance to win a title for Vince Lombardi. They gravitated toward a corner of the locker room: Gregg, Jordan, Nitschke, Davis, Starr, Dowler, Kramer, Skoronski, Thurston, and McGee. For Fuzzy and Max it would be the last time they wore Packer uniforms. Ten men who had come all the way. They vowed to "play the last thirty minutes for the Old Man," bestowing the Navy term of endearment on the captain who had charted a happy and profitable course for them over the past nine years. Acknowledging that they had made more than the usual number of mental mistakes purely out of excitement, they spread the word that the entire team would have to settle down to the accustomed pattern of cool, calculated play in the second half.

And that is pretty much what happened. We held the Raiders to minimal yardage and one more score late in the final period. Meanwhile, Starr's bomb to McGee and a run by Anderson

## PACKER DYNASTY

gave us one touchdown, Herb Adderley's sixty-yard runback of an interception gave us another, and Chandler added his last field goal for the 33–14 outcome. About the only question on anyone's mind in the final minutes was the whereabouts of fullback Ben Wilson's contact lens. He spent the last eight minutes on his hands and knees looking anxiously for the $43.50 piece of plastic while the Super Bowl management was filling out a fifteen-thousand-dollar check in his name.

At the final gun—of the game, and, as it would turn out, a Packer coaching career—Lombardi was expertly elevated to the shoulders of Jerry Kramer and Forrest Gregg. "One more time, Coach," said Kramer, beaming, and Lombardi grinned back, "This is the best way to leave a football field."

Back in the dressing room, he mixed his usual frank comments with the expected praise: "This wasn't our best effort—we let up too much when we got ahead. But I have to say we moved the ball very well. We didn't get into the end zone often, but we scored almost every time we got down there." By then newsmen were pressing him about his career, but he just smiled and said they would have to wait.

Only a professional football coach could end a third successful quest for the ultimate crown by worrying over a few little imperfections. Everyone else added to the almost embarrassing chorus of hallelujahs to the team. "The difference is not between the leagues," said the managing general partner of the Raiders, Al Davis. "It's between the Packers and anybody else." Similar praise came from sportswriter Red Smith, who opined: "The Packers are better than the Raiders. They are also better than fifteen teams in the National Football League. It's as simple as that."

When the plaudits and the celebrating were over and the annual league business had been transacted in Miami, the players left for family vacations, rounds of speaking engagements, visits to business interests, or just plain well-deserved rest. Vince and I returned to Green Bay to make some hard decisions.

"I sit here and marvel," he sighed, looking out at the slow

traffic on ice-rutted Highland Avenue outside Packer headquarters. "I marvel that I tried to do both jobs for all those years." He had just pronounced our formal agreement to realign the operation, with him as full-time general manager and me moving up to head coach. He reiterated his ever-growing role, as the equivalent of team owner, in the details of merging the two leagues and dealing with increasing player-management problems. He also discussed his new enterprise with a group of businessmen involved in the building of housing for low-income groups. After pacing and talking a while, he sat on the edge of his huge wooden desk and looked at me placidly, smiling. "You know, everybody is going to be second-guessing us. We're both taking a pretty big leap. But I think we both kind of do what we feel we have to do. The sporting end of football is almost all emotions; the business end has to be hard practicalities. Right?"

I nodded in agreement, and before I left his office, he told me he would prepare a news release announcing the changeover, probably for delivery at a sports dinner on the first of February at the Oneida Golf and Riding Club.

All hard practicalities? No emotions?

When Vince called eighty-three-year-old Ray Lombardi to tell him the news, his father pleaded: "For what you have given up coaching? You should coach forever, Vinnie." Vince choked back emotions and tried to explain the hard practicalities.

After the final decision had been made, my wife and I sat in the two large reclining chairs in our family room and talked much later into the night than usual. I mentioned the hard practicality of the generous insurance policy that would be part of my Packer compensation. "Remember what Dad Bengtson used to tell you during the thirties?" Kathryn mused. "'Football is too uncertain a business; you should go into something solid, like insurance.' What do you think he'd say now?"

The day of the announcement, Vince's secretary came into my office and sat down. "I've never seen him so nervous," she confided. "The door has been closed for more than an hour with the telephone off the hook." Vince was working on his statement. Meanwhile his staff was making last-minute preparations to accommodate more than a hundred sportsmen and newswriters at what was to have been a more or less intimate dinner for a selected few. It was getting to be as tense as the kickoff of a championship game.

At the dinner, the moment for the announcement finally came, and Vince stepped up to the battery of microphones. Hands trembling, he pulled a packet of five sheets of paper from his breast pocket and spread them on the speaker's lectern. He had handwritten his remarks in huge script letters three-quarters of an inch tall with a grease pen like the ones he always used to sketch play patterns on a notepad. He looked around the crowded room, lifted a clenched hand to his mouth for a brief moment, and then forced a small smile.

"What I have to say is not completely without emotion," he began. "Because of the emotion involved, I felt I could not trust myself to say what I must say unless it was written." (Vince Lombardi, who had bellowed at and berated men twice his size, demanding subservient excellence, tolerating no rebuff.)

He outlined very briefly the growth of pro football and the Packers, and the increasing responsibility of the general manager's job. Because they had been a part of that growth, and because they knew what Lombardi was leading up to, the rapt audience of newsmen and Packer corporate officers waited breathlessly for the final words.

"I believe it is impractical for me to do both jobs, and feel I must relinquish one of them. . . ." A moment later he read the last words on his paper: "Gentlemen, let me introduce the new head coach of the Packers. . . ." The written words ended there. When he spoke my name, I rose, and he led the applause. There were tears in his eyes, and as I stood there, I felt more drained of energy than after the toughest game I could remember. When you make your living telling other men to maintain their poise while performing near-impossible tasks, it's strange to suddenly find yourself thrust into the same situation. The torch had been passed.

In answer to the inevitable question, I responded, "I hope we will be able to continue the winning tradition of the Green Bay Packers." I knew what a challenge that would be. But like every Green Bay Packer, I had learned to love that challenge.

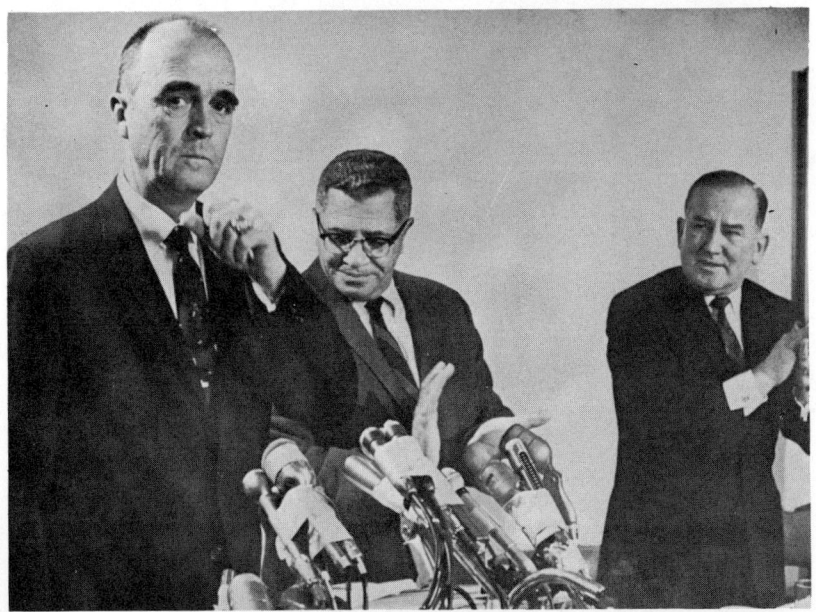

CHANGING OF THE GUARD — When Vince Lombardi took over at Green Bay in 1959, he was backed up by six assistants: (from left) Norb Hecker, Bill Austin, Pat Peppler, Red Cochran, myself, and Tom Fears. Nine years later, following his emotional announcement, I took over the head coaching job from Vince. Packer president Dominic Olejniczak is at right.

PHOTOS BY VERNON J. BIEVER

SURE COMBINATIONS — Here are superstars who spelled success for the Packers in the 1960s. At left, quarterback Bart Starr confers on the bench with fullback Jim Taylor and halfback Paul Hornung. Below, Starr holds as Don Chandler puts another three points on the scoreboard.

ENDLESS SUMMER — Behind December's glories are July's labors. In an early year, Coach Austin positions a swinging dummy for rookies running through a blocking drill, while I look on. More recently, assistant Bob Schnelker watches his receivers taking turns on a pass drill while I exercise the head coach's prerogative of expressing vehement displeasure.

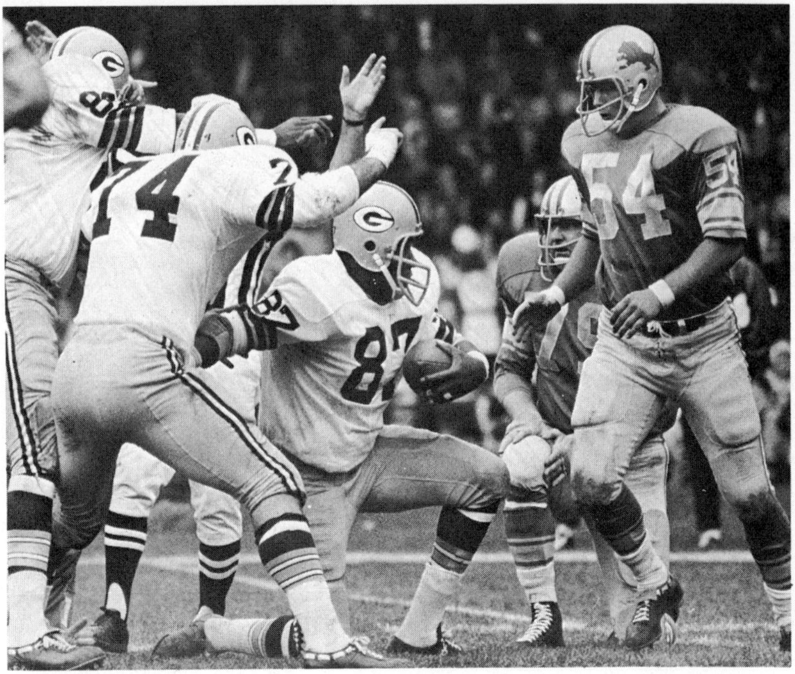

DEFENSE AT WORK — Nothing could make a defensive coach happier than the scenes on these two pages. Defensive end Willie Davis, above, has snapped up a loose ball that belonged to the Lions a moment earlier. Tackle Henry Jordan (74) is optimistically indicating the direction to the end zone. Cowboy Don Meredith, below, has notions about handing off to Don Perkins for a big gain, but tackle Ron Kostelnik is bursting through the line with something else in mind. This was one of our big defensive plays in the 1966 championship at Dallas.

MOTION DEFEATED — Linebackers are a beautiful sight as they deny the opponent a gain. Lee Roy Caffey (60) smothers a Lion while Ray Nitschke burrows up from underneath to see if he can jar the ball loose. Below, Caffey comes in from Fran Tarkenton's blind side, a move that will prevent the tricky Giant signal caller from passing or escaping for one of his famous scrambles.

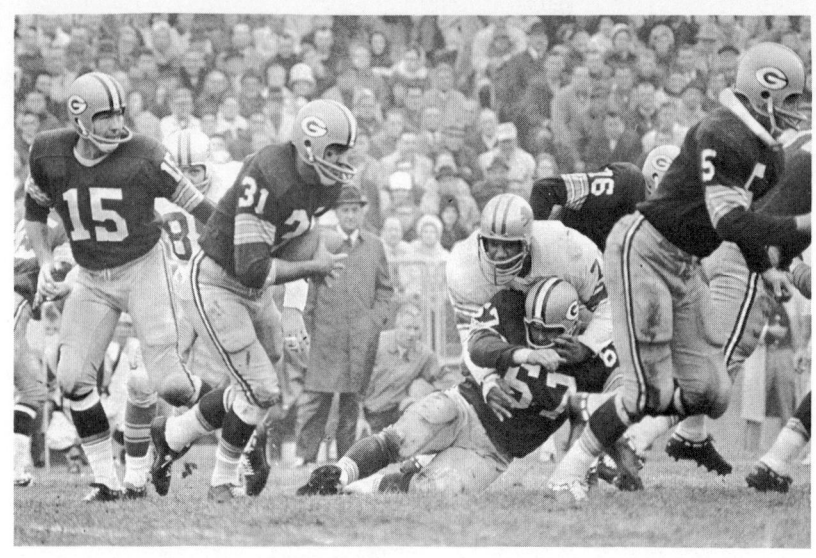

TWO CLASSICS — Here are the all-time Packer bread-and-butter plays. In days of old it was Starr handing off to Taylor, above, with Hornung running ahead to block for him. In recent times, the format, below, is Gale Gillingham (68) and Jerry Kramer (64) pulling to the left as Starr hands off to Donny Anderson.

MAGNIFICENT MOMENTS – A second glance at these apparently hopeless tangles reveals the essence of "basic" football as the Packers play it. Above, Jim Taylor finds a momentary hole in the line, opened by guard Kramer and tackle Forrest Gregg (75). In the play that won the cliff-hanging 1967 championship against Dallas, below, Starr hurls himself over the goal line through the hole opened by Kramer. A jubilant Chuck Mercein (30) signals victory.

SIDELINE CONFERENCE — Head coach and quarterback must communicate constantly to keep pace with defensive adjustments. When a great field general like Bart Starr is in charge of carrying out the game plan, the coach rarely needs to send in a play. Our sideline conferences are mostly exchanging of information and ideas.

PHOTOS BY VERNON J. BIEVER

# PART TWO

# THE MEN, THE MACHINERY, AND THE MYSTIQUE

## 13 · THE BIGGEST LITTLE MAJOR LEAGUE CITY IN THE WORLD

"**P**RO FOOTBALL can't possibly stay in Green Bay," wrote a famous New York sportswriter thirty years ago, after the Packers had leveled the Giants 27–0 for the league championship. The wise scribe explained that the game was, unfortunately, growing too fast for the small Wisconsin city to continue supporting a team.

As recently as 1961 a newspaperman in Toledo wrote, "It seems silly to play a National Football League championship game in cold and remote little Green Bay, Wisconsin." A few days later, he admitted his mistake in the same column, citing an eloquent rebuttal by a former Packer living in Toledo who said: "Maybe I sound corny about Green Bay, but ask any of the guys who played there . . . they'll tell you exactly what I'm telling you. It's the biggest little major league city in the world."

More recently, when Coach Lombardi warned fellow NFL managers that athletes like Jim Taylor who played out their options might start a trend for players to seek out "fun cities," a reporter asked him whether he considered Green Bay a fun city. "No," he replied, "it's not a fun city, it's a *great* city."

Lombardi, who has grown steadily more intrigued with the business aspects of football, commissioned a Washington research firm to conduct an economic survey subsequently issued to the public under the splendiferous heading, "An Official Statement of the Green Bay Packers' Contribution to the Communities of Green Bay and Milwaukee and the State of Wisconsin during the 1967 Season." The survey showed that the Packers meant more than 8.5 million dollars in measurable income to the state of Wisconsin, in addition to the considerable indirect economic stimulus provided by a major league sports attraction.

The researchers found that, in addition to the two million dollars spent by the Packers, visiting teams, and the press, more than five million dollars was spent by fans. Vince, always the stickler for details, asked for a complete breakdown, and the firm—thorough as an NFL coach—gave us every individual profile of imaginable use. We learned, for example, that the typical resident of Green Bay spent $2.08 per home game, while the average nonlocal fan spent $4.63. We even learned that the average fan at Lambeau Field spends 14 percent of his football budget for beverages, contrasted with 5 percent for the Milwaukee fan—which apparently indicates the relative celebrating capacities of our two sets of fans.

More important than the measurement of fan characteristics, however, was the "prestige factor" cited by the survey. The researchers found that the Packers have not only made Green Bay the best-known city of its size in the United States, they have made its name synonymous with excellence. The cities of Green Bay and Milwaukee both benefit from "the image of success conveyed, an image of teamwork, efficiency, and precision," the survey concluded.

The research report merely translated into cold statistics what anyone who visits Green Bay soon learns: Pro football there is business, entertainment, culture, social life, and chief conversational topic all rolled into one. The town fairly lives and breathes Packers.

In how many towns of its size do the yellow pages of the telephone book list "Football Clubs" between "Foot Specialists" and "Foreign Cars"? How many towns have restaurants that suggest you start the day with a "Linebacker Special"

## PACKER DYNASTY

(hearty breakfast topped off with a steak) and commence an evening with a "Quick Opener" (appetizers)? Where else could you turn on the radio one frosty morning in January to hear this all-points bulletin: "There is a cocker spaniel missing in the vicinity of Chateau Drive and Oneida. Will anybody who has seen the dog please call the following number so that Cherry Starr can leave for the Super Bowl. . . ."

Where else can you raise a football fan from infancy than in Green Bay? Flatow's Infants' and Children's Wear sells one-piece terry cloth pajamas in Packer colors with the team insignia on the front, starting with size one. When the kid grows out of that, Prange's department store has an official Packer Shop where he can be outfitted in a Packer cardigan sweater ensemble complete with the team insignia on tie clasp and cufflinks.

The Packer green-and-gold combination is virtually the official color of Green Bay, enhancing delivery trucks, signboards, doormats, cigarette urns, waiters' vests, and most everything else that has been replaced or renewed within the past decade. It is no accident that there is a green bench and a yellow fireplug on every major street corner. True, park benches are green and hydrants are yellow in many a town, but in Green Bay it strikes the observer as conscientious exterior decoration. When the new team headquarters were constructed adjacent to Lambeau Stadium, the contractor rejected brick-colored bricks. Nothing less than specially ordered yellow and green bricks would do for the castle at the end of the yellow brick road now known as Lombardi Avenue.

The most humble eateries in town pay allegiance to the team with Know Your Packers placemats. Middle-range supper clubs like the King's X, favorite meeting place of Hornung, McGee, and friends in the early 1960s when it was owned by defensive back Jesse Whittenton, ring the room with spotlighted pictures of Packer greats and mounted footballs inscribed with dates and scores of famous games. The most pretentious dining facilities, like Bilotti's Forum across Oneida Avenue from the stadium, offer a more subtle tribute in the form of planters full of green hedges softly backlighted in yellow. Somehow the effect gives prominence to the yellow-labeled green glass bottles of Cutty Sark lined up next to the emerald cash register.

And anywhere you go in Green Bay, there are the ubiquitous Packer souvenirs. Instead of the cheese, sausage, birchbark tomtoms, and Made-in-Japan "Hi! from Wisconsin" trinkets found elsewhere in the state, the visitor to Green Bay can choose from piggy banks in the shape of a pot-bellied lineman, yellow balloons that inflate to the shape of a football bearing the "Go Packers" legend, half an official helmet mounted on a plaque (only a few available, at twenty-five dollars apiece), sheafs of autographed portraits available in complete sets or individually as premiums from gas stations, placemats printed with newspaper accounts of championship games, drinking glasses covered with team signatures, headscarfs, keychains, lighters, pen and pencil sets, sweatshirts, and most anything else that can be manufactured in yellow and green, imprinted with the Packer name and labeled "official." For the fan who has everything, there's even a "Packer Backer" recording. Sheet music is also available.

More substantial are the "souvenirs" presented to the Packers by the fans of Green Bay after the championships of the early sixties. For the first title we each received a huge silver tray with an inscription in the center. In subsequent years we received other mementoes, including rings and billfolds. The practice was eventually discontinued, not for lack of appreciation by the fans, but because we finally got to be "harder to buy for than old Uncle Charlie at Christmastime," in the words of one member of the Chamber of Commerce.

Another link between town and team is the annual intrasquad game each August. The local police and firemen discovered a few years ago that football is more attractive than the charity ball. So the traditional dances that nobody attended but to which everybody bought a couple of dollars' worth of tickets have given way to the prepreseason game. The uniformed services find the tickets are not only easier to sell and bring in considerably more money, but most everyone uses them. There were thirty-five thousand in the stands last year, more than some professional football teams draw for a league game.

No goal is too big for Green Bay where football is concerned. When it was learned that the U. S. Post Office plans to issue a football stamp on November 6, 1969 to commemorate the hundredth anniversary of the game, a group of citizens convinced the Green Bay Philatelic Society to convince the Green Bay postmaster's advisory committee to convince the federal government to feature Green Bay on the stamp. Undaunted by opinions that Rutgers University, site of the first game, or Canton, Ohio, home of the professional football hall of fame, might be chosen, the citizens made the crux of their appeal the fact that "everybody knows that Green Bay is now the football capital of the country."

# 14 · SUPERFANS:
# THE PACKER BACKERS

IF YOU want to go on a wild goose chase in Green Bay, ask somebody where you can meet the biggest Packer fan in town. Each person you meet admits that he is "maybe the second or third biggest fan in town" and then nominates a friend or neighbor as the Packerphile to end all.

The usual starting place is Holzer's Drug Store at the corner of Pine and Washington in the middle of downtown Green Bay, where genial John Holzer dispenses Packer history along with aspirin and razor blades. Sitting in a booth and munching Vitamin Salad (shredded cabbage, lettuce, carrots, and celery), you scan an entire wall of football memorabilia, including a copy of the original NFL franchise granted to Green Bay on August 21, 1922, and pictures that start with Curly Lambeau's gladiators tussling in the dust of old Hagemeister Park and end with the "Changing of the Guard" on February 1, 1968.

The focal point of the display is Holzer's fragment of the goalpost from the 1961 championship, emblazoned with the 37–0 final score. If you want, John can cite most any other statistic from that and other games. If you're something of an expert yourself, he'll be more than happy to delve into such fine points as comparing the receiving styles of all-time greats Don Hutson of the forties and Bill Howton of the fifties.

If the argument is a standoff, Holzer will doubtless suggest that you drive a few blocks over to North Broadway to let Paul Massellini cast the deciding vote. At Paul's Standard

Oil station, they'll probably tell you to look for him a few doors up, at Martha's Cafe.

When you walk through the door of Martha's you're sure to get a cup of coffee, a slice of Americana and, whether you order it or not, the lowdown on the Packers. Martha's is a typical midwestern lunch counter-restaurant: waitresses in ankle-length socks and tennis shoes, pie of the day, choice of potato salad or mashed with gravy, a Dr. Pepper clock sharing the wall with calendars from two banks and a machinery company, adjacent racks of Sanka, Kellogg's cereals, and Bromo-Seltzer packets, bulging dispensers of paper napkins, varicolored plastic water pitchers, checkered oilcloth tablecovers, plastic roses in cut-glass vases, a rampant philodendron trailing from a pot on top of the cigarette machine, and next to the door a bubble gum vendor sponsored by the Kiwanis Club.

But as you take closer note, you realize that there is more to it: On the south wall hangs a placard bearing two portraits and the legend "Sponsored by Martha's Coffee Club." Pictured are Franklin Ricardo of Colombia and Tse Lai Ngor of Hong Kong, "adopted" through the contributions of club members. At one side of the room, several tables are pushed together to form the arena for an outsized kaffeeklatsch. It is here that the Monday-morning quarterbacks meet to analyze one Sunday's performance and offer prognostications for the next. Matchbooks on the tables at midweek are inscribed with Martha's predictions (Packers 27, Steelers 10), which usually are fairly accurate.

If you find Paul Massellini there, it won't take much coaxing to get him talking about the Packers. He knows the players and staff well, servicing many of their cars and offering us the use of his pickup truck to haul equipment from stadium headquarters to training camp every summer. And he is a part of the club's history. When the new stadium replaced old City Stadium in 1957, he and his friends lovingly and painstakingly dismantled the fence around the old facility and divided it up among the faithful, thereby making them all "plank owners."

If Paul's memory fails, he'll advise you: "Just stick around;

PACKER DYNASTY

the biggest Packer fan of them all will be here any minute." And before long you'll meet Howie Blindauer. Howie, who runs a roofing, siding, and heating firm with his sons, could probably claim and defend the title as well as anybody. He has his own projector and films of Packer games which he takes around to any school, club, or civic group that wants a football program. The show is free, and in recent years he has put it on more than two hundred times, often twice a day. At the beginning of training camp each July, he prints up handbills with the player roster, the season schedule, rules of conduct for spectators at the practice field, and a plug for the Green Bay Packers Hall of Fame. The "program" carries a personal greeting to visitors and is signed: "Howie Blindauer, a sports fan who likes all sports." Last year Howie handed out twenty thousand of them, personally welcoming and aiding almost that many people.

Howie and Paul are great friends of many of the players. A Packer who's looking for a house, needs repair work, or can't get his car started usually finds someone from Martha's Coffee Club coming to his aid. When I mention casually to Paul as he's filling my gas tank that we have a piece of equipment out of order at the office or need emergency construction at our training facilities, I usually get back to the office to find Howie's truck parked outside and workmen already tackling the project. Certainly other pro teams have a good relationship with businesses in the community, but I've never seen anything like the fervor of a Green Bay merchant who finds he can do something to help out the Packers.

When the long confab at Martha's finally recesses, you could head across town to the East Side, where Biebel's Market is as good a place as any to pick up Packer lore. Ray Biebel makes some of the finest sausage in Wisconsin right on the premises; the only thing that attracts more people to his counter is when Bart Starr comes in to buy homemade wieners. "The customers get excited, and my clerks go all to pieces," Ray laughs, shaking his head.

Now that his son can run the operation, Ray likes to travel.

## PACKER DYNASTY

But wherever he goes, he ends up talking Packers. When he was in the St. Louis area, he drove thirty miles out of his way to see the Cardinals at practice. "The equipment was shoddy compared with ours," he reported to friends upon returning to Green Bay. "And the discipline was terrible—the players and onlookers mingled on the field." Ray, like most Packer fans, knows how a taut ship is run and takes pride in every detail of the Green Bay operation.

On a trip to Europe a few years ago, Ray and his wife Dorothy found themselves getting personal attention from the captain of the U.S.S. *Constitution* at his reception. After perfunctory greetings to assorted doctors, lawyers, and industrialists, the skipper took Ray aside and pumped him for the latest dope on Paul Hornung. On their return to the United States, the Biebels found that the Packer stickers on their luggage had the customs man so enthused over their acquaintance with the Packers that he waved them on with only a cursory inspection.

Ray's nominee for top fan goes to Leonard Liebmann, who has a complete scrapbook of Packer clippings for the past decade. His prize possession is not a local paper, but rather the January 3, 1966 issue of the Miami *Herald,* whose sports editors featured an account of the Packer championship higher on the page than the story of their own local game, the Orange Bowl. Len makes an annual trip to the Orange Bowl, and in 1958 he came back from the Clemson-Colorado game with exiting news of the performance by Colorado's Boyd Dowler, which he relayed to Packer headquarters. "I'm practically a scout for Green Bay," he proudly asserts.

Len is a typical lifelong fan who inherited not only his tickets —part of a block of seats bought by the family firm—but the love and understanding of football that comes from attending games over a period of thirty or forty years. "Len's like most Green Bay businessmen," says his wife, Ruth. "They don't have ulcers, because whenever they get together they end up talking football. It's an outlet. That's why Green Bay has grown so phenominally: The businessmen are all relaxed, happy, and able to do a good job. All because of football."

## PACKER DYNASTY

Another happily successful businessman-fan is Eugene Sladky, vice president of one of the biggest banks in Green Bay. In addition to serving as a volunteer door guard outside the Packer locker room during games, he travels with the team and keeps "minutes played" statistics on the individual players—a useful kind of information that most teams don't have the luxury of receiving. He even calculates "seconds played" for the "suicide squads" that come into action only for covering kickoffs. Trivial as the information may seem, it can come in handy for planning. In order to make the best use of personnel, you have to know who is getting what kind of workout and will be in condition to perform the various tasks. Gene gets a genuine kick out of providing that highly specialized information for the Packer machinery.

He has also helped the ticket department for years, drawing on his banking experience when it's needed. When we played our first NFL championship in Green Bay in 1961, nobody had any idea how to handle the flood of ticket requests. Gene and his colleagues came to the rescue, volunteering to work out a ratio system of allocating championship tickets fairly to our season ticket holders in both Milwaukee and Green Bay. Only the publicly owned Packers with two "home" stadiums would face such a problem, and only the Packers could get volunteers to solve it.

The top honors for sartorial splendor among our superfans must go to Clifford Chaulkline, who has a full-length fur coat (and matching cap) which he wears open to display a special Packer vest of yellow leather, covered with autographs of all the players, coaches, and other superfans. When the Packers went to the first Super Bowl, he and his wife Ann designed special warm-weather vestments, including gold sweatshirts bearing green hand-stitched slogans appropriate to the first AFL-NFL meeting. The Chaulkline (the name is punningly appropriate) outfits spend the off-season in a display case in the Packer Hall of Fame museum.

A commendation for being the most unflappable fan should be given to businessman Bill Berger. While on a Wisconsin trade mission to Japan, he received a telephone call from home with news that his plant had caught fire. Before hanging up, he asked for the Packers-Browns score, which he thereupon posted in the Osaka hotel lobby as a public service.

A week later, on that same trip, there seemed no way of getting the score in Hong Kong until Governor Warren Knowles decided it was worth calling his office to find out. The next week, in Bangkok, even a phone call was impossible, so another member of the party who knew an Air Force major stationed nearby managed to arrange a radio hookup to someone who had heard the Packer score over the military network. No matter where in the world they may be, Packer fans want and get their score on Sunday night.

There are probably seventy-five thousand superfans in Green Bay—half again as many as the stadium now holds. A few, like "Old Ed" Longteau, ninety-three, have gracefully retired to a less demanding brand of fanaticism he calls "Packer watching." Ed's home in De Pere, Wisconsin lies right on the route from the dormitory to the dining room which the players walk three times a day in July and August. Sitting in front of his house, Old Ed greets the players, taking note of which veterans are missing this year, which rookies look promising, and who's wearing a cast or a sling today. He no longer gets to the games, but he follows the team by radio after they cease to "check in" with him personally come September.

Most Packer fans are as hardy as the team they cheer, however. When we left for the second Super Bowl in Miami, 250 of them gathered in the windy, ten-below-zero weather at the airport to give us a sendoff.

They're loyal fans. I was dismayed, while watching a televised game late last season when the race in our division was tight, to see the partisans in another NFL town booing the decisions of their quarterback in a losing effort. Only the week before we had lost an important game when we missed three field goal attempts in a row, and there was not a single boo or catcall in Lambeau Stadium. That kind of support can be the crucial difference for a team in the difficult final weeks of a hard race.

## PACKER DYNASTY

That's not to say our fans aren't vociferously adamant about some things. When CBS decided before the 1968 season to end the practice of assigning various sportscasters to teams on a regular basis, it meant that popular Ray Scott would no longer be the exclusive "Voice of the Packers." Green Bay fans were furious when they heard about the rotation of announcers, and in the campaign that followed, thousands of signatures were gathered on petitions and sent to the network's sports director. It was, unfortunately, one of the few efforts by Packer fans that was doomed to fail.

The best measure of fan loyalty, of course, is ticket sales, and that's another department in which Green Bay is among the league leaders. It wasn't always so. Back in the 1940s, it took a concerted effort to sell even a few thousand season tickets in a special campaign. With only three home games scheduled, the club was in danger of losing its franchise. Special intrasquad games at midseason were held to bring in enough capital to keep the club alive, and nonprofit stock drives in 1949 and 1950 salvaged the franchise by turning it over to the public.

Through the lean years, all kinds of gimmicks were necessary to fill the seats at City Stadium. One year it was a prize drawing for season ticket holders. Among the prizes were candy, butter, food baskets, Wisconsin cheese, and permission to sit on the bench during an intrasquad game and be "co-coach" for one quarter. As late as 1956, local merchants took full-page advertisements in the *Press-Gazette,* urging, "Let's fill all the seats for all the games. Unlike every other competitive team, the Green Bay Packers are more than a football team. They are also a city, stubbornly and courageously hanging on to a big-time membership some people think they should never have had. They belong to no millionaire. They are not backed by any wealthy sports group. They are financed by ticket sales, the people who pay to see the Packers in Green Bay and in America's biggest cities."

In tougher times, local businesses were pressured to buy blocks of tickets. The owners would then pass them out to employees or give them as business favors to other concerns. It was the nearest thing to charity.

But all that changed after 1959. By the third year of the new regime, the *Press-Gazette* ad ran, "Please don't write for tickets! Ever try to put 500,000 people into a stadium that seats 38,600?"

Suddenly Packer tickets were the hottest item made and sold in Green Bay, including paper towels. A season ticket costs six dollars times the number of home games, and preference is given to those who have bought in previous years. For eight years now, that has meant virtually no room for new subscribers, and the resulting scramble is legendary. Businessmen who used to begrudge the annual "contribution" now cherish the right. Most of them keep the tickets in the company name and pay for them with a cashier's check so that the ticket privilege will pass on to their children, or at least their co-workers, when they die.

People who finally make it after years of waiting usually find some way of ordering the tickets so they will be assured of having them *in perpetuum* by not ordering them in their own name. One Packer custom is the kids' section of the stadium, reserved for children fourteen years and younger. Some parents go directly from the hospital to the Packer ticket office to get an infant on the kiddee list, and the most agonizing thing that can happen to a boy is to have a fifteenth birthday fall right before the opening of the season.

In Green Bay area divorce cases, the worst haggling is over the kids, the dog, and the Packer tickets. Judges have been known to consider the ducats equal to a car or a family pet. Desperation even leads some who covet tickets to stoop to the ultimate in bad taste: inquiring at a wake what disposition the widow intends to make of her dearly departed's fifty-yard-line seats.

All around the league, the Packers are famous for their drawing power. It's been years since we played to a single empty seat, and when we played the Rams in Los Angeles in 1967, they had a sellout in advance of the game day for the first time since they moved from Cleveland. Attendance was 76,637, and the ticket windows never opened. What's more, that game took precedence over Lynda Bird Johnson's televised wedding on many stations around the country, including the Johnson-owned station in Texas.

June 15 is the deadline for buying season tickets to Lambeau Stadium for previous customers; the date is better known and more closely observed than the income tax deadline. Every year, despite the reminders in the paper and on the radio, and despite the fact that most people talk about nothing else for two weeks, a few hapless souls forget to mail their applications. They might as well join the Foreign Legion once their family learns of the horrendous oversight.

By July 1 last year we were oversubscribed by five thousand seats and had to start returning applications. Two weeks later the "sorry, try next year" pile had mounted to fifteen thousand. Every year disappointed fans ask why we don't add more seats to the stadium—a second deck if necessary. We've given it thought in some headier moments, but in the end we come to the conclusion that there's such a thing as an ideal-sized facility for pro football. If you have too big a stadium, people know they can get in and they'll wait until they know if the game is attractive, the weather's good, or the team is doing well. That means the weatherman, unfortunate injuries to star players, or weakness around the league can wreak havoc on your finances.

But if the stadium is just the right size, the advance sale will fill it to capacity. All the new stadiums around the country —in St. Louis, San Diego, and Minnesota, for example—are the same size as ours, in the fifty to fifty-five thousand range. That's just about right for football's law of supply and demand. When our new stadium was built, the planners wisely set the initial seating at thirty-two thousand, just four thousand more than the old facility. Subsequently one section at a time was added to increase the capacity to fifty thousand. That ended the complaints of other clubs, who get a percentage of our gate, but in an orderly way it kept us from sabotaging our financial base.

Green Bay fans are aware of the financial considerations

and support our moves. In fact, awareness of the operation is a hallmark of our followers. Most of them can quote our profit from last year: It's printed right in the program. Most can give you the numbers and assignments on our standard plays, and Green Bay women pride themselves in being able to describe the functions of a pulling guard or a blitzing linebacker if the cocktail party discussion turns to football. For the Packer Backer is not just a fan. He has probably been a student of the game since childhood, and football is part of his life style.

The local paper summed it up in describing the "somewhat sophisticated, but obviously happy" throng of three thousand who jammed the airport to welcome the team after the second Super Bowl: "The usual banners and shouts of encouragement were there, but the delirious receptions of past championships were not. Instead a certain amount of maturity characterized the crowd. One fan said, 'I guess in a way we're getting like the players in the locker room. They don't whoop it up any more. But we're awfully proud of the team. If we weren't, we wouldn't be out here tonight.'"

## 15 · THE DRAFT: PLAYING FOOTBALL'S STOCKMARKET

**H**E'S HOT stuff at fullback for State Tech: the team's leading ground gainer all season, three touchdowns in the homecoming game, forty-six-yard average on punts, etcetera, etcetera. It means his mother had to start a third scrapbook for his clippings. It also means that the man up in the pressbox for the last game of the season, armed with a blunt-tipped pen and a thick pad of ruled paper, is Pat Peppler, director of player personnel for the Green Bay Packers.

A couple of seventy-five-yard runs from scrimmage and an afternoon's worth of key blocks and fancy fakes won't have Peppler knocking down the locker room door with a bonus-fattened pro contract. He doesn't even carry the Packer checkbook on scouting trips. But he does have that potent pen, and he uses it to record a set of mysterious digits to feed into a leased IBM machine in Philadelphia.

As he scans the herd for some choice sides of football beef to supply the Packers, he can award a top score of 1.0 to the local hero even before the game starts: The young man's tall, square-cut, and muscle-laden frame is just right for a running back, and he gets top rating for "size," one of twenty-three categories. A telephone conversation with the boy's high school coach confirms that he is kind, cheerful, brave, clean—the whole Boy Scout list—so he also gets a high rating in "character."

If he goes out on the field and breaks his arm on the first play from scrimmage, he'll be jeopardizing his "injury prone" mark. But if he has spunk, he can earn it right back in the "play when hurt" category. He's not playing for Mom's scrapbook now, he's producing for our computer. At stake is a lucrative career for him and the insurance policy on a multimillion-dollar business for us.

Each year the Packers and the twenty-five other American and National Football League teams scan the rosters of the more than six hundred colleges which field football teams, and designate approximately two thousand young men as candidates for pro stardom. Fewer than five hundred will be offered pro contracts, and only half that number will be on the rosters when the season begins in mid-September.

Talent scouting used to be a casual operation. Coaches, sportscasters, and retired players sent handwritten reports on various players to professional teams in return for small payments, or just for the thrill of helping out the big leagues. That system still works for obscure small college games. But when two major college gridiron powers like U.C.L.A. and Southern California meet head-on, the pressbox is glutted with pro scouts. Their attaché cases spill over with computer sheets carrying spring practice grades and evaluations on the likes of USC's Ron Yary, Mike Taylor, Tim Rossovich, Mike Hull, and Earl McCullough, and hotshot U.C.L.A. quarterback Gary Beban. Those gentlemen received impressive grades in the 1967 meeting between the two teams. And when the season was over and professional football held its draft—the kind of draft a college boy wouldn't think of picketing—the six were among the first thirty players tapped.

In the early 1960s, when professional football began to eclipse baseball as the national pastime, clubowners turned to data processing as a means of cataloging and sorting out the collegiate storehouse of potential players. Since it costs over a quarter of a million dollars a year to gather and store that all-important information, various teams agreed to pool intelligence. In 1965 the Packers joined with six other teams—the Cleveland Browns, Baltimore Colts, St. Louis Cardinals, New

York Giants, Washington Redskins, and Atlanta Falcons—to form the largest of the three NFL talent operations.

How do we get a player's number?

Our rating system goes from 1.0 (absolute tops) to 5.0 (nothing special), and all players are rated in twelve basic categories: "size," "speed," "strength," "agility," "toughness," "football intelligence," "attitude," "injury prone," "play when hurt," "character," "leadership," and "aggressiveness."

Each position has its own checklist. A fullback, for example, will be measured in eleven areas that evaluate his capabilities at that position: "acceleration," "power runner," "elusive runner," "outside runner," "inside runner," "receiver," "block run," "block pass," "run pass," "balance," and "fumbler."

A 3.2 player is no superhero, but certainly worth watching in spring practice. A man who averages 2.5 in our books is doubtless being watched by many teams, and the fellow we rate 1.5 or better is probably an O. J. Simpson. There is also a place on our IBM listing for general comments such as "Good power runner; good quickness into the line; can also punt." Throughout the ten-game college season, noteworthy players are watched by scouts from our pool. Each grade on our "Final Alpha Listing" in January is a composite of at least ten evaluations.

Of course athletic abilities aren't the only thing we're interested in. The office staff also feeds other information into the machinery: home and school address and phone numbers, education, marital and military status, and anything else that might have bearing. American Telephone & Telegraph is working on a system whereby all the information—including film clips of the players in action—can be transmitted by Picturephone. In the future we'll be able to "dial-a-player" for the complete rundown on anybody who interests us.

When my assistants and I begin to prepare for the combined NFL-AFL draft in January, the conference room in Packer headquarters takes on the appearance of a network studio on the night of a presidential election. Status boards are the name of the game. There is a huge depth chart on one wall showing our present personnel and indicating how many players we'll have at each position. There's another board along one entire wall with the name of each professional team and space to list its draft picks in the order they are taken.

Along the biggest of the walls, blotting out two windows and several shiny plaques, is the big board itself—the pot of goodies for this year. Each player's name is written on a strip of cardboard with grease pen, along with his school, position, and his computer grade. For days we play with those strips like kids setting up toy soldiers.

"Move him up higher on the board," says offensive line coach Ray Wietecha. "We've got to get some youth in that forward wall."

Then the assistant coach in charge of receivers, Bob Schnelker, who played for Lombardi with the Giants, makes a good point: "Look, there are only about five top ends in the whole mess this year. We didn't keep any the last time around, so we've got to put one high on the list this time." He's right, of course, so we move some more strips around to get a pass receiver higher.

Up until a few years ago, the pro draft was conducted in the proverbial smoke-filled hotel room, with each team's representatives huddled around their own table poring over charts and records, with clerks at a giant blackboard recording the picks as they were made. The tension was strictly Las Vegas, with all the brains in pro football closeted in one stuffy room for eighteen-hour days of hushed and hurried conferences, frantic long-distance phone calls, and incredible eyestrain.

Now, thanks to the telephone company's system for joining more than two dozen offices on one super party line, the draft is carried on in civilized fashion, with each coach and general manager occupying the chair in which he is accustomed to making momentous decisions. In the crucial earlier rounds when the best players are on the block, we have thirty or forty minutes for each selection. As the pile grows smaller and the seventeenth and final round approaches, only a few minutes are accorded each decision.

PACKER DYNASTY

In recent years, we have been blessed with several extra choices, received from other teams in trade for our expendable players. In the 1968 draft, for example, we had extra picks in five of the first ten rounds. So we play the draft game like some people play the stock market, buying up commodities which we know we can trade later at a good gain. A football power is built at the draft meeting and in off-season trades, not just at training camp and on the gridiron. The men who build it are not just good football strategists; they must be careful planners and shrewd traders.

A glance at our top picks in 1968 gives an idea of the thinking that ran through our minds when we looked for new cogs to put in the machine that had ground out championships for three years running.

All-American Fred Carr from the University of Texas at El Paso, which had a phenomenal team, scored the highest in our ratings and was our first pick. He was tops in every category, and the choice was borne out in July when *Sport* magazine polled all the pro teams to find the "rookie most likely to succeed" from the 1968 crop. The unanimous choice was Carr. In addition to filling the physical mold perfectly and being able to run a hundred yards in just a fraction over ten seconds in football gear, Carr had the potential to play defensive end, linebacker, tight end, or safety. Getting him was like drawing the wild card in poker.

Our second choice, offensive guard Bill Lueck from Arizona, caught some people by surprise. The talent pool that includes the other three teams in our Central Division, the Chicago Bears, the Detroit Lions, and the Minnesota Vikings, had rated Lueck in the "questionable" range. But we saw a lot we liked in him: his 235-pound frame could quickly be beefed up to a pro-sized 255, and he had the speed and moves we need for our running plays that call for the guard to pull from the line and run interference for the back. He clicked on all the personality traits, too: He's a big, rugged young man who operates his family's cattle ranch, and he has a brother playing ball in the Canadian league who we were sure he'd like to impress.

## PACKER DYNASTY

Bill Stevens, also from Texas at El Paso and our third pick, is a quarterback with quick delivery, a strong arm, and a penchant for passing. He holds twenty-seven of his school's records. In a league that depends on superstar quarterbacks, he would be excellent trade bait, we reasoned, and he would be excellent competition for our present quarterbacking corps. (That competition was inadvertently suspended early during the 1968 training season when third-string quarterback Don Horn was activated for six months' military duty, creating a vacuum that Stevens quickly filled.)

Our fourth selection also caught many by surprise, especially the man himself: Dick Himes, offensive tackle from Ohio State. We were one of the few teams that didn't outwardly demonstrate interest in Himes; in fact, the Dallas Cowboys called him the night before the draft and told him they expected to tap him early in the selections. But we had our eye on him . . . and on our depth charts, which show we need someone to back up eleven-year veteran Bob Skoronski. Himes is quick, strong, and full of hustle. Our checks at Ohio State showed him to be a good student who maintained a B-or-better average and was both respected and liked by his dormmates, who called him "Giant." Despite a switch in positions during his senior year, he made the postseason teams. To all of that we added the customary extra credit for coming out of Woody Hayes' renowned Big Ten mill, and we knew we had a player with potential to make the team.

Our draft has to be well-rounded if we are to plug the unforeseen holes that may appear in July and August when some of the veterans don't come back. It also has to contain some trade material so that we can maintain a strong position in the preseason bartering that is sure to transpire. And it's always nice when our top picks pan out, justifying our faith, our hopes, and our large bonus contracts. In most of the past decade's years, from six to eight rookies have made the team, which is the optimum number for orderly attrition. Back in 1962, our top four choices all made it. In 1966, eight rookies made the roster, four each on offense and defense. Three years later all but one of them is playing for us. That kind of job security makes everyone in the Packer organization happy—labor and management both.

There's not much of a hiatus between the midwinter draft and summer training camp. If we are to know and appreciate what talent is developing around the country, we have to do as much scouting in the off-season as we do during the autumn. During the spring practices, when college coaches drill next year's squad in fundamentals and give freshmen a crack at making the team, the pro coach and his assistants make the rounds. They watch practice sessions, talk to the coaches, and take in the annual spring scrimmages and alumni games. When my assistants and I fan out for our spring look, I take the Southwest, an area which has been contributing an increasing percentage of fodder for the football mills over the past decade.

I first started watching Donny Anderson on my trips to Texas Tech in 1963. Because coaches can get out to scout only in the spring, I never did see him in a game. Most of my information was gathered from his school, other schools in the league, and by watching their films. But I did get to watch him playing varsity baseball, and I could tell that he was a natural athlete. He was a good, strong hitter, and his speed was obvious. You can scout a football player to a certain extent by watching him play another sport, and what I saw was enough to convince me that we ought to make a strong bid for him. We drafted him as a future pick in 1964, his junior year. It's seldom that a team can afford that luxury. The Packers hadn't done it since 1945, but it was well worth it.

After his junior year, Anderson was named to the All-Southwest Conference team for the second time. He was also named the conference's Back of the Year, and he made most of the All-America selections. He didn't let us down in his senior year, when he gained 705 yards rushing and caught passes for 797 yards. He scored seventeen touchdowns, including a one-hundred-yard kickoff return. Voted the collegiate Co-Player of the Year (the "Co-" was our 1965 top draft pick, Jim Grabowski of Illinois), he also was the outstanding player in the Gator and Hula Bowls and a unanimous All-America selection.

The tapping of Anderson in 1964 was probably the most exciting draft pick during the decade that Lombardi managed our club. His coach had told us that Donny could play flanker and defensive back as well as running back, but we knew that other teams would be looking at him as a runner, and that's what we needed for the future, too. The scouting report read: "Outstanding toughness, an elusive runner, a game-breaker . . . could be another Paul Hornung." That meant he *had* to be a Green Bay Packer.

We didn't have a high pick, because of our winning record, but we did have the seventh choice in the first round because of a trade obligation from Philadelphia. We watched all the top running backs fall in the first few choices: Tucker Fredrickson to the Giants, Gale Sayers to the Bears, and Ken Willard to the 49ers. That meant anyone wanting a star running back would have to wait a year—or spend a "future." Because we were still competing with the AFL, the gambling was twice as precarious.

The fifth pick belonged to Dallas. The Cowboys, of course, had their eyes on Anderson. He would have an almost irresistible hometown appeal in the Cotton Bowl. We waited nervously while they thought over their decision. Finally the word came: "Dallas picks Craig Morton, quarterback of California." That meant we would have a shot at Anderson. When our turn came, Lombardi announced: "Green Bay picks, as a future, Donny Anderson of Texas Tech."

The Cowboys were terribly upset. "You'll never sign him, not a Texas boy," they told us. "Yes, we will," Lombardi replied. "I talked to him last night." Vince had called Donny at home to make sure he would accept the idea of playing in Green Bay. Anderson was shocked. He asked Lombardi three times if he knew who he was talking to, but he said he was willing to play for whomever drafted him. He had expected San Francisco if not Dallas, but he was genuinely thrilled when Vince told him we wanted him to wear the gold and green of the Packers.

## PACKER DYNASTY

Houston of the AFL also tapped Anderson, and there was worry in some quarters that Texas would lure him from the NFL. But Donny elected money and a championship team over sentiment. There were also rumors that we had bought him to trade with Dallas, and they became so persistent that Vince had to call Donny and assure him we wanted him for ourselves.

Again in 1965 our finish put us far from the head of the draft table, but our trades had brought us a higher pick. We took Jim Grabowski, who had spent his senior year breaking not only the records he had set as a junior, but many long-standing marks of Red Grange, J. C. Caroline, Alan Ameche, and other collegiate greats. Again there were dozens of rumors about what we intended to do with this valuable piece of property, but again we wanted him for our backfield and nothing else.

The publicity that followed the Anderson and Grabowski drafts and signings could have been detrimental if it hadn't been for the Packer way of doing things. Some clubs allow the personalities of players, and even of the owners, to emerge too strongly. The personnel become celebrities around which publicity and fan appeal are built. Eccentricities are permitted, and egoism abounds. The Packer image puts the *team* at the center of things, and each member must accept his role as part of that team. Thus there was no chafing between the Taylor-Hornung backfield and the newcomers. Nor was the defense unhappy. Two good, young running backs means more bench time for them in the future, so they had nothing but good things to say. Nor did the matter of the huge sums paid to keep the AFL from grabbing the "Gold Dust Twins" bother incumbent players. "We don't want to play against them in some future Super Bowl," was the prevailing attitude. All players want to be on a winning team, so they look upon glamorous rookies not as competitors for attention, but as men who can help them bring home Superchecks.

Will Grabowski be the leading rusher in the NFL some day? And will Anderson be the leading scorer? We thought so when we chose them, and we still think so today. They've grown up together in the Packer backfield. With apprenticeship and injuries behind them, they're ready.

A player who doesn't get selected in the draft or make it as a rookie in his first training camp may still wind up with us if he's good. Sometimes we waive a man because we are deep at his position or we don't feel he can develop fast enough to be of use to us. But the situation may change, and he can get a second chance as a free agent or in football's minor leagues. We picked defensive end Bob Brown up from the Wheeling, West Virginia, Ironmen, where he went after two tryouts with the 49ers and one with a Canadian team. Chuck Mercein played for the Westchester, N.Y., Bulls and rode the Washington Redskin taxi squad before coming to us. Dick Capp, who played for the Lowell, Mass., Giants, came to us in midseason when injuries sent us looking for replacements. Seemingly destined to languish in the minors, Capp and Mercein suddenly found themselves getting partial shares of our Super Bowl winnings.

I was asked by the editors of a young people's magazine last year to show their readers what it takes to be a professional football player. After "Could You Make It with the Green Bay Packers?" appeared, I received a number of letters, including one from a young man in Nebraska who said he was ready and willing to replace Bart Starr. Since Bart wasn't ready and willing to step aside, I had to turn the lad down. But Willie Wood became a regular after writing us a letter. Willie had been passed over in the draft, which proves that the draft, while highly scientific, isn't an infallible way of finding talent. And that's why we read our mail, answer the telephone, and listen patiently to the guy who buttonholes us after the Elks Club smoker to give us a hot tip: "You ought to see my Johnny; he can pass a hundred yards with his left arm."

If he can, we'll put his name on a computer tape and start watching him.

## 16 · THE DAY OF DAYS

As a kid I lived just a few short blocks from the Minnesota State Fair Grounds in St. Paul, and the biggest excitement as the summer grew long was anticipating the arrival of the carnival. Two weeks before the fair opened, posters went up on dozens of neighborhood billboards proclaiming "Royal American Shows—World's Largest Midway." A week later, wooden stakes suddenly sprouted in the packed earth alongside Commonwealth Avenue, and we defied fairgrounds guards to sneak down and get a better look at the legends: Octopus ride . . . Tunnel of Love . . . Ferris wheels . . . Freak show . . . Penny pitch.

Sure enough, a few days later those marvelous rides, sideshows, and games of skill mysteriously took shape almost overnight, rising from the earth to lure a boy and his hard-earned lawn-mowing money. The day the fair opened, I would tromp through the fresh sawdust clutching a strip of tickets "Good on all rides and for all shows except the Sally Rand Extravaganza." What a thrill to stand gawking, the pungent aroma of roast peanuts and fresh caramel apples in my nostrils, and then finally work up the courage to stride forward and conquer the Dodgem Cars, the Chamber of Horrors, and the vexing Over-21-or-Under-11-Wins-a-Panda game. It was truly The Day of Days.

I don't get to the state fair and the midway any more, but I still have the excitement of a Day of Days each summer—the opening of training camp in mid-July.

For a professional athlete, training is a year-round duty,

and when the six feet of frost finally works itself out of the ground at our training field sometime in May, the veterans who make their home in Green Bay gather almost every weekday morning at 10 A.M. to work out. On a typical day, half a dozen players will be there: perhaps Starr, Dowler, Weatherwax, Nitschke, and Bowman, plus an assistant coach or two and a free agent we've agreed to take a look at. They start with ten minutes of calisthenics mixed with good-natured chiding about everything from middle-aged waistlines to middle-priced stocks.

Then, like sweatsuited substitutes for the Harlem Globetrotters' farm club, they stand in a circle and toss the football around: "Hey, hey! . . . Watch it, Ken, baby. . . . Keep it moving, Wax. . . . Save your arm, Bart. . . . Hey, hey!" If the day's turnout includes a center, an end, and a quarterback —Bowman, Dowler, and Starr, for example—they may run a few patterns while the others jog around the field two or three times. Suddenly Nitschke breaks away and streaks alongside Dowler yelling, "I'm open, I'm open," and Bart drops a thirty-yard shot into his arms. "Now you know how insecure your job is," Ray lectures Boyd with mock severity at the same time he is firing the ball back to Bart with accuracy and grace belying the fact that he is not a quarterback himself. After a half hour to forty-five minutes of work and play, they head for a shower and an afternoon of business pursuits.

Late in June, advance signs of the impending bivouac can be seen wherever you look. The Milwaukee paper carries a picture of Lionel Aldridge running up the steps of County Stadium; since a national magazine showed Paul Hornung scaling the plateaus of Lambeau after his year of inactivity, the shot has been a sports page cliché. A few days later the wire services have a picture of Carroll Dale flopped on his back flailing the air with his sinewy legs, getting in shape while serving on the faculty of a football camp for boys.

In the publicity office, Chuck Lane is on the phone every ten minutes assuring writers and editors that the printers will have the Press Book ready any day now, and across the hall the secretaries bemoan a 300 percent increase in what they call

## PACKER DYNASTY

the brat mail: requests for autographed pictures of the players, "espeshully Bartt Star and enclossed is my 10 sense, thank you."

The stadium lawn crew begins daily sprinklings of the practice fields, joining huge sections of perforated pipe together to soak half a gridiron at a time. Somebody repaints the sign on the watchtower installed by Lombardi: "Keep Off—Police Order." Mothers with station wagons full of kids pull to the curb and ask, "When do the Packers start to practice?" and the sweating, shirtless lawn tender looks up long enough to shout back, "July tenth, according to the paper, but some of them were down here this morning." Attendance picks up at the Packer Hall of Fame, and outside of town fresh posters beckon tourists on U.S. 41 to "Visit the home of the Green Bay Packers."

Early in July the sports magazines and football annuals blossom on the newsstands, and we note with relief that Don Meredith is on the majority of the covers. The year they all featured Unitas and asked breathlessly, "Is This the Year of Johnny's Big Comeback?" . . . it wasn't. The next year Bart was the big attraction: "Year of the SuperStarr?" and he had what amounted to a mediocre season, for him. So this year Don Meredith will be the victim, we reckon, and maybe next time it will be Roman Gabriel. The only thing worse that can happen is if *Time* puts you on its cover in the tenth week of the season. Then you've had it for sure.

A few days before the rookies and veteran backs report—the veteran linemen get a short reprieve—we finish working up the room assignments. Rookie roommates are paired to bring out certain qualities. A shy fellow will be matched with a braggart so they can learn from each other. Geographic areas are balanced, so two southern boys or two big-city fellows don't wind up reinforcing their ingrained values. There are always some special cases. Anderson and Grabowski were roommates in their freshman year, not because they were unalike, but because they both came to camp late, after the All-Star game. And each year we look hopefully for a snorer to put with Ron

Kostelnik. Since his old roommate, Dave Hanner, another horrible snorer, joined the coaching ranks, we've been looking for a suitable companion. Usually the best we can do is put him with Doug Hart, who is our deepest sleeper.

The first day of training camp is taken up with physical exams, issuing equipment, and opening remarks by the coaching staff. Then comes the Day of Days, when eighty men begin the rigorous preparation that will reduce their number to forty and start them on the long road to December . . . and perhaps January.

Clad in white shorts and T-shirts, they jog out across the wide expanse of parking lot that will be the site of a thousand tailgate picnics come September. Once on the grassy field, they strain for a few minutes at the tension exercisers next to the equipment shed, then form up in ranks at midfield for calisthenics and cadence. The exercises that follow are performed with all the seriousness and ritual of an Olympics ceremony. One coach, attired in baseball cap and baseball-type pants topped with a dun-colored windbreaker, steps forward to lead the drills, and the others patrol the ranks, shouting at laggards and noting progress. Nothing is haphazard or extemporaneous —one of us is carefully maintaining a minute-by-minute log sheet that details who did what for how long . . . and with how much success. In the third week of camp I may ask Dave Hanner, "How much time have the defensive linemen had on the reaction machine?" He'll check his charts before giving me a precise figure in minutes, accompanied with man-by-man evaluations.

Some of the exercises push and punish. Grass drills! "Run in place. Pick 'em up. Hit it." Offensive line coach Ray Wietecha has the most abrasively effective voice for this one. "Down on your face. Get up. Run, run, run. On your back. Up, up. Down, down. Up. On your face. Up. Run. Stop."

Others are more subtle. Hanner, an ever-present enormous chaw of tobacco distending his right cheek, chants the litany like a parish priest: "Awright, toe of right foot at heel of left and one-two-three toe touches, gentlemen, that'll be seven times and I want to see the torsion on that abdomen, awright, on the count, a-one, two, three. . . ." It's the first time, and a hapless rookie who has aligned his feet wrong starts to waver, so the coach nearest him calls a halt, and Hanner recites the litany over again. The rookie does it properly.

Some exercises are sloppy because they're new to the rookies, but soon we hit a standard one and all eighty men perform with the precision of a chorus line. Lying on their backs with raised legs crisscrossing in the air, they look like an aquacade in the grass. It's a special thrill to the coach, because for the first time he is seeing his men move and act as one. And that, of course, is the final objective of the training camp.

To end the exercise period, the drillmaster shouts "south!" or "north!" to indicate which goalpost he wants the entire group to storm *en masse*. Usually it's Ray Nitschke who leads the pack, grabbing an upright with both hands to arrest his headlong dash and then striking a Geronimo pose, yelling "onward and upward" to those who follow in his wake.

Next, the players line up in ranks of eleven—not just linemen, but all of them—and we run from an imaginary line of scrimmage. On the count, the first group charges off the mark explosively and noisily. It's as smooth and hard as the last rush of the previous season, and the coach feels a tingle running up his spine. The second group lines up, the coach counts cadence, and the entire right side of the line bolts at the wrong time. That breaks the spell. The coach starts barking numbers again, and everyone realizes we have weeks of hard work before we'll be a dependable machine again.

We log the four-minute segment and move on to group work. Receivers and backs work on play patterns, the lines get a workout on the blocking dummies, and the kicking specialists go off with their tees and shag boys to practice placements. Someone who had not watched a pro team in training might expect to see the offensive and defensive squads lining up in scrimmage and running through tricky plays. We might have more fun that way. We'd also have many more injuries. And

## PACKER DYNASTY

worst of all, we wouldn't be a very good team, because training is something much more fundamental than "practicing at playing." It's a coach watching an individual player run through a kicking, blocking, or receiving drill, diagnosing where his technique could be improved, then explaining it to him in such a way that he can learn and perfect it. Some people come to our practices expecting to watch a football game. What they see instead is a laboratory, a kind of football diagnostic center in action. If they come back for the afternoon workout, they'll see us in uniform and pads, and before the day is over we'll run a two-minute beat-the-clock drill that at least partly approximates game conditions.

That's not to say that those who turn out for our practice sessions—frequently as many as two thousand a day—don't get a kick out of it. Our sideline viewing area is a show in itself. Half an hour before practice begins, cars start arriving, many of them bearing out-of-state license plates, and some pulling boats or camping trailers. Among the hundreds of kids are several wearing pint-sized versions of the official Packer regalia, and the most popular jersey number is Bart Starr's 15. Hardly a day goes by that the real 15 doesn't have to take time to autograph a couple of dozen scrapbooks and footballs thrust at him by the cluster of miniature quarterbacks waiting excitedly for him to come to the railing near the spectator benches. Others sit patiently with Packer yearbooks logging a sighting of Forrest Gregg, the number of passes caught by Carroll Dale, or some other personally important statistic.

Two policemen patrol the crowd. The junior man has to endure the kids along the rail, while the senior man posts himself as gatekeeper, where he can rub elbows with the heroes and greet the bigwigs who come and go.

The *Press-Gazette* photographer comes early for his obligatory start-of-the-season shot, and soon his colleagues from the television stations arrive. One sets up his movie camera in the middle of the vast parking lot, starts with a shot of the empty stadium, and then pans 180 degrees to zoom in on the players. You can just about anticipate the script for tonight's six o'clock news: "Today Lambeau field stands empty and quiet. But just one short month from today. . . ."

Old-timers who haven't missed the opening day of practice in years, greet each other and earnestly compare information on the rookie crop.

Two women who stopped on the way to the Laundromat watch silently, and finally one says to the other with awe: "Look at the legs on that one."

Every bread, diaper, soda pop, and potato chip delivery man in town seems to have arranged his route so he'll pass the practice field with time to slow down and watch, as does the white Cadillac with four businessmen on their way to some important meeting, the state patrol car, and the taxicab.

When the practice session is over, the kids who have been selling ice cream and pop walk the sidelines with burlap sacks, picking up the debris left by their customers. "This is the Packers' field; I want it 100 percent clean before you leave," admonishes their employer, who runs the concession stand across the street. "You've got to have *pride* in your job."

Lunchtime after the very first practice session finds the coaching staff beginning evaluation of the rookies. The new men may all have looked the same to the fans on the sidelines, but from the moment they stepped on the field, we began to see important differences. From the way one man jogs along we can tell that he's in shape, while another who has just as good a college reputation is already disappointing us because he obviously didn't report to camp in top form. The first day is none too soon to evaluate spirit, ability to learn, and team play—characteristics which, if lagging, can have a rookie marked for failure before the first scrimmage is run.

We almost always keep a rookie beyond the time when we realize he won't work out for us, just on the chance that he may show us we were wrong. The day he is finally cut, it won't be his fumbling of a ball that morning that killed him. We may have decided after the first week that he was one of those players who peaked in his junior year of college—reached a threshold of ability and desire beyond which he is incapable of passing. If so, he'll never make it as a pro.

This Day of Days ends for almost every player and coach in total exhaustion. Even those who professed to have come to camp in shape feel the tightening muscles in calves and backs that haven't had a real workout since last January. The first few hours of paging through the thick playbooks and the opening session of film watching tax the brain, especially for rookies who never knew the game was so complex. So by mid-evening, the second and the third floors of our dormitory at St. Norbert College are quiet, and everyone is sound asleep. Except, perhaps, Kostelnik's roommate.

# 17 · IT'S LIKE GOING TO SCHOOL AGAIN

"**O**KAY, YOU guys, I've got a *plan:* Everybody out for a pass."

That brand of genius has won many a Sunday afternoon touch game in the park, not to mention a great number of high school and college contests. But any pro who doesn't want to spend the entire day either on his back or receiving the other team's kickoffs must log countless hours each week planning for the next opponent. In order to mount a winning effort, each player will have to augment the coaching sessions and team drills with sufficient personal preparation. Once the season is under way, the gladiator who supposedly uses his brawn to earn a living spends much of his time at a table or desk, racking his brains as hard as any doctor, lawyer, or merchant chief.

The number one planning tool of the Packers and every pro team is the film. It's the coaching staff's job to spend the Monday after a game in the projection room so that when the players return from a day's rest the information to be found in the movies is ready for them to absorb. The screening usually involves four games: official NFL films of the opponent's last two games, plus our own films of our last game and the most recent game we've played with the opponent. In the case of infrequent foes, such as the Washington Redskins, we don't bother with the film from our last game together, since it will be too outdated to show today's personnel in action.

Each game is divided into three reels: offense, defense, and kicking. The two defensive coaches analyze their own films plus reels showing our opponent's offense, while the offensive coaches look at the opponent's defense. Usually the reels are more or less the same size, each carrying about seventy plays in a closely matched, evenly fought game. But it's not always the case. After our 1965 championship game against the Cleveland Browns, Lombardi looked at the Packer defensive reel, representing only 39 of the 108 plays in the game, and snorted, "Humph, and to think your men got paid eight thousand bucks the same as the offense." On the not infrequent Mondays when the reel representing my men's work was twice the size of the offense's, he just smiled and murmured, "Thank God for the defense."

The pair of coaches analyzing a reel sit at a table just six feet from the screen, one operating the projector and the other charting plays on notepads by the light of a high-intensity lamp. Our team photographer shoots the films in black and white at the standard twenty-four frames per second, and we project them at four frames per second slower, which is halfway between standard and slow speed. That gives us the necessary advantage of drawing out the action, but without the unnatural movements of true slow motion. Our films don't resemble what you see on television because the shot is at less of an angle, and we frame nearly a third of the field. All twenty-two players are in view until the ball crosses the scrimmage line, because unlike the typical video fan who wants to watch the quarterback, the runners, and the receivers, we are every bit as interested in the pattern run by the defensive back or the rush put on by the end. Only when the play has fully developed does our shot "zoom" in slightly to get a closer view of the blocks and tackles that terminate the action.

The projectors we use are special heavy-duty machines with forward, reverse, stop-action, and a hand crank for advancing one frame at a time. Using a hand-held control button, the analyst works his way through the film at a pace that would unnerve anyone other than a football coach. On a typical complex play, he runs the film without stopping for the five to ten seconds' duration. Then he goes back and runs it at least once for each position he is charting, which means no less than eleven more looks—if he is able to spot the moves the first time, every time. When he's completed that phase, he'll run it three or four more times just to make sure he hasn't missed anything—a total of fifteen to twenty times per play. In analyzing how a player made the critical move necessary to burst through the line, he may "rock" the film back and forth through a four- or five-frame section until his eye spots the twist of the hip or the thrust of the balancing hand that is the key. To an onlooker, it is as if he were compelling the celluloid puppet under his control to perform a weird, undulating dance. Sometimes more can be learned about an opponent's unfamiliar play by running the film backward to see where everybody came from to get where he wound up.

When all the films have been charted in rough form, the entire coaching staff gathers to run through them and make general comments. It's in these sessions that the years of experience either as a player or as a coach show. A good memory is the coach's best asset, and it's not uncommon to hear someone say: "Look at Marv Fleming; he's giving the same move at the line of scrimmage on the down-and-out as he did two years ago in our first game against the Lions. We'll have to tell him about that." Sometimes, however, we may not be sure of what we're seeing even when we look at our own films:

"Here comes a forty." (A trap to the weak side).

"Yeah, Bart said he planned to use it after whatsisname had gotten in there a couple of times."

"Wait a minute, that's not forty: Look where he's got the guard."

"Oh, hell, that was the busted play."

"Well, what was it *supposed* to be?"

"I dunno. We'll ask him tomorrow."

Sometimes watching a play can be a delight:

"Look at those silly Giant ends just standing around."

"Yeah, they think it's a thirty-six and the play has stopped, but there he goes. . . . Well, we know what they'll be writing down when they watch their copy of this one."

Sometimes it can be misery:

"Well, here it comes. . . ."

"Damn."

"How does that dad-blamed Tarkenton get out of there?"

Sometimes it's just plain frustrating:

"That play is jinxed. It's a hell of a play, and someday we're going to get a score out of it, but they always screw it up somehow."

"We'll run it again this week. The trouble is, they always do it okay in practice right after we talk about it, but stick it in a game and it's all loose shoelaces and runny noses."

After the coaches have thoroughly analyzed the footage, it's ready for screening with the players. First the kicking reel is shown to the entire team; then offense and defense split up to study their own reels and those of the opponents. If we've just come off of a big victory, the atmosphere can be somewhat jovial. Dave Hanner loves to use his advance familiarity to work a man over verbally: "Good grief, Pittsy," he chides our running back as he is nosediving into the corner of the screen to the delight of thirty-nine teammates, "get yourself in shape, will you?" A minute later Pitts is streaking down the sideline thirty yards for a score, and Hanner chortles: "Well, I see you finally took my advice and got in shape."

After a squeaker or a loss, the comments are likely to be more to the point:

"Come on, Grabbo, don't hit and splatter; keep those legs going."

"Marv, you're making your cut two steps too soon. One of these days it's going to mean six points for that guy defending against you."

"What's going wrong on that play, Bart? We haven't gotten five yards off of it all year, and the hole has been there every time."

There's more to the films than just showing them and making appropriate comments. Each player must study his opposite number until he knows exactly what to expect and how to counter it. After the first session with the films, each player compares what he has seen with a detailed report form he filled out the last time the teams met. The offensive ends, for example, scan earlier replies to the following questions: 1. What are the charges and forces of defensive personnel encountered against the run? 2. Diagram the three most frequently used pass coverages against your position; 3. Describe the individual defensive techniques of the secondary, including any changes other than what we expected; 4. What running plays do you suggest against this defense? 5. What pass plays do you suggest?

On another form which is kept in our files, he finds an evaluation of the opponent made earlier by himself and others, rating from one to five such qualities as: ability to diagnose plays, quickness, speed, tackling, ability to cover man-to-man, pursuit, and one-on-one blocking.

"My gosh," remarked one rookie as he retired to his room with a bundle of forms to study and another set of reports to fill out, "it's like going to school again. This is tougher than some of the tests we got in college."

The first-year man has only the paperwork to study. The veterans also must draw on their personal memory banks for stored information that will be of use, especially if they are meeting a man with a big reputation. Preparing for the big defensive stars was one of the things Fuzzy Thurston did so well. He'd come out the week he was going to play against Roger Brown and just knock himself out. By game time he was ready to do a great job. It was strictly a case of studying Brown's every move on film, then mentally preparing himself, building up confidence, convincing himself that he was going to improve his own techniques sufficiently to do a good job against the best in the league. And he usually did.

Preparing for Alex Karras is always a formidable task for our offensive line. Along about Tuesday morning it suddenly occurs to each one of them: "Oh, my God. That thunderbolt is going to start striking at 1:15 Sunday." After our 17–17 tie with Detroit in the season opener of 1967, Jerry Kramer made a pact with himself to avenge Karras's performance. The insolent Lion left tackle had gotten through to Starr seven times in the first game, stopping that many passes, at least one or two of which might have won the game for us. Kramer admitted at the time that Karras had enjoyed "a lovely day," primarily at his expense.

Jerry watched the films of the first game and other games over the years for hours, critically assaying what he had done wrong and analyzing how Karras's quick moves might be contained. In the rematch, Karras got to the quarterback only twice. "I knew what I wanted to do today, and I did it," Jerry told the press happily afterward. "I'd say *I* had a lovely day today."

Some players have personal duels that date back to their college days, like Bob Skoronski's matchup with the Rams' Lamar Lundy that goes back to their Big Ten days at Indiana and Purdue, respectively. They know each other so well that it's not a matter of studying one another each time, but one of getting properly psyched up for the renewal of professional hostilities. Each time they meet, there are two outcomes: the one on the scoreboard and a new chapter in a private history of two adversaries.

Sometimes a special rivalry will emerge for the duration of one game; it happens when a veteran's pride is hurt by a poor performance in the first round of a home-and-home series. After our regular 1967 game with the Rams in Los Angeles, they awarded their game ball to offensive tackle Charlie Cowan in recognition for his effort at containing our Willie Davis. Nobody talked about it, but it was obvious all the next week that Willie was thinking, planning, reliving the encounter, and readying himself for the Western Conference playoff in Milwaukee. The rematch found Willie atoning for his bad day. That's the value of a proud veteran in what the Packers have come to call "the championship days" at the end of the season, when men meeting for the second or the third time that year show what they have learned.

There are various ways for a coach to handle his players'

concept of an opponent. He can go down the roster and build each man up, giving his players a challenging goal. Or he can tear the opposing players down, convincing his men that they are superior and should act accordingly when they get on the field. The Packer policy has been to tell our men the strengths of each opponent, making our players feel they're playing another good team that is worthy of being considered their equals. This pays off in the long run, because if they win, they have a feeling of accomplishment, and if they lose, they don't feel as discouraged as they would if we had shrugged the other team off as a patsy. Often in the Packer dressing room you'll hear more compliments about the team we face than you will from that team's own fans and its local press.

Part of the players' pregame duty is to look over their counterparts during the warmup on the field. That can be the time for a little bit of psychological warfare, although it's mostly a matter of the defensive backs looking to see how loose the receivers and passers are, while the safetymen keep an eye on the kickers to see what lift and distance they're getting under the prevailing conditions. Sometimes we have to check out the fitness of key players on the opposite team, although that information is supposed to be made available through the league office. Prior to the second Super Bowl, for example, all the papers said Oakland's defensive tackle Tom Keating wouldn't play. We looked him over and made up our minds that there wasn't enough trace of limp to believe the rumors. He turned out to be a starter, played practically the entire game, and did well. It's the coach's job to prepare the players for every aspect of the game. If what the coach tells the players does indeed develop, the players gain confidence, and the chances of winning are greatly improved. If, on the other hand, they encounter all sorts of things they didn't expect, it erodes their confidence, they feel uneasy, and the result may be mistakes or a half-baked effort.

The most complex planning and preparation task befalls the quarterbacks, who have projectors in their homes and do virtually as much or more work as their coaches. Bart Starr and Zeke Bratkowski are personal friends, and they spend a couple of nights a week in Bart's basement recreation room watching the films and testing each other on defenses, effective calls in various situations, and the variety of options on different plays.

The quarterbacks, like the coaches, make considerable use of a special file for opponents' patterns, the Unisort card sort system. The coaches' charts from opponents' films have all been transcribed to 8-by-11-inch cards in four different colors, one each for offensive running patterns, offensive passing, pass defense, and rush defense. Along the top margin of each card are forty-three holes, each corresponding to a fact about or a characteristic of the individual play. On the pass defense card, for example, one hole is notched fully to the margin to indicate that the play was used in the first meeting of the year. Another is notched to indicate the year, 1966. Another is notched to indicate that the "red right" offensive formation was used against the defense. Farther down the card, a notch replaces a hole to indicate a 4–3 positioning of linemen and linebackers. Another notch tells that the secondary was man-to-man. And so on, cataloging each important characteristic of the defense. There's a card for every play in the game, and every game for several years is in the file case.

So, if the quarterbacks want to know how many times on second and long yardage in a 4–3 defense facing a red right offense the opponent tends to blitz or go man-to-man on receivers, they insert long "wands" or rods into the Unisort file through holes which correspond to all those prerequisites. Only the cards with holes notched out in every single one of those categories can drop out—the rest remain suspended from one or more rods.

Some teams use computers for this recalling of information, but we like using this manual system because the large cards carry our own sketches of the plays, complete with annotations and information that can be studied visually for greater retention. After trying out the computer for a while, we decided to use it for handling ticket sales, but not in game planning, although each year we review our decision and consult with computer men on the latest developments.

The information that the coaches and quarterbacks must come up with is called the "tendencies," which are recorded on a frequency chart. It's a definite weakness if you fail to keep an up-to-date profile of yourself, too, in order to know what your opponent is thinking about you. Bart is a master at "double-psyching" the opponent and coming up with a few surprise choices in every game. And our defense is caught by surprise once in a while when an opposing quarterback decides to rewrite the chapter in the book that tells what he is most likely to do.

When we have done all the research that is humanly possible within the few days available, the coaches and quarterbacks put together the "game plan" which will be given to all the players on Wednesday.

Sometimes it's hard for the fans to understand why, when they have watched a team come out on the field, play poorly for two quarters, lose the ball on breaks and fail to score, the coach will say in the postgame interview: "Well, the first half went pretty much according to our game plan." How can it be? Wasn't it the game plan to come out and start rolling, devastating the opposition and running up a fat margin?

No, not in professional ball, where two teams are evenly matched and the outcome probably won't be secure until the final gun goes off. The game plan is a sixty-minute proposition that we hope will result in victory, or will at least keep us within striking distance until the final two minutes when fate, poise, and other intangibles come to bear. The game plan is no bag of tricks and surprises. It's mostly the selection of plays from our repertoire that the coaches and quarterbacks think will be the most successful against the defense we expect to encounter. Of our 150 running variations, for example, we'll make up a "ready list" of about a dozen, based on our evaluation of the films, scouting reports, and past encounters. Those are the plays we drill in practice sessions Wednesday and Thursday. From our hundreds of pass patterns, we select fifteen—fewer, if possible—and our receivers bone up on their routes for those particular plays. The number and types of plays selected is smaller if we're facing a familiar team with a standard defense, larger if we're meeting a comparative stranger who likes to mix up the alignment of the defensive forward wall.

Now and then we do have a special play for a certain team. Not a trick or a gimmick, really, but something out of the past that nobody associates with the Packers. And we never do it out of sheer caprice; it's usually because we've seen where we can take advantage of a weakness. If we notice that they've been lining up consistently in anticipation of a pass for long yardage play, and nobody has stung them on it yet, we may dust off a straight-ahead running play that by rights would be a ridiculous call. If we have noticed in our own profile an exaggerated statistic that is undoubtedly in their scouting reports, we'll probaby work up an uncharacteristic play to defy the statistics. If you can catch an opponent relying too heavily on the tendency charts and take advantage of it with a big gainer, you've probably struck a blow to their confidence in their own preparation. That, of course, would be a genuine psychological coup.

Sometimes you spot an individual player in their defense who you know for sure isn't as capable as the man you'll be sending out against him. Instead of getting greedy and trying to take advantage of him instantly, you instruct your man to "run out there during the first couple of drives and let him get the feeling he's containing you." When your man reports back that his defender thinks he's got the situation in hand, then the special play is set up. You take the reins off your man and he shocks his defender—and the spectators—by completely outrunning the opposition and making it look like a minor miracle has happened. That's why the Packers so often pull out the victories in so-called "squeakers." They know that the game is sixty minutes long and they don't have to show everything in the first quarter. Like the cagey poker player with his bluffs, the Packers opt to rake in the chips at going-home time.

Special plays occasionally are inserted in the second half of the game plan after the players report back and make suggestions for halftime adjustments. Those various individual suggestions have to be quickly processed by the coaches and translated into second-half plays. That's why the first and second halves of some games are in reality two different contests —and why the Packers have gained a reputation as a second-half team. Hollywood movies to the contrary, halftime is not so much a time for fiery oration and sudden inspirations as a time for processing and updating information based on reports from twenty-two players and six coaches. It comes closest to being a fast-paced caucus and board meeting, with the necessary amount of ministry and medication conducted simultaneously.

The danger in using special plays or preparing an inflexible game plan is that when they don't work, the players begin to wonder why. If the coaches have let them build up a particular play or a particular strategy in their minds and then it backfires, the breakdown of morale could be disastrous. It all comes back to the reasons for installing "basic" football as the way of life in Green Bay ten years ago. Of course if the key plays are going wrong because an individual is executing poorly, the coaches in the pressbox will phone the explanation down to the bench, and we'll try to correct it. Once we do, the players realize that the game plan was sound, and we should be back on the track.

Some of our critics maintain that the Packers traditionally "waste" the first play of the game by running smack into the center of the line for one or two yards. These, of course, are the folks who like to see the first play from scrimmage go twenty or thirty yards to assure everyone that it's going to be a good day. Fortunately, our sophisticated Green Bay fans are now educated to basic football, and they watch the game with an eye to how strong we look, where we are wearing down the opposition, how much time we are controlling the ball, and how we maintain good field position. Our fans don't boo, be-

## PACKER DYNASTY

cause they're watching the line play; fans who only know how to watch backfields and receivers are the big booers.

We had an assistant coach a few years ago who became disgusted after a while because he had the feeling we never passed on first down. We went back over a year's worth of plays and gathered statistics showing that we passed as often on first down as two-thirds of the teams in the league. It just wasn't a part of our "image." We would like, ideally, to make six yards running on the first down. That puts the defense in an awkward position, because we'd certainly use at least one pass play if we had to make seven or eight yards in two downs, and we'd probably keep it on the ground if we had only a single yard to make. But two downs to make four yards creates the "overlapping statistics" that are the ideal situation in pro ball. That's why so often on first down we send a back over tackle, where he is bound to make four yards before a linebacker grabs him, and he'll fall about two more yards, giving us the gain of six we like.

We frequently discard certain plays without seriously altering our approach. The game plan is like a specially designed vehicle that has to be test driven, adjusted, and sometimes modified. It's how soon you get it settled down and running smoothly that makes the difference in how far you go with it.

Our very first Lombardi era game plan, against the Bears in 1959, was one of our simplest. The basic plays were the end run and the Packer sweep. The defensive plan was to force long-ball receiver Harlan Hill to the outside, and to key on Willy Galimore on the kick returns.

Nine full seasons later, the game plan going into the NFL championship game—our second against Dallas—was very much the same. Again our defense was concerned with a long-ball threat in Bob Hayes and powerful, quick runners in Perkins and Reeves. Since their defensive tackle Bob Lilly had a reputation for busting through any offensive line he met, our game plan emphasized quick passes to the backs rather than trying to set up long passes to the ends in the precious extra seconds that might not be there. We remembered that in our previous game with them they had keyed on our ends and done quite a good job; comparatively, they neglected our backs. Since we had been our characteristic selves during the weeks leading up to the championship, we were confident that they would be consistent in their attention to our ends.

The prime concern of our defense was to present a stable picture, refusing to be forced into unnatural alignments. The Dallas offense shows the widest variety of attacks in the league: man-in-motion, rollouts, all sorts of things you usually don't see in three successive weeks of meeting other teams. The idea is to force your defense to meet them on the Cowboys' terms. The team that beats Dallas is the team that can come up with a strong, basic defense that is equally effective at denying options.

Although we were playing for our lives in the final minutes of that thriller, we had not by any means thrown our game plan to the wintry winds of Lambeau Field. Our passes from Starr to Anderson were planned—although only as a one-time variation. The basic pattern called for a deep-running end to be the primary receiver, with Anderson the alternate. What happened was that Bart had to, and was able to, use his safety valve more than once. It's really a pretty standard system, but it was a tribute to Starr's canniness and Anderson's running ability that they were able to make it click under such tremendous pressure. Any team can make it work once; only the best can set it up and march with it.

A year earlier, in our first championship game with Dallas, a special play set up by Lombardi opened our first drive spectacularly. It was a counter play, perfectly chosen to take advantage of the Cowboys' great pursuit, and when Elijah Pitts gained thirty-two yards on it, we were off and rolling. We were "high" at the beginning of the game, and when our special first play broke for such a long gain, the feeling was electric. We just *knew* we'd score on that drive; that's how big a lift it gave us.

Once a game is moving along, it's very rare that we'll send a play in. Information from the coach in the pressbox, yes, but not a play. Many college coaches send every play in, and even some pro coaches like former signal-caller Norm Van Brocklin prefer to send in the third-down orders. But both Lombardi and I have felt that by game time all of our knowledge has been passed on to the quarterbacks, and the men on the field have that up-to-the-second information that nobody else does. With a young team we might be less confident; with veterans and champions, it's the only way to run the club.

It often seems that the Packers and other clubs are trying to sell more tickets by letting the game go down to the last few minutes before pulling it out with some near miracles. But we're not really interested in theatrical finishes, and we really don't think it's the dramatic last-second play that won the game, even if it did produce the go-ahead score. If you get down to the final two minutes of play with a tie or a slim margin, then you've established that the contest is virtually equal. Now it's up to the team that's just slightly better to react to the extreme tension by quickly reviewing the entire game in their minds. You must capitalize on the stored information to strike at the opponent's weaknesses, catching him in a place you knew you could exploit when it came down to a last-ditch effort. The tendency used to be to throw the ball deep four times in a row when you were behind, but now the defenses are so improved that there's very little chance of being successful that way. After fifty-eight minutes of cool, poised football you'd be foolish to throw it away, so you have to try the draw, the screen, short sideline passes, or even an ordinary running play in hopes of gaining yardage and forcing the defense to be "honest."

We've pulled them out in the final minutes so many times that the fans and writers called it a "Packer finish" when we beat Dallas in the championships. But it doesn't always work out that way. In our 1967 season opener, we were moving down the field in the final minute with every intention of breaking the 17–17 tie we'd precipitated by coming back from a 17–0 deficit at halftime. (They call that a "Packer second half"!) With eight seconds on the clock, Starr hurled a quick one to Dowler on the eastern sideline, in a move to stop the clock and give us time to set up for a field goal in what we expected to be the remaining three or four seconds. Dowler caught it, and players from both sides swarmed around him, each man hurrying over to see firsthand if he'd gotten out of bounds, which he had. But suddenly, during the ensuing hurly-burly, the gun went off. The game was over.

Lombardi looked for a moment as if the gun had fired a bullet through his heart. Then he shook his head and said, "That was the quickest eight seconds I've ever seen. I can't understand it." Reporters quickly ran up to him and asked if he thought he had been robbed, but he refused to complain. "Have my publicity man get your statement from the officials," he told them and stalked off the field. As he walked back to the coaches' room, he stopped at the door to the officials' dressing room, stuck his head in the door, and said gruffly, but with half a smile: "You guys sure make us look like lousy coaches out there."

When the reporters asked referee Norm Schachter about the hesitancy over the time, he explained that it was the job of field judge Herman Rohrig to ascertain the moment when the player carried the ball across the sideline stripe. He had depressed the button on his stopwatch without looking at it because there was a good bit of jostling on the field. When he was sure that the play had stopped and there was no threat of hostilities in the electrified atmosphere, he looked down at the face of his stopwatch and saw that time had elapsed. We were busily giving instructions to Don Chandler and sending him on the field with his tee when the end was signaled.

That was one time when it didn't turn out the way the coaches said it would, not because the officiating was bad, but because it was precise. And that is just one more area where a coach must be sure of adequate preparation. Each year the officials seem to be emphasizing some facet of the game we've all been taking for granted or they've been a little lax on previously. It's up to the coaching staff to note these trends and inform or instruct the players accordingly.

In 1968, for example, the officials seemed to be paying closer attention than ever before to face mask grabbing. They had found that head and neck injuries had increased in recent years as a result of the violent twist a grab at the face guard can give a man. Early in the season the fifteen-yard penalties cost many teams heavily, including the always clean and fair Green Bay Packers. I had my assistants single out the filmed shots of face mask infractions—ours and those of other teams—and we studied them to see how it happened. As a result, we discussed with our players ways to prevent their hands from trailing over an opponent's face in such a way that the fingers inadvertently became entwined in the mask. There's no sure way of preventing an accidental *faux pas,* but we felt that by studying the plays and talking to the players, we could make them more alert to the problem and cut down on the personal fouls.

We also noted last year that the officials were blowing plays dead more quickly than they had in the past, again to prevent injuries that result from piling on or late tackles. We coached the players on the problems created by that development. There would be more penalties for unnecessary roughness or unsportsmanlike conduct against men who "came in late," which meant they'd have to concentrate on vaulting over or sidestepping the ball carrier if they couldn't stop in time to avoid the place where he lay. And it also meant there would be fewer fumble recoveries, since more of the balls that squirted out just after the carrier was stopped would be ruled dead. We had to make sure our players recognized that so they wouldn't lose their tempers after an apparent fumble recovery and earn us a penalty, or even get themselves thrown out of the game.

Come to think of it, I envy the touch football quarterback whose "plan" involves sending everybody out for a pass. If his brainstorm doesn't work, he can always come back with that great fooler, the ball-inside-the-sweatshirt ruse. There are days when I wish *we* had it on our ready list.

# 18 · OF MUSCLES AND MISERIES

It is paradoxical that the physical fitness of pro football players and the number of injuries are both at an all-time high. But if you stop to think about it, there's no paradox at all. Both phenomena stem from the fact that we're trying harder than ever to play excellent, winning football. We've built bigger, stronger, quicker, and physically better-equipped players, and when they clash, the result is "football knees," bruised ribs, popped shoulders, and hairline fractures. It all adds up to professional football's biggest dilemma after half a century of working to perfect the game.

The popular notion a generation ago was that the best summer job a football player could find was one that involved the most rigorous physical labor. Most of my teammates on the mighty Bernie Bierman teams of the thirties sought work in the grain mills of Minneapolis or on highway construction crews, the idea being to build up strength and stamina through hard work. Praise from coaches and families, along with the admiration of college girls and ninety-eight-pound weaklings, helped perpetuate the myth.

Now we know that hard work builds character, but not necessarily muscle or strength. And it certainly doesn't develop the tone that an athlete needs. So today's Green Bay Packer looks for off-season employment that offers him three things: interest and excitement (after an NFL campaign, most jobs are routine and dull); a business opportunity following his football career; and most important of all, hours which permit regular, sound physical training. We encourage our players to train scientifically with weights three days a week through the winter and spring, mixed with sports such as handball and basketball that hone coordination and stamina. For the athlete who can't participate in such team sports, the answer is a program of jogging and running.

The Packers started a regular program of isometric exercises during our second year, 1960. We were to a great extent responsible for the publicity accorded the "nonsweaty" muscle-against-muscle approach. Jim Taylor was a great advocate of weight-lifting, and he also used isometric exercises he had learned as a college star at Louisiana State University. The isometric principles had been around for years and were part of mail order courses like the Charles Atlas ("Don't let that bully kick sand in your face.") "dynamic tension" system. LSU was a leader in developing a program combining isometric and isotonic (with movement) exercises, and Taylor urged us to look into their methods.

After our first season at Green Bay, I made a trip down to Baton Rouge and visited the operator of the health studio where Taylor and other LSU players worked out. He showed me through his operation, demonstrated the methods he had developed in conjunction with LSU's trainer, and suggested ways of adapting his devices to our program. At the opening of our next training camp we installed fixed bars at knee and chest level in a space adjacent to our dressing room. Taylor demonstrated how to strain against them for ten-second periods, alternating with complete relaxation of the muscles. The players liked the system and were amazed at how much could be done with such a simple approach. A brief visit to the isometric bars became mandatory before going out on the practice field.

For too many Americans, isometrics were a passing fad, but we have stayed with them. We now use improved methods made possible by an ingenious device first marketed about five years ago under the brand name Exer-Genie. The device was an outgrowth of an opera star's fear of hotel fires: he drew on basic principles of gears and friction to come up with a rope coiled inside a small cylinder that he could use to lower himself from a window if necessary. The developers of the Exer-Genie modified the device to include a calibrated dial which is used to select any amount of resistance. A rope passing through the cylinder can move as easily as the cord on a set of venetian blinds, or as reluctantly as an anchor mired in a lake bottom.

The beauty of the device is that it can isolate any muscle you want to exercise, and it can also exercise the entire body with just a few minutes of work. It offers both isometric and isotonic work in one set: after straining against the hand bar on the rope for ten seconds of isometrics, the rope is released to feed through the cylinder, giving the same isotonic effect as lifting weights. The first part of the exercise tires an entire group of muscle fibers so that they will respond to the second part. The result is effective building of both strength and tone.

We used to start every practice session with three laps around the field, followed by calisthenics. Now we've cut down on the running and jumping around. After two laps, everybody reports to one of the ten stations at the side of the field for a short session with the Exer-Genie that includes the Big Four combination exercise and the equivalent of running, bicycling, and doing situps. Various players also make specialized use of the device. The running backs, for example, strap on a shoulder harness and burst away on foot in a thirty-foot tug-of-war against the little gadget. (It can give a coach delusions of grandeur to stop a Pitts or a Grabowski dead in his tracks with a slight increase of the index finger's pressure on the rope.) We can exercise the entire team in about ten minutes, and they love it because it not only improves the cardiovascular system, it works out the stiffness resulting from the previous day's practice. It has made remedial calisthenics for the limp and the lame virtually unnecessary.

We were the first pro team to use the Exer-Genie, but lately I've seen others using them before the game to drain their players of tension. And during the televised portions of the Apollo space missions, the astronauts gave demonstrations of the little machine's usefulness to space crews. Last year a similar apparatus was made available to the public under the name Exer-gym, and it now carries the endorsement of the entire Bart Starr family, including wife Cherry and son Bart, Jr. At twenty-five dollars, it is by far the best investment in physical fitness a family could make.

The fitness of players who are one hundred percent "well" depends mostly on personal dedication, but when a player is hurt, his physical rebuilding is in the hands of trainer Carl W. (Bud) Jorgenson, who has been with the Packers for forty-five years, and team physicians Dr. James W. Nellen and Dr. E. S. Brusky. In the past two years, they have had more players under treatment and rehabilitation than ever before. There were days last year when they reported more players under treatment than well and able.

The field of diagnosing and prescribing therapy for football injuries has made considerable strides in recent years. Dr. Nellen recently wrote a booklet for the Upjohn Company entitled *Medicine and the Green Bay Packers* to pass our knowledge on to college and high school teams. The publication deals primarily with the treatment of musculoskeletal injuries, discussing and illustrating such problems as Jim Grabowski's knee injury against the Colts in that medically disastrous 1967 game, and Tom Brown's bruised shoulder from the Halloween game in St. Louis. It pictures the extensive bandaging required by center Ken Bowman—"Rag Doll" to his teammates—when he suffers his periodic popped shoulder. Not surprisingly, almost half of the forty-nine color illustrations in the booklet depict knees and legs, for that's where the injury rate has soared in recent years.

Unlike physicians who treat an injury and then prescribe "lots of rest and stay off of the leg for a couple of weeks," football doctors must treat casualties so the patient can return to the battlefield. So the booklet discusses such specialized treatment as preventing swelling during the game through use of oversized icepacks, local injections of steroids to prevent inflammation, and strapping joints with elastic tape in such a way that strength and protection are provided at the same time that the movements demanded by the player's position and assignments are not retarded.

Players with bruises or chronic conditions of the joints and limbs have daily sessions with Jorgenson and his assistant, Dominic Gentile, in their impeccable medical room adjoining the locker area. In addition to the traditional linament, tape, and words of encouragement they have dispensed for decades, they now offer hydro- and electrotherapy. It's not uncommon after a particularly hard-hitting game to come in on Monday morning and find a man in the large whirlpool, another with a knee or elbow in the smaller one, and three or four more players waiting for the relief that comes from ultrasonic generators. Dominic has relieved the operating room appearance of the room somewhat with a small Victorian nightstand he brought in, painted white and placed against the back wall for a touch of home. In the drawer he stores electrotherapy local pain applicators that look like microphones, and a variety of headstraps for the traction device attached to the wall nearby. When he gets a 220-pound halfback trussed up with his head in a sling, his knees taped, and the buzzing vibrator pressed to the small of his back, it looks like something straight out of a torture chamber scene in the movies. But the player usually comes away from the session with the feeling he'll live to play again.

The medical room and locker area are a not unpleasant place to relax and recuperate. The area is carpeted throughout —even on the platform of the scale—with lush, green, indoor-outdoor carpet. We have a ventilating system that sweeps away the sweatsocks aroma generally associated with locker rooms, circulating fresh air every six minutes.

Borne on the air is the players' own selection of music, piped in over a hi-fi system purchased out of the fine fund. You can usually tell who arrived first by the selection of records stacked on the turntable: Roger Miller, Ernest Tubb and "All Aboard the Blue Train" with Johnnie Cash is a fair indication, for example, that big Lee Roy Caffey, the rancher and linebacker from Thorndale, Texas, made the choice. An extended medley of The Temptations, Righteous Brothers, Ray Charles, and "Soul Sauce" with Cal Tjader, on the other hand, would indicate that Travis Williams was the earlybird. Soothing Julie London means the offensive line is in the whirlpool; the Tijuana Brass indicates the defensive backfield has dropped in for a supply of Cepacol lozenges. By day's end, Jorgenson, Gentile, and Frank Sinatra are the only ones still around.

Much of the trainer's work, however, is done outside the antiseptic confines of his dispensary. The single toolbox full of bandages of yesteryear has swelled to three huge medical supply lockers that go with the team to the sidelines at home and away, along with an oxygen tank and a thermolocker for ice. In my day a man played as long as he was physically able and then limped off to the locker room to salve his wounds. But in today's highly specialized game, a player comes off after performing his kick, his runback, or his series of downs to be rejuvenated and readied for the next call. The protestations of sixty-minute football advocates aside, today's fast-moving, explosive game would not be possible without the continuous sideline ministrations of the trainer and his assistants.

The trainer has to be alert off the field, too. On the bus to the airport after a recent game in Los Angeles, huge Willie Davis (six-foot-three, 245 pounds, fifty-one-inch chest) suddenly turned blue-gray in the face and began to shake violently. Players sitting nearby were horrified, but Bud Jorgenson diagnosed it quickly as dehydration, which can result when a big man plays so hard that he sweats off fifteen pounds in one game. Jorgenson pumped a fistful of salt tablets into the defensive co-captain, grabbing half a cup of soda pop from another player to help Willie wash them down. A huge, hard lump had swelled up on Willie's abdomen, but moments after he downed the tablets and liquid, it began to subside, to the relief of his shocked teammates. By the time we arrived at the airport, Jorgenson had him sitting up revived and almost back to normal.

Off-season injuries and ailments are also a source of worry, especially when players are active in other sports where there is a high likelihood of injury. Jerry Kramer is our biggest worry, because he's a skiing enthusiast, and he's the most accident-prone player on the squad. I don't know what could be worse than an accident-prone skiier, and frankly, I hate to think about Jerry when it snows. Marv Fleming is one of those guys who pitches himself headlong into anything he does, and just before training camp in 1967 he hurt a tendon while playing basketball. It hampered him throughout the season, but fortunately he was able to get back in condition the following year by skipping rope.

The club must give permission for a player to participate in another pro sport, and thankfully more and more of them seem to be choosing singing and acting sidelines these days instead of the old favorite, wrestling. Now our biggest fear is the annual spring alumni games at some schools and the charity dogsled races and basketball games that some players get involved with because they're celebrities. We and they both have too much at stake in their careers to risk throwing a pelvis out of whack in a supermarket's Grand Opening stunt.

When a player suffers a serious injury such as a fracture, we're concerned not only with mending the break, but also with the important job of keeping the rest of his body in top shape so that he'll be ready to go the minute the injured limb has healed. Our insurance policy in that department takes the form of a twenty-two-hundred-pound behemoth just down the hall from our sauna. Called the Universal Gym, it looks like a cross between a piece of playground equipment and a mammoth drill press. It sits in the center of the room and projects seven different pieces of exercise equipment out of a core filled with hanging stacks of weights.

Nine men can use the device simultaneously, moving from station to station and exercising each part of the body individually. One segment works the arms, another the legs, another the torso, and so on. Vince discovered it in 1967 at a coaches' convention in Atlantic City and ordered one on the spot. In addition to versatility, the machine is 100 percent safe because no weights can accidentally fall on a user. It's a valuable time saver because weights can be changed in two seconds with the twist of a selector pin. Forty men can get a workout in less than half an hour.

Healthy players use the machine to pursue the PTA program: PTA for the pain, torture, and agony that come from following the thrice-weekly regimen of rapid successive exercises without rest. Linemen lift the heavier weights to improve endurance and power—especially the explosive power they need to get off the ball quickly. The running backs lift lighter weights to build and strengthen tendons and ligaments, and to put on extra weight without losing any agility.

Players with serious injuries use the machine for a modified program that helps them retain stamina even though they cannot run or use their entire body. That's why defensive end Lionel Aldridge was back in the lineup less than two months after fracturing a leg bone in a preseason game. The machine had kept him at playing weight and condition, and he used a special set of exercises to rehabilitate the injured leg in less than half the normal recuperation period. Last year another defensive end, muscular Bob Brown, broke his arm in practice before the exhibition season began. While it was mending, he worked on building up his legs, getting to the point where he could push six hundred pounds with his legs. He returned to the lineup, played a few games, and then suffered a leg fracture. Gamely rationalizing two bad breaks in a single season, he went to work on his arms while waiting for the leg to heal.

According to league statistics, the average NFL club in 1966 had five players out of action at any one time because of knee injuries. Some were on the disabled list for part or all of the season, and others were in uniform but too seriously hobbled to play well. In the last two years the situation has worsened, with a number of teams falling from championship contention because of knee injuries to key players. Recently the league subsidized a study of pro football injuries by a team of California doctors. Their recommendations for improved helmets and further investigation of the benefits of playing on artificial turf should lead to some improvements.

But as long as the game features spectacular pass plays and lightning-quick runners, the fractures, popped shoulders, and bruised ribcages will persist. Would the public go for a no-passing game that legislated against the more dangerous running plays? If that happened, football would degenerate to little more than wrestling and a tug-of-war.

And yet, if players like Gale Sayers, Bart Starr, and Johnny Unitas must sit out half a season, the fans are denied some of the action they paid to see when they plunked down forty dollars for a season ticket. So the day may soon come when we'll have to tinker with the game to prevent some of the injuries that have reached epidemic proportions. If it does, I hope we can protect our players and still give the fans the all out effort they've come to expect. I'd hate to see football bog down, and I certainly couldn't in good conscience be associated with a team that held anything back when a championship was at stake.

## 19 · NITSCHKE, AND OTHER THINGS IN MY DEFENSE

**W**HEN I first began coaching the pros twenty years ago, I handled training of both the offensive and the defensive lines in a system that had its roots in collegiate sixty-minute football. It seemed sensible, since it merely meant teaching the same principles to men who would make positive or negative use of the information. But throughout the fifties, the concept of a defense with a philosophy of its own began to evolve, and consequently, by the time I joined Lombardi in Green Bay, I considered myself a defensive specialist.

In the early days of football, you "defended" against an opposing line by stringing out your own eleven in front of them in a sort of horizontal tug-of-war where each player was his own anchor man. When offenses got a bit trickier and the forward pass was born, a corresponding "secondary" was set up in the form of a string of defensive men farther back to thwart aerials.

That left an open area in the defense, and slowly the idea of the linebacker evolved. In a 1929 contest with New York, Packer founder and coach Curly Lambeau created a sensation by pulling one of his linemen a step back of the line and giving him "roving duty." The man could wait for the play to develop and then bolster the imperiled segment of the line. He could arrange to let a tackle or end bolt forward at the snap to rush the passer, while he stepped in to fill the vacated hole. Or, he could leap through himself and attempt to astonish the passer.

The tactic resulted in a 20–6 victory over the Giants and foretold of things to come.

In the early 1950s, the Giants made a big step in the development of the modern defense by pulling three players back from the seven-man forward wall and creating the basic linebacker corps as we know it today. The trio had the duty of "reading" the play quickly and then either bolstering the line or dropping back to prevent the pass completion, thus covering both bets.

We developed the linebackers at San Francisco, too, and our most successful teams included such defensive stars as Hardy Brown and Matt Hazeltine. In 1957, heading for a conference tie and facing the then-champion Giants, we developed a new tactic to use against the strong pass attack of assistant coach Vince Lombardi's offense. After studying the New York films, I decided that if we were to stop the deadly arm of veteran Charley Conerly, we'd have to do it in the pocket rather than at the receiving end. I pondered the calculated risk of shooting two, or even all three, of the linebackers across the line at the moment of the snap, gambling on dropping the quarterback before he could cock his arm and release the ball. Failure, of course, could mean only four defenders covering as many as five receivers. We tried it, and it worked spectacularly. "Red dog" was the code name our players gave it, and now it's also known as the blitz, a standard threat against the pocket quarterback, and highly effective if not overused.

When I came to Green Bay as Lombardi's defensive chief, there was only one way to go. The preceding year had been a disaster for the defense, which led the league in most of the negative statistics—for example, a pitiful average of five yards each game in the category of trapping the quarterback for a loss behind the line of scrimmage. Analyzing the personnel we had to work with at the key linebacker positions, I found that the Packers had three capable veterans in Purdue All-American Tom Bettis, Dan Currie from Michigan State, and Bill Forester from Southern Methodist. And a converted Illinois fullback named Ray Nitschke, who was in his second year, promised to be the roughest and toughest of them all: "He might even move into middle linebacker eventually," I predicted at the time, probably the understatement of my career. All four of them were strong, speedy, and possessing of leadership qualities; they were the equals, if not the betters, of my linebackers at San Francisco.

So what was wrong? They had been coached to play a cautious, waiting game, doubtless the result of having been burned so many times in the lean years. They were a defense in every sense of the word: the Switzerland of pro football. All I had to do to remedy the situation was to explain that in the modern game of football, the defense *attacks*. The defense has plays, formations, strategies, and it can even produce points by making touchdowns and safeties. Most important, the aggressive defensive squad must have a morale of its own: a goal, a leader, and a reward. It all comes under the heading of Pride, which is what I tried to instill in my defense that long, hot summer of 1959 when they had none.

Mixing the red dog in more frequently, we surprised many a team in 1959, dropping hotshot quarterbacks like Earl Morrall and Johnny Unitas with regularity for a total of 248 yards —an improvement of better than 300 percent over the previous year. The more aggressive play in the season opener against the Bears, especially by Forester, had led to a containment of feared Chicago back Rick Casares. By the middle of the season the defense was working like a machine, and we came up with the first Green Bay Packer shutout in ten years, a 21–0 victory over the Washington Redskins. The last one had come in 1949 against the New York Bulldogs. That is precisely the kind of reward a defensive team needs. In our finest year, 1962, we held three teams scoreless and allowed only 148 points while our offense was racking up 415.

The ideal defensive team is a mirror image of the offense it will meet. Take stock of the defender and you'll know most everything you need to know about his personal opponent. Scientists theorize that for every particle of matter there's a corresponding negative particle of *antimatter*. They might well be theorizing about Ray Nitschke, a dynamic manifestation of the antiquarterback. Do you want a lightning review of all the plays and formations the Cowboys will use against us next Sunday? Ask Don Meredith. If he's unavailable, ask Nitschke. What signal is being called out there at the line of scrimmage? Both the quarterback and the opposing middle linebacker have switched to audibles, and there's a good chance they'll both wind up at the same call. If they do, it's a standoff, which is a victory for the fast-guessing antiquarterback.

More than once in intrasquad scrimmages I've seen Bart drop back into the pocket, cock his arm, switch his eyes to a deep receiver, recock, and let fly with the bomb—forty-fifty-sixty yards in the air. Down in the end zone where the ball has rolled to a stop, Nitschke runs over, picks it up, and easily tosses it back forty-fifty-sixty, even seventy yards, right on target to the center standing next to Bart. Nitschke loves the feel of the football. And he can handle it just about as well as he can handle a charging fullback. If all of our offensive backs came down with the flu on the day of the game and I had to create a quarterback-for-the-day, the nod would go to Nitschke.

Most defensive backs were offensive halfbacks in college, and they store up all their old knowledge to use along with their new defensive maneuvers. Herb Adderley, for example, was starting halfback and tricaptain for the Michigan State Spartans. An All-American, he played in the Hula Bowl, the East-West Shrine game, and the All-Star game. When he intercepted a Daryle Lamonica pass in the Super Bowl, he scooted through the Raiders as if he were giving them a free offensive running demonstration. With only Lamonica between him and the goal line, he faked the quarterback one way, then the other, and flashed past him to put our final touchdown on the board.

Defensive backs must be able to run backward even better than they run forward. They backpedal furiously at the same rate as the offensive back or end who is rushing at them, ready to shoot to one side or the other when the man makes his cut.

When they're not running backward or sideways, they must run "out of gear" like a flywheel that can suddenly catch hold and take off in any direction. That's why you see the defensive backs working their legs madly in place and pumping their arms out in front of them. The maneuver helps them to maintain their balance, and if they should opt to run forward into the line, the perpetual gyrations become part of their pummeling, pushing, shoving fierceness that makes up for the fact they weigh twenty or thirty pounds less than the man they're trying to stop. Defensive backs spend more time than any other players running the ropes, drilling until the furious leg action is second nature. When they intercept a short or medium-length pass, they often make it into the opponent's end zone without being touched, simply because they can be heading in that direction before anyone else even processes the information.

The defense's job is to prevent a score, not necessarily to prevent a gain. Norm Van Brocklin likes to say, "You can run all day against the Packers," and he's right. We have a defense that permits short gains and tries to deny the long ones. The main objective is to *minimize* the gains, forcing the opponent to play our slow game rather than his fast game. Make him run lots of plays, and when he makes his share of mistakes, capitalize on them.

Some teams, hoping to draw us in and to change our defensive game plan, try to tantalize Adderley and cornerback Bob Jeter by throwing quick passes in front of them for short gains. When they do, some of our players get excited, especially if the opponent completes a series that includes a couple of passes that look as if they could have been intercepted. But we've coached our defensive backs to permit the short gain in situations like that and to prevent the long bomb. If they get overeager—especially when our own bench is yelling "Come on, you guys, grab that thing"—they may fall prey to a clever quarterback's wiles. It's terribly frustrating for them to do what I have told them is right when their human nature, their buddies, and their fans all tell them differently. Like patient fishermen, they have to wait until just the right minute to make their catch. If they do, the quarterback is eventually going to misthrow a pass they can pick off without getting out of position or committing themselves to the ball instead of the man.

A few years ago in Los Angeles the Rams started right out picking on Jeter early in the game. I kept telling him "Forget it, just forget it," when he came off the field dejectedly after the first series of plays. About four or five plays later they popped it right into his hands, and he ran it back seventy-five yards for the first touchdown of the game. "See," I told him, "they come your way eventually, so just wait instead of worrying." We won the game, 27–23; his patience and alertness to the break constituted the margin of difference.

Sometimes we have to adjust our defense to move a man with certain qualifications to a spot where he can contain the opponent's strongest thrust. After studying films of Oakland in preparation for the Super Bowl, for example, we saw that the standard approach of matching up a defensive end against their explosive tight end was not sufficient to contain him. So we had our end concentrate on the pass rush, and we kept a linebacker on their tight end. With more time to react and greater mobility, the linebacker was better able to neutralize the Raiders' bread-and-butter plays.

Since defense is akin to Army intelligence, it's not too surprising that a certain amount of counterintelligence goes on, too. I have used various systems to communicate with Ray Nitschke, who passes it on in the brief defensive huddle that transpires when the ball is placed. I may call a change in formation, based on the "tendencies" we have charted. I also give the word to blitz—something we have not chosen to do much in recent years, owing to our strength and our lack of desire to commit ourselves to "their game." At one time I used a system of wigwagging my fingers to Ray, but eventually that became too obvious. In recent years when we met teams in our conference who were quite familiar with us, I worked up special signals for any particular game: adjusting the brim of my hat, straightening my tie, tossing a tuft of grass as if testing wind direction.

In a game with Chicago, the Bears thought they had my signal picked up, so they'd wait for me to give it and then send a substitute in with a new play. When we realized what they were doing, we just waited a little longer and put the burden on the offensive team to get the play off in time without getting a five-yard penalty for delay of game. Soon it was self-defeating. At halftime, anticipating their adjustments, Ray and I threw in a curve of our own: I would give two signals, and depending on whether my hand was in my pocket or not, the second signal pre-empted the first.

Once in a while we see an assistant or an injured player across the field making a play-by-play record in an attempt to decode our signal system. But it's an awful lot of work for something we can change quickly. The only fear we have, really, is that they'll figure out our blitz signal. That one's really worth having, because if they know we're going to commit ourselves, they can spring a play that could have a disastrous effect: a draw or screen for ten, twenty, or even thirty yards before we can recover. So the blitz signal is changed frequently even if we don't get the feeling we're being watched.

Most of the football spy work is "fair" espionage that falls under the category of careful preparation. The league forbids us to send scouts to other teams' practice sessions, but it doesn't forbid psychological warfare. George Halas frequently used to tell his players he had "special dope" on the opponent's practice and preparation; he did it to give his players the feeling that he was doing everything possible to help them win, and I have no doubt it gave them a boost.

Papa Bear was overly cautious; he even had the contents of his wastebaskets destroyed at the end of the day. Once when we had a big game coming up with the Bears, I sat at my desk pondering whether I, too, ought to burn, shred, or swallow the evidence. Instead of worrying about it, however, I just sketched half a dozen bogus plays on some slips of paper, dropped them in the basket with the rest of my discarded charts, and went home to get a good night's sleep.

## 20 · LOVE, HATE, AND OTHER USEFUL EMOTIONS

THE PACKERS have gotten along with the press as well as any team in pro sports. We've tried to be cooperative, and we think we've been treated fairly most of the time. The infrequent occasions when we have had differences of opinion almost always were precipitated by someone's attempt to analyze our emotions. When we let it be known that we teach our players to *hate* an opponent—for one week, that is—some writers jumped on us as if we'd desecrated the Bible. When Lombardi said that what made the Packers great was their *love* for each other, some of the same writers accused us of being just plain corny.

The simple truth is that the player draft and the financial arrangements give every football club approximately the same amount of talent and manpower. What the club accomplishes with its resources depends upon the emotional climate that is fostered by the coaching staff and perpetuated by the players. Respect, team spirit, and submission of personal ego are hallmarks of the Packers, and we're unashamed to label what these amount to: love.

It's rarely expressed in a physical way, although Willie Wood and Ray Nitschke are most certainly the biggest huggers in the world. Each time we have a successful goal-line stand or block a punt or recover a key fumble, I brace myself on the sidelines for huge bearhugs from that effervescent pair.

Instead, it's the brotherly affection that comes from living, working, and literally growing up together. As Jerry Kramer put it in our 1967 season highlights film, "Brothers can criticize each other and fight among themselves, but just let somebody outside the family say it and he's in trouble." The entire Packer family was profoundly disappointed after an article in *Esquire* magazine portrayed Vince as a slave driver and his players as groveling, torture-wracked *misérables*. The profanity was what upset Vince the most. We had given the author *carte blanche* to live with us in training camp for a week, and his unrepresentative selection of quotes made the coach sound like a perpetually foul-tempered bully. Many of the players were furious, and they came to realize that remarks often appear different in print. Most of them know that in order to be successful in football, the leader has to be strong and demanding, and they submit willingly to the criticism that's dished out. There may be some profanity when forty hard-charging men and six demanding coaches are mixing it up on the field, but frankly we didn't expect to see it in print any more than we expect a photographer to take pictures of us in the locker room with our pants off.

An indication of each Packer's admiration for the others is the remarks they make in public. When Nitschke accepted the award as the most valuable Packer of 1967, he spoke mostly of "the other thirty-nine players who should be accepting this award." He cut short his speech when he felt the tears starting to come. Bart Starr is the same say: The reporters ask him about how it feels to be the NFL's top quarterback, and his reply usually has something to do with the offensive line or the running backs or the receivers.

Another measure of the love and respect of our players is their attitude toward themselves and society. The Packer experience has made most of them realize that they have a responsibility to others. There's no better example than Willie Wood, a native of Washington, D.C., who took part as a boy in the violent street warfare in that city. Now he returns to those streets in the spring and early summer as a "roving leader" for the Recreation Department, working with youngsters and running a football clinic for the boys. Drawing upon his sociology degree from Southern California and the character developed as a Packer, Willie has earned the trust and respect of the boys and has managed to achieve a stalemate between the rival gangs.

Other Packers, like Carroll Dale and Willie Davis, have worked at summer camps because they find it a rewarding way of using their ability to get along with people. "The Packers believe in themselves as individuals and as a unit," says Carroll, "and that's what I try to get across to the boys I counsel." Davis attempted during his stint as a boys' camp physical education counselor to demonstrate that personal dedication and group effort are vital to success in any endeavor. When he left, the boys lined up in formation, holding aloft a banner bearing one of Willie's favorite admonitions. He says it was one of the biggest thrills for him in a year that included playing in the Super Bowl and earning a master's degree.

Is *hate* the right word for the mental attitude we try to inculcate in our players each week? Perhaps not, but somehow "enthusiasm" or "incentive" or "motivation" don't seem to convey the intensity of feeling we need to create in pep talks as the game draws nearer. Football is a contact sport with rugged hitting, and you can't hit a man with all of your physical ability unless you have worked up a synthetic hatred. When we're facing a team with a superstar in its lineup, we're going to have to stop that man in his tracks in order to be successful. If *he's* more successful at building up a reservoir of pent-up fury than we are, he's going to have a good day, and his team is going to win. Some say football is a contest of wills. It's also a contest of won'ts.

It's not enough to get up every week and tick off a list of the opponent's attributes. Week after week we meet fine teams with great players. We need something to make the men angry, and press clippings on the other teams are an effective burr under their saddle. Did Roman Gabriel tell Jim Murray of the Los Angeles *Times* this week that the Packer front four is old and tired, he doesn't expect much of a pass rush Sunday?

That column, with the injudicious remark underlined in blood red, goes up on the bulletin board. No amount of coach's lung power could say and do as much. Is Gale Sayers bolting across the goal line on the cover of *Sports Illustrated* with a pleased expression on his face? Tape it on the door to the equipment room and demand in inch-high grease pen letters: "Why is this man smiling?" Has a Viking defensive back called Dowler "average"? Slip the clipping in Boyd's shoe, and he'll use it to run circles around the man on Sunday.

I don't have much time to think nice thoughts about mean old Alex Karras of the Lions, but I do love him for one thing: He always pops off to the press after our first game of the season with something like, "The Packers are just another team." Lee Remmel of the Green Bay *Press-Gazette* always obliges us by recording the intemperate outburst word-by-word for later use in a "prelim" story before the rematch. That's all our offensive line needs to hear. We don't think of ourselves as just another team, and it becomes part of our game plan to remind Karras that he is wrong.

We don't let off-season bravado slip by unnoticed, either. I have a drawer in my desk for clippings from out-of-town papers that will be of use next year. We know, too, that anything we say to the media can provide our opponents with temperament injections. So one of the first items I cover in training camp each year is advice against making statements deprecating the abilities of other players and teams. We've provided very little inspiration of that type, and I think it's because we are a happy team and a close team. It also helps that we have limited coverage: a few papers in Green Bay and Milwaukee, plus some space in the Chicago press. Teams in Los Angeles and New York are badgered by as many as a dozen reporters, all working to get a different slant, and their prodding eventually shakes loose a comment from a player or coach that the club will regret later.

Our players are genuinely sensitive about their press image. Following the 1967 championship win over Dallas, Ray Nitschke was singled out to appear on the CBS postgame show. "And now," announced former Eagle Tom Brookshier glibly, "we bring you the *madman* of the Packers, Ray Nitschke." Ray's prompt reply was "What do you mean, madman?" and he disavowed the choice of words on the spot. To his discouragement, many writers picked the term up, just as they had jumped on Cowboy Dan Reeves' earlier description of the fierce middle linebacker as "an animal."

Ray was a bit of a terror on and off the field in his younger days, and his early teammates jokingly called him "wild man." Now a family man who doesn't drink and who builds his private life around a wife, two adopted children, and the community's youth program, he doesn't ask for or appreciate the bestial appellations some writers conjure up for him. He admits that as a younger player, his behavior was a carryover of hostilities developed in a turbulent childhood. But today he approaches his job from a completely professional viewpoint: the middle linebacker is the man who thinks fast, communicates to his teammates, then draws on his physical assets to contact and stop the runner. He enjoys the rough play, no doubt about that—but only as a means to the very important end of helping his teammates win.

Ray, like all players, has learned that his press image can be used by his coaches to demand top performance. When he missed a shot at the fullback in training camp scrimmage a few years ago, Vince called the entire team to attention and addressed Ray: *"Mister* Nitschke, I read in the papers that you are the best linebacker in the National Football League. After watching that last play, I find it rather difficult to believe. Run it again." The instant replay was a different story: Ray knocked his blocker stone cold and stopped the fullback without a gain.

What are the underlying psychological reasons for using hate and love as tools of the coaching profession? In recent years the social scientists have been examining the game of football with an eye to explaining its function as that of 1. a paramilitary organization in a militaristic society, 2. a manifestation of the "family" approach to societal grouping, and 3. a tribal folk religion.

There are more religious aspects than the mere fact that people flock to the center of (hero) worship on Sundays, the psychologists say. There are ritual chants: "We want a touchdown; we want a touchdown." The coaches function a bit like bishops, the officials like deacons, and the sportswriters like prophets (false and otherwise). And we have a shrine or two. Fine, the analogy can be pushed about as far as you want, and it probably has some relevance for cultural anthropologists.

The "family" parallel appeals to me even less. The explanation is that the head coach is a father figure, the assistant coaches uncles, the players brothers. The father, like an Indian chief, readies his sons for manhood and gives them authority to hunt, to kill, to take their place in the councils. The brothers have rivalries which they must subjugate in the face of threats from outside the family. The father's word is the law; the youngest brother is given the most odious tasks, for which he receives the hindmost portion of the reward. Again the parallels between the patriarchical family and a football team are somewhat relevant, but the theory isn't entirely sound. I don't really believe that a professional football player does well "for the coach," even when he himself believes he is. The player produces for himself, and for the team in the sense that the team is an extension of himself. That's what made Lombardi's approach so successful: he pushed each player to push himself, prove himself, reward himself. Even when he spoke of team pride and performance, the basic appeal was to individual pride and performance. The final rewards in professional football—after the last hurrahs have echoed—are monetary, and the checks are made out to the order of individuals.

The theory with the greatest validity in the case of the Green Bay Packers is the military parallel. Although Vince was never in the service himself, he coached at West Point under Colonel Red Blaik. There he learned the value of military discipline, as well as many of the military catch-phrases he used to inspire his players. Vince became a friend of Douglas MacArthur when the general retired to New York. He used to go up to MacArthur's suite at the Waldorf-Astoria to visit with him, exchanging opinions on football regimen and politics. Frequently in his speeches to civic organizations, Vince draws analogies and makes points that mirror MacArthur's beliefs.

My coach at Minnesota, the great Bernie Bierman, thought of the football game as a war, and he exhorted his players to "take away the enemy's will to win. You do it by punishing him, by denying him the territory he needs to achieve victory. When you must give ground, your tactics must be to give him only temporary gains." My experience as a naval officer confirmed what I had learned. The leader, whether military or football, constantly imposes a regimentation that superficially may chafe, but in a more fundamental way prepares the individual to give all he has when the crucial moment arrives. A good military officer reports "all in readiness" to his commander and must be confident that his men will perform to the best of their ability because of their training. A football coach comes on the field at game time knowing that he has already done 99 percent of what he can. The play on the field confirms or refutes his ability to marshal his forces.

The following remarks appeared in a fan's letter to Lombardi:

"I have begun to notice something just as important as your winning games. Self Respect! The attitude you have instilled in your players is amazing. Too often conceit and a boisterous personality are symbols of stardom. If so, you have no 'stars' on your team. I think the 'quiet' performance of the Packers shows confidence and respect for the other members of the team and is just an extension of the attitude instilled in them. You are doing more than just winning football games; you are teaching many more to compete in the game of life."

We posted the letter on the locker room bulletin board two years ago, and it's there to this day. We like that explanation better than any the psychologists have come up with.

# 21 · "WHAT MEN OR GODS ARE THESE?"
—KEATS

**A** GREEN BAY housewife, driving through a local shopping center with an out-of-town family, suddenly pointed wildly toward the door of the supermarket.

"Quick, look!" she shouted, as if there had been an unannounced eclipse of the sun. "There are some of the Packers with sacks of groceries."

The children in the car were sufficiently impressed, but their mother only murmured something about "I suppose they have to eat, too." Her callous indifference cost them all an opportunity to be driven past Bart Starr's house.

Approximately half of the Packers have made their permanent home in Green Bay; most are listed in the telephone book, attend local churches, and belong to community organizations. Somehow they all manage to be hero and the guy next door at the same time.

Being a Green Bay Packer for the past decade has carried with it the burdens and the pleasures of living a legend—the *saga* of the Lombardi era, as the Hall of Fame narration puts it. Sports history is verbal history, living history, chronicled from day to day, and season to season. There is an atmosphere every time the players enter the locker room or step out on the field, that what is said and done there will add to the legend. No factory worker, barber, teacher, or insurance man gets that feeling when he arrives at work each day. And no professional football player comes home at night with "just another day at the old grind" behind him.

Out of this crucible come men who bear remarkable similarities in their behavior, their preferences, and their emotional makeup.

Most of the players count other players and their families as their closest friends. The Starrs and the Bratkowskis are a frequent golfing foursome. A regular postgame dinner group consists of the Greggs, Dowlers, Gillinghams, Caffeys, Grabowskis, and bachelor Donny Anderson. Jerry Kramer and Henry Jordan are good neighbors on aptly named Careful Drive. (Both have nursed injuries in recent years.) In the old days, Hornung, McGee, and Thurston were practically an inseparable trio. The friendships come about not because of a disdain for neighbors with less colorful occupations, but rather the close bonds that grow between men who fight side-by-side through the long season, and wives who have a six-month widowhood in common.

In the environs of their work, the players have an almost uniform vocabulary and mode of expressing themselves. Virtually the same conversation can take place a dozen times on a single day, a thousand times a season:

"How ya doin', old man?"

"Never felt better. Little soreness in the shoulder, but I'll be hitting out there."

"Whataya think of those Bears?"

"We'll kill 'em."

"How about tossing me that tape."

"Sure. Never use the stuff myself."

Most of us in pro ball have heard the same "jock talk" since we were on the high school freshman squad. It's first of all a masculine bravado. But there's another more important reason why locker-room exchanges are often less original and meaningful than a United Nations debate. In football, deeds speak for themselves. No player wants to be a talker, he wants to be a doer, to perform on the field. At the same time that he is bandying clichés with a teammate, he's conversing much

# PACKER DYNASTY

more profoundly with his inner self. He's reviewing what he has done before, what he hopes to do today, how he will feel if he doesn't succeed, what success or failure on his part can mean to the team and to his own career. Most of us can get through a day without pondering job security from dawn to dusk, but the football player is constantly proving himself. If he falls down on the job, he knows he'll be replaced immediately. That's why each football player is to some extent a brooder, no matter what his external image.

When the season is over, perhaps a few football people retreat to quiet islands or remote spots where they can lick their wounds and commune with nature. But most coaches and players prefer the excitement of Las Vegas, New York, Los Angeles, San Francisco, New Orleans—or a goodwill tour of Vietnam. The pent-up emotions of a football season don't drain too well on a good book or a game of shuffleboard. Football players like the fast pace, the gaiety, the challenges of the livelier holiday spots. And most of them crave continued competition, because it's in their blood. It's impossible to be competitive for six months of the year and then turn it off like a faucet. A week after the second Super Bowl, Starr and Nitschke were competing against each other in a five-lap race on Sunday afternoon at the "All-Pro Snowmobile Championships" in Eagle River, Wisconsin. Not too many years ago the immediate postscript to the season was a challenge match of hockey, with Nitschke, McGee, Thurston, and Jesse Whittenton heading up the squads of madly flailing amateurs. Most of us—players and coaches, too—want to match brawn, wits, skill, luck, or whatever we have at our command against someone else. The will to win doesn't end in January. My own particular outlet is gin rummy. Not the kind your grandmother taught you, but the ultra-invigorating Hollywood system of triple-column scoring. I love it; I love to win.

And then there's golf. If the Packers were not in the NFL, they'd be in the PGA, believe me. An avid golfer, Vince shoots in the eighties. (When he played Jack Nicklaus in an exhibition match a few years ago, he had a respectable 82 to Jack's par

## PACKER DYNASTY

72.) His assistant, Tom Miller, won a *TV Guide* Celebrity Tournament with a near-par performance. Zeke Bratkowski is the best golfer among our players (partner Bart Starr is *his* backup man in that category). Kicking specialist Don Chandler bought a set of golf clubs for his seven-year-old son with his Super Bowl earnings. Last February, Jerry Kramer won the American Airlines Astrojet golf tournament, and Ray Nitschke also finished in the top money.

Because they are heroes, the men realize that what they do is imitated, and their behavior is emulated. We stress constantly that the players and coaches contribute to the Packer image in everything they do, and we must be better than average citizens in every respect. One of my few nervous habits is lighting up cigarettes—far more than I actually smoke—while I'm at the sideline. After a televised game last year, I received twenty letters from high school kids questioning or reprimanding me. I decided to make a concerted effort not to appear dependent on the things the next time we were on the air. I made it until the fourth quarter of the Dallas game without reaching in my pocket and lighting up. Seven or eight years ago, Paul Hornung endorsed Marlboros in a television advertisement, but the league has since forbidden players to lend their names to tobacco or alcoholic beverages. If they ever forbid coaches to smoke in public, I guess I'll have to hang up my clipboard for good.

Making endorsements is a major sideline for the most successful players. At one time Hornung was a regular Betty Furness. When he wasn't adjusting his Zenith television for the folks, he showed up in a Jantzen cabana set or golf sweater. Now Bart Starr is the team's leading plugger, lapping up his Dinty Moore beef stew so he'll have the energy to go ten minutes on his Exer-gym and then take it off, take it all off with Noxzema. ("Men, if Bart Starr takes it off with Noxzema, shouldn't you?") This year the entire team is eating Nestlé chocolate bars and drinking Stokely-Van Camp "Gatorade" quick-energy fruit drink. At the end of the season, the players fan out on various commercial ventures: Boyd Dowler and his wife lead an AAA tour to Hawaii . . . Ray Nitschke promotes hairpieces, a home care concern, and a housing development . . . Elijah Pitts is part owner of an employment agency in Milwaukee's Inner Core . . . Willie Davis spreads the good word for Schlitz.

Lacking the appeal of a star quarterback or a rugged linebacker, I didn't expect too big a slice of the endorsement pie even when I became head coach. But I was wrong. Salesmen for a national fertilizer distributor got their seasonal "pep talk" from me on film—blackboard and all, even though we haven't used a blackboard since we got our overhead projector. A bedding company (they instructed me not to say "mattresses") put my picture on their "Posture Power" extra-length model and brought me to the annual furniture convention in Chicago to enhance their booth. "Meet Phil Bengtson, Head Coach of the Green Bay Packers" said the banner across the display, and all of the firm's representatives wore green Packer blazers. I was the one in the middle wearing a gray suit. We bought the mattresses for use in our training camp, and each Packer went to sleep with me under his sheets, although none of them ever discovered it. They're old hands at endorsements, but I'm just getting the hang of it.

Anyone needing confirmation that football players are mortals would receive it at approximately 9 P.M. the night before an away game at whatever motel the Packers are calling home. The game day will bring a strict dietary regimen (brunch, exactly four hours before kickoff to permit complete digestion: a twelve-ounce steak, baked potato and/or scrambled eggs, fruit juice, coffee or tea, toast—no milk allowed because it may not digest fully by game time.) So bedtime the night before is the last chance for satisfying personal cravings. After watching Jackie Gleason in my room (his particular brand of mania takes my mind off the upcoming game), I order a cheese or chicken salad sandwich. Zeke Bratkowski wants—needs—a piece of pie, preferably fruit pie. The younger players have a passion for hamburgers, while the veterans like to retire with a small steak under their belts. Some of the southern boys, like

Texan Doug Hart, don't rest well unless they have a little soup, beans, and corn bread in their bellies. The corridors of the motel are a frenzy of bedtime snack activity until about 10 P.M. When we make arrangements for our accommodations in other cities, I always have publicity director Chuck Lane check to make sure the kitchen facilities are open at night and offer a wide variety of items. It would be silly to upset morale by something trivial like no fruit pie or split pea soup. After the game we're all ravenous from not having eaten for seven hours. On the planes we get our steaks, but on the bus trips back from Milwaukee we have a catered sandwich lunch.

Occasionally we are asked why, in all those years of winning playoffs, championships, and supergames, the Packers never reveled in the bubbling froth of victory champagne. Well, in the first place a player who has given his all on the field is too tired to act boisterously. But more to the point, we feel it's unbecoming. The baseball teams all do it, the AFL's Kansas City Chiefs did it in 1966, and it doesn't do them much credit as professionals. Vince and I both believe the professional image is as important in sports as anywhere. Before the opening of training camp last year, one of the television newsmen called to ask me if he could come out and take shots of himself doing exercises with the team to show how rigorous it is. I knew he would be unable to resist the temptation to clown around, so I turned him down. Nothing we do should cheapen our image.

The image of professional football has been carefully and consciously improved over the last fifteen years. Nobody thinks of NFL players as ignorant simians who are little more than highly paid gladiators. The postgame interviews have shown our players to be intelligent, well-spoken gentlemen who are proud of their craft. Everything else the players do contributes to the image, including the wearing of tailored suits, the evidencing of business acumen, and the off-season guest appearances on television.

Men or gods? Men, of course. But godlike men, each one of them.

## 22 · THE PLAYERS' PLAYER: BART STARR

First-round 1968 draft pick Bill Lueck reported to camp three weeks late because of the All-Star game; his first training session was our Sunday evening postmortem. After the films, other rookies and a few veterans were introducing themselves to the heavy-set Arizonan when a familiar figure left the group of quarterbacks and coaches at the projector table, thrust his hand out, and said: "Hi, Bill . . . Bart Starr. Nice to meet you." The introduction struck Lueck about the same way a freshman congressman would feel if he heard, "Hi, Dick Nixon's the name . . ." at his first White House reception. The astonished rookie managed to mumble an awe-struck "Hello" as Mr. Quarterback himself smiled and pumped his hand.

Football players are probably the best-mannered of all athletes, the Packers are among the most affable gridiron gentlemen, and Bryan Bartlett Starr is *the* Nice Guy in Green Bay. He's a coach's player, which is to say he understands all facets of the game, is instrumental in the planning process, acts as a team catalyst, and executes with near-faultless precision. He's a players' player, too—a man respected by every single teammate because he puts the game before personal considerations, devotes much of his training time to helping others develop, and is a spiritual leader as well as the field general. From 199th draft pick in 1956, he has risen to number one on just about everybody's list.

## PACKER DYNASTY

Starr is the most efficient passer in the National Football League's history. Despite his injuries last season, he completed 63 percent of his passes, raising his lifetime percentage to 58, ahead of such all-time greats as Sammy Baugh, Otto Graham and, yes, Johnny Unitas. His 294 consecutive passes without an interception is far and away the league mark. Three times he has led the league in combined passing statistics, and since 1961 he has never fallen from among the leaders. The statistics and the awards—most valuable Super Bowl player twice, All-Pro and Jim Thorpe Award winner in 1966—are nice, but they're not necessary to prove his reputation. One out of every three Americans watched the Packers move down the field on December 31, 1967 in a four-minute testimonial to his greatness.

Starr's difficult apprenticeship was so methodical that he can pinpoint specific plays and games when a lightbulb turned on over his head—just like in the comics—and he gained another measure of confidence or football knowhow. It was in the last game of the 1959 season, against San Francisco, that Starr says he permanently gained the ability to step up to the line of scrimmage, read the opponent's defense, and make his crucial decision of whether or not to alter the play with an audible. A "revelation" is his description of the way all his laborious study suddenly fell into place.

That same game has been recorded as the first time Bart *asserted* himself. When Max McGee interrupted his thinking in the huddle by urging "Throw it to me; I'm wide open," Starr talked back to a veteran for the first time with a forthright "Hush up," the southern equivalent of "shut up." The elation in the huddle over the emergence at last of Bart's personality took the form of such uproarious laughter that offensive captain Jim Ringo had to call a time out to prevent a delay-of-game penalty.

Even while setting records and playing in the Pro Bowls of 1961–62–63, Bart was still unsure whether he had developed enough confidence to carry the team over the rough spots. In our early-season 1964 game with the Colts, who were destined to dominate the conference that year, he threw an interception which ended a last-minute drive that could have pulled out the 21–20 loss for us. Walking off the field dejectedly, Starr says he realized for the first time that a football player survives even the most disastrous mistake if he hopes to come back and win. He marks that day as the moment when he decided never again to let defeat depress him.

Bart's ability to pinpoint crucial moments in his life may seem like an incredibly intense personal historical awareness, but I think it explains why he has succeeded where others of considerable ability have faltered. Vince Lombardi once summed up Bart's mental approach to his role in the game of football as "coordinated efficiency." Colorful Fuzzy Thurston refrained from his usual witty rhetoric to label it "infallible logic." I like to think of it as "premeditated excellence."

As one of the most sought-after speakers on the postseason banquet circuit, Bart has developed an acronym on the word *success* to explain what those who would emulate him must have: S–Sense of direction, U–Understanding, C–Charity, C–Courage, E–Esteem, S–Self-confidence, S–Sense of humor. Starr has developed in the last two of those categories to the point where he even works in a few jokes about his coaches and about himself.

Bart no longer lets anybody get the best of him. He shows up at contract time to make his case. "Gee," said Vince a few years ago, shaking his head as he looked at Bart's fresh signature on the papers, "I spend six years building up his confidence, and what happens? Finally he's got enough confidence to come in and argue for more money. I've created a Frankenstein monster."

He also has courage on the field. In a scrimmage last year, he was upset when Dave Robinson intercepted his pass. As the linebacker thundered up the field worrying about who might be pursuing him, Bart tackled him, completely upending the burly 240-pounder. On the next play, Bart threw a thirty-five-yard touchdown pass in retribution.

The newest off-season sport for football players is acting, and even gentle Bart was intrigued enough to accept a role on "Gentle Ben," the television serial about a pet bear. While he was on location at the Ivor Tors studios in Florida in April of 1968, the rumor somehow was started that "Bart Starr is dead." It spread wildly, and before long the switchboards at Packer headquarters and at the *Press-Gazette* were jammed with calls from anxious fans. We finally had to call the studio, where we learned that Bart was not only very much alive, but performing credibly before the cameras.

I don't worry too much about losing Bart to the movies, but of course the twilight of his career in football is approaching. I hope that we can keep a strong line in front of him for another three or four years, because without the protection he could suffer the same fate as Y. A. Tittle. The Giants' trades in the early sixties left the grand old quarterback to take the punishment of the rushing defensemen, and he was forced to quit. With an adequate bulwark, his able arm could have seen another year or two of valuable action. Bart has suffered sore ribs and an injured hand in recent years, so he'll have to make a season-by-season assessment of his ability to continue. Quarterback durability is a strange thing: A good quarterback can bring up the level of the entire team to the point where he can extend his career by a few years.

When he finally hangs up jersey number 15 for good, Bart can just about do what he wants and be assured of success. He'd make an excellent coach, and I'd give anything to have him, but unfortunately economic reality comes into play: The superstar in football can hardly afford to become a coach because it's such a drop from his finishing salary to the starting pay of an assistant. Tittle, for example, would have loved to coach for the 49ers, but his thriving insurance business was too lucrative. He had to settle for helping out at San Francisco on a part-time basis. Paul Hornung, too, would have stayed on at New Orleans or returned to Green Bay as an assistant, but he could command a much higher salary in the broadcasting business, where he could capitalize on his fame, reputation, and personality. Bart has the opportunity to take over a soft-drink bottling franchise any time he's ready, and he is also involved in myriads of endorsement and business deals. In fact, he could just about run his finger down Standard & Poor's list and be assured that any place he stopped would yield a company with room in its lineup for a man whose life spells s-u-c-c-e-s-s.

## 23 · RELIGION AND THE GREEN BAY PACKERS

**P**ARISHIONERS at the Shrine of the Immaculate Conception in Atlanta, Georgia were unaware of the crisis behind the scenes on a Tuesday morning in May of 1968. The assigned altar boy had failed to show up, and mass was scheduled to begin in a few minutes.

When the priest emerged on time, the last-minute substitution trailing in his footsteps had a round, beaming face befitting an altar boy. It was a familiar face, that of Vincent Thomas Lombardi. A visitor to Atlanta during the National Football League owners' meeting, he volunteered to play the not unfamiliar role. And the following day, when a mass for all the deceased of the NFL was said, Lombardi again came off the bench to participate in the service.

Religion plays an important part in the private and professional lives of the Packers. If the decision has to be made, we feel it comes ahead of football. But usually a member of our team finds that his religious and professional lives are inseparable, because moral and physical strength are equally important in the course of a long gridiron campaign.

The habit of praying together before playing together is formed in training camp at St. Norbert College in De Pere, Wisconsin, where the rigorous schedule makes provision for attending mass before morning practice. It is not uncommon to find one of the coaches or players serving as altar boy, and the celebrant often works the Packers into his prayers.

Before a game, we join in the Lord's Prayer, coaches and players kneeling on the locker room floor. If it is a Sunday, we have usually prayed together in church services earlier that morning. We never go into a game without praying for a worthy performance, for the ability to play our best, and for protection from injuries.

One of our strongest opponents in recent years has been the Los Angeles Rams, and Lombardi often invoked the teachings of religion to prepare the players for the tough contests. In 1966, when we met the Rams after clinching our conference race and there was a temptation to let up, he told the players:

"If you go out on that field and give anything less than the best you have in you, you are not only cheating yourself and your team, but your very Maker, who gave you the ability to succeed. If you give Him anything less than the very best He gave you, then you are cheating Him."

They went out on the field and won, 27–23.

A year later, when we faced the Rams in the Western Conference playoff, it was bound to be one of our toughest games of all time. Only two weeks earlier quarterback Roman Gabriel had directed a masterful game and beaten us by three points with a score in the final minute of play. In the Friday squad meeting before the game, Lombardi emphasized the importance of the game by quoting from St. Paul's Epistles: "Know ye not that they which run in a race run all, but one receiveth the prize. So run that ye may obtain." The Packers gave the Rams a 7–0 head start and then went on to silence Gabriel's horn, 28–7.

Even when we are in a remote motel near an NFL city on a Sunday morning, the Packers worship together. In one room Bart Starr conducts a service for the Protestant players, while down the hall Zeke Bratkowski helps the priest brought in to say mass for the Catholic members of the squad.

In Green Bay, where devout football fans have come to speak of "the Gospel according to St. Vincent" and there once were bumper stickers bearing the legend "God is alive and coaching the Green Bay Packers," religion and football fanaticism are quite compatible. There is even a specialized local form of humor in making Packer jokes out of Bible passages: "Coach Lombardi bought five hotdogs and two Pepsis and fed the fifty thousand at Lambeau Stadium."

During the height of the craze, publicity director Chuck Lane dusted off an old Bear Bryant joke and convinced the usually reticent Starr to use it in a talk to the Fellowship of Christian Athletes, an organization to which many of our players belong. "Did you hear about Lombardi's accident?" the joke goes. "He was taking his usual morning walk when he was hit by a motorboat."

Local clergymen don't mind the slight irreverence at all. In fact, some of them are the leading Packer backers. At the beginning of the season, all denominations are likely to hear special sermons worked around the theme of the Packers. When players of visiting teams come to worship, the finest Christian charity is extended to them, at least until 1 P.M. "It's nice to see members of the Bear family in our congregation this morning," said the pastor of a downtown parish one Sunday. Another Sabbath, after a particularly long service had the parishioners restless, their spiritual leader stepped into the pulpit, bowed his head as was the custom before a long sermon, then raised his hand and said: "We're running late; see you at the game," and made a hasty exit.

During the football season, Catholic churches in Green Bay change the regular baptism time from 1:15 P.M. to 5 P.M. on game days. When one family inquired if there might be another alternative, the priest suggested: "Well, you can baptize him a Lutheran until next week when the Packers are on the road."

Even when the moment is not lighthearted, religion and football mix. When the founder of the Green Bay Packers, Earl "Curly" Lambeau died, his body lay in state at St. Francis Xavier Cathedral, and he was fittingly surrounded by the greens and golds that are the Packer colors: gold on the vaulted ceiling, the sanctuary railing, the trim of the celebrant's seat; the

## PACKER DYNASTY

green of velvet cushions at the rail, missals in the pews, and ferns around the altar.

The pastor of St. Xavier, Monsignor Gehl, had been a Packer fan for years, and he embellished his eulogy with gridiron references: "The games are played by men with great ability, and each plays to his very limit. But when the games are finished, we return to respect and love each other. We are all a Christian people. I ask that you remember Curly Lambeau in your prayers." And later: "The final gun has sounded for Curly Lambeau. . . . May God leave him with a winning score."

When my oldest son was wed recently in the same church, the priest's message to the couple ended with the admonition, "Unless you accept God as your coach, general manager, and owner, your team will not succeed."

At least once a year, the Church even goes so far as to complete a forward pass in Lambeau Stadium. The exhibition game played in Green Bay each September is designated the Bishop's Charities game, and the bishop himself traditionally tosses out the first ball.

But the finest indication of what religion means to the Packer coaches and players, I think, is reflected in the concept we have of ourselves and of each other. I am proud to know that when rough and rugged linebacker Ray Nitschke was asked at the 1968 Columbus, Ohio, Touchdown Club dinner to comment on Coach Lombardi, his summation was: "He is a tremendous Christian."

That is more important than any trophy or championship.

## 24 · WHAT IS VINCE LOMBARDI REALLY LIKE?

NBC TELEVISION's Hugh Downs used to lament the frequency with which he had to answer that same old question during his years as the announcer for Jack Paar on the "Tonight" show: What is Jack Paar *really* like? I know how he felt. From February to May every year I choked down the last bite of roast beef and peas, stood up before the Kiwanis, the Boy Scouts, or the Moose Junction Athletic Association, and tried to convince them of the simple truth: Vince Lombardi is a hardworking, practical, religious, dedicated, fair-and-square businessman who happens also to be a football genius and a leader of men. Most people are disappointed that the explanation isn't more complicated.

The secret of Vince Lombardi's success is that he used every type of persuasion known—charm, anger, laughter, tears, nagging, pleading, coaxing, demanding—to make every single person in his organization do the best job he was humanly capable of performing. One day about a year and a half ago a young woman named Sarah McLain joined us as a receptionist in the front office. She recalls her early days on the job:

"The first day Mr. Lombardi came out, shook my hand, and told me, 'I'll be yelling at you.' I was so scared I couldn't let go of his hand. The assistant coaches stood over in the corner and nearly died laughing. I told myself: 'That's the way he is; that's the way he gets things done. So, whatever he says, I'm going to do it and do it right, and if he says it's wrong, I'll do it over again his way.' Right away I could see it was going to be the best job I ever had, because there's no communications problem around here. Everybody gets the word; that's why things run so smoothly.

"I went one week, two weeks, three weeks and he didn't yell at me. Then I had a dream one night: His special fountain pen that fills like a hypodermic needle had run dry. I was so nervous when I woke up that I came to work half an hour early that morning and went right into his office to check it. Sure enough, it *was* dry. That's Mr. Lombardi; he even gives you orders in your dreams."

He can terrorize a fullback, but he can clown around, too, when he wants to. I've seen him beat his hat out of shape and weave down the aisle of the plane like Crazy Guggenheim just to loosen everybody up. After a loss, the same man who yelled and prodded all week long would walk through the bus to the airport talking gently to each individual and uplifting sagged spirits. If I were lost in the middle of nowhere with only one dime for the pay telephone and needed a doctor, a lawyer, a priest, and a friend, I'd call Vince Lombardi. As a child might say, he can make everything all right.

If I've fallen short in explaining Vince Lombardi, look how many have tried . . .

Red Smith in the Chicago *Sun-Times:*

"Depending on which author you read, the coach of the Green Bay Packers is either Thomas de Torquemade or St. Francis of Assisi. In any case, his brain is obviously a transplant from Leonardo da Vinci."

AFL official Tony Veteri after the second Super Bowl:

"He misses nothing, not even the slightest detail. I remember one play when I thought Jerry Kramer threw a good block. But Lombardi snarled at him, 'If you'd executed it the way you were supposed to, the runner would have made an extra yard.' An extra yard? It wasn't an important yard, either. This and other things I heard and saw showed me why he is such an extraordinary coach. I was never more impressed."

Guard Fred "Fuzzy" Thurston:

"He's a totally dedicated man. Somehow you don't mind it

from him. He demands 125 percent and that way he gets 95."

Halfback Donny Anderson, interviewed in the Milwaukee *Sentinel:*

"Sure, everyone gets pressure from him, but he's not harsh in training or anywhere else. . . . He's an iron man when it comes to getting people in shape, but that's the first rule in football. I enjoy playing for him. Anyone in his right mind would feel that way. He's a very dedicated person."

Wife Marie Lombardi, interviewed by CBS television:

"He says he's made some football players out of men and some men out of football players. He's prouder of the latter."

Colonel Red Blaik, former Army coach:

"He is volatile, enthusiastic, and given to degrees of emotion not likely to be found in coaches. He is motivated to succeed, to win if you will, not for personal glory, but rather for the personal satisfaction that comes with great accomplishment."

Tackle Steve Wright:

"If Vince had been born two hundred years ago, he'd have conquered the world. He's the kind of guy who rallies people behind him. He's a leader. But he is just plain terrible to play for."

Defensive end Lionel Aldridge:

"Coach Lombardi makes the rules, and you go along with him or else he rips the corner off your paycheck if you're wrong. If you're wrong again, the corner gets bigger."

Lombardi himself, after reading of a rumored trade:

"They say I'm ill-tempered. How can you help but be ill-tempered when you keep reading such guff?"

Defensive end Willie Davis:

"He always hits you with the unexpected. When you lost or play badly and expect to get chewed out, he'll come in and say, 'Why is everybody looking so sad?' But when you play well and think everything is all right, that's the time he comes in looking for heads."

Quarterback Bart Starr:

"He gives you confidence, a method to go and win, the proper mental attitude, and I think that's 90 percent of it because everybody is even physically. He does a tremendous job of keeping that sharp edge."

End Ron Kramer:

"He rules. He's the leader. You do it his way or you don't do it at all. And it's a good way. He's a great leader and he hates to lose. He makes everybody feel that way."

Tackle Bob Skoronski:

"His approach was so perfect it was unbelievable. He's been so emotional that he's been down on his knees with us. He's laughed with us, kidded us, and suffered the things we've suffered and enjoyed the things we've enjoyed."

Jim Murray in the Los Angeles *Times:*

"Vince Lombardi, like Ben Hogan and golf, just knows something about his game that nobody else knows."

Green Bay *Press-Gazette* writer Bob Woessner:

"He is respected, admired, looked on with awe as if he were some great natural phenomenon like the Grand Canyon or the Rocky Mountains. He has become, in this part of the land, an epic hero—a man who will always find a way to emerge triumphant."

Text of Fordham University Insignis Award:

"Untried kids and tired old men have learned from him. They have learned that men like Vincent Lombardi know how to fight, how to win, how to lose. Above all, they and all of us have learned that only with such men is the whole greater than its parts, that a team, a real team, is like all creations of love—a thing of wonder."

Defensive tackle Henry Jordan:

"The Packers are great because Vince Lombardi teaches and preaches absolute professionalism and makes us believe it."

Chicago *Sun-Times* columnist Bill Gleason:

"Given the opportunity, Vince Lombardi could have saved the Studebaker, revived the Edsel and brought off the Tucker Torpedo."

Milwaukee *Sentinel* sports editor Lloyd Larsen:

"Because he sets a rugged pace, his players soon fall into the hard work pattern, and because they work harder, they are in better condition and are more likely to come up with superior execution."

But, of course, Vince typically has the last word:

"I don't care what people say about me, just as long as I win. That's what I get paid for."

And that's what Vince Lombardi is really like.

## 25 · SLEDS, HORNS, AND OTHER TOYS FOR GROWN MEN

WHEN Vince Lombardi took over the Green Bay Packers, the first thing he did was to rule out gimmicks. No scrambling, no double reverses, no shotguns or alley-oops.

But gadgets? And innovations? Ah, that is something else entirely. There's not a football coach alive—not even those of us who believe in playing "pure" football as a contest of will and ability—who is not obsessed with mechanical gadgets and ideas for tinkering with the game. A reporter once asked me what I do in the off-season, and I replied that there is no off-season for a professional coach. He pressed me to tell him what I do when I'm not thinking about football, and I had to reply: "I'm always thinking about football." Even when I make my annual vacation getaway to Arizona and Nevada, I find myself lining up eleven blue poker chips against eleven red ones and trying a new maneuver. At banquets where I have to wait through the presentation of a few hundred merit badges before giving my talk, I sometimes find my napkin doodles turning from aimless lines to the basic sketch for a new piece of training equipment.

A pro coach is always on the lookout for devices to improve the training of his players, whether the ideas come from fellow pros or a high school coach. And as a result, equipment has changed considerably from the simple blocking dummies we charged at back in the thirties.

A tour of the Packer training field across Oneida Street

from our headquarters takes in most of the latest equipment. The plain old stuffed dummies are still there. The offensive backfield assistant coach may hold one in front of him and wiggle it at charging halfbacks, but mostly the dummies have become makeshift sofas for tired newsmen. The two-man sleds are in use, along with an outgrowth developed by the coaches at Tulane, the seven-man sled. We bought one of the earliest ones, but now every pro team has one, as do all the colleges and even some high schools. The Tulane coaches used to have them turned out by a small foundry in their area, but the idea was eventually bought by a training equipment manufacturer in Ardmore, Pa., who supplies the entire country.

In 1967 we were the first pro team to use a new machine developed by a high school coach to simulate a realistic rush for tackling practice. The device looks like a cow exerciser, with a big boom extending from a tripod base. The coach, standing at the end of the boom, releases a trip which sends a dummy sailing down the rail toward the player, who is standing in the tripod. When the player sees it coming, he rushes at it, throws his block, and pushes the simulated opponent back out to the end of the boom, where it locks in place. There's a sway in the boom and two springs for tension that make the dummy feel almost like a real rusher. Although there's no device that can completely simulate game conditions, we feel this one does a pretty good job while minimizing the chance of injuries. If we didn't have to worry about injuries, we could probably get along without any equipment at all.

The Reaction Machine, developed by an Idaho coach, is near and dear to me as a former defensive coach. First demonstrated by its developer at various coaches' conventions, it is now produced by a major equipment firm and has sold in the thousands. This device tests the ability of a defensive lineman to "read" the intention of his opponent according to his moves, and to react accordingly. The coach stands behind the device and manipulates a helmet perched on two shoulderlike wings. He can move the helmet forward to simulate a straight drive, back to indicate that the "foe" is dropping into a pass protection block, or to either side, as if a play were developing in that direction. The player he is drilling must move in the proper direction and then move the dummy-sled part of the device as if he were fighting through the resistance. We do a lot of work on it with our men, and we feel it's one reason why they're the most alert we've seen through the years.

Sometimes the evolution of a particular apparatus is a bit difficult to trace. A gadget we call The Shield is an inflated device about thirty inches long and eighteen inches wide that defenders push with in light contact scrimmage to prevent hard collisions and needless injuries. When two manufacturers of the device wound up in court over which owned the patent rights, I was called upon to give a deposition for the trial. My testimony didn't really favor either one of the parties: I explained that it was *I* who first invented the device when I was at Stanford. My only regret was that I hadn't carried through with the marketing of the successful gadget.

Back in 1963 and 1964, when our fortunes were a bit below what we considered par, we were working doubly hard on drills designed to improve our timing. One thing that irked Vince was that he just couldn't simulate a realistic pass rush for his quarterback in the receivers-and-halfback segment of the practice session without using both defensive and offensive lines. That virtually amounts to a full scrimmage, and takes the lines away from their important drills. And when the lines wanted to drill, the backs were usually otherwise occupied. After a particularly unsatisfactory workout, Vince asked, "Can't we come up with some sort of timer device that's reliable and accurate?" I decided to work on it.

First I checked into the timers on stoves and washing machines. The problem: they were set to tick off minutes. We needed to have an alarm go off precisely three seconds after the snap, signifying to the quarterback that the defense has begun to penetrate the offensive line and it is time to start moving around in the pocket to avoid being nailed behind the line of scrimmage.

I followed up a tip and went to a local camera store to find out if darkroom timers might be the answer. They sent me to people who develop X-ray film, and there I found the split-second accuracy we needed. The problem: split-second accuracy doesn't come from wind-up springs; you have to be plugged into a power source. It would take either a portable generator or an extension cord three city blocks long for us to use the laboratory timer.

Next I tried Tom VanderZander, the town's leading watch repairman. After talking to fellow watch men at a national convention and writing a half dozen letters to experts around the country, he concluded that nothing like what I needed existed. But he was intrigued with the idea by then, and he started tinkering with batteries, mechanisms from old timepieces, and various noisemakers. After four months of work ("At 25 cents an hour, I'd have to charge you a thousand dollars to break even," he told me), he came up with something that worked.

I took the device to practice, and we decided to try it out on the drill between the offensive and defensive lines. Usually line drills are dull and unrealistic because they amount to a lot of grunt-and-puff work without any reward other than the coach's "Awright, line up and do it again." After setting up the machine, I explained to the players what would happen:

"Okay, you'll line up and move when you hear the snap, same as before. Precisely three seconds later the horn sounds, which means that the defense should be into the pocket and the passer should be on the move. This will give us an accurate indication each time of whether the offensive or the defensive line did the better job."

I was certain that the new element of competition would make the drill more successful. And the coaches would be freed from the nuisance of trying to observe a stopwatch and their players at the same time.

Fourteen burly men lined up on the ball—seven against seven. When the center moved the ball, I pushed the lever on the machine. A thousand one, a thousand two, a thousand thr-HONK! Nitschke doubled over with laughter just at the spot where he should have been shooting into the pocket, and Fuzzy

Thurston collapsed convulsively, tears filling his eyes. Both lines ground to a halt, stopped not by one another but by the incongruity of the noise. When we finally restored order, I did what I should have done in the first place: demonstrated the device and let them hear the squawker a couple of times.

"All right, back on the ball," I ordered. "Remember, three seconds and the passer should be under pressure. Let's see which team is stronger."

One-two-three-Honk! The horn went off with the offensive men firmly standing their ground. "That was no three seconds," came a voice from the defensive side.

Again, one-two-three-Honk! Again the defense had not penetrated. A linebacker griped: "I counted myself, dammit. That was only two seconds."

Another time, one-two-three and the defense was spilling over and around the line. A moment later and I was surrounded by seven offensive men: "Coach Bengtson, that thing's out of whack. . . . How do you know it's *exactly* three seconds?" The protesting linemen were even supported by a wary offensive coach, so we got out the stopwatch and ran a test half a dozen times. The new timer proved accurate. Back to the trenches. The gadget was a success.

Subsequently we made some changes, and my partner and I decided to try marketing them in a modest business venture called the Coaching Aids Company. Our first "Football Instant Timer" was simply a battery-operated horn with a regular stopwatch attached. When the big hand was on three, it made contact with the horn; it was that simple. We sold a few, and we got complaints about "sticking." The problem was traced to a buildup of carbon deposits on the contacting hand, so we sent along instructions on how to clean it with a paper match from time to time. Later we eliminated the offending part and replaced it with a transistor. At one hundred twenty-five dollars apiece, the orders were starting to come in.

Then I got a call from Tom Fears in New Orleans: His timer didn't work. I worried for four days while it was in the mail, wondering if all of them would be coming back with an inherent weakness. It turned out that the battery had merely come out of its holder and was loose.

"Gee, Tom," I chewed him out over the phone. "If you bought a flashlight and it didn't work, wouldn't you check out the battery first?" I was rather exasperated.

"When I buy something exotic and it doesn't work, I figure something exotic is wrong with it," he replied.

So we improved the battery housing and added "Check batteries before using" to the instruction sheet. To date we have sold about a hundred of the things, and all over the country grown men are pushing each other around waiting for the horn to go off.

The innovation that has coaches talking today, of course, is the new artificial turf. We first tested the base portion of 3M's Tartan surface in 1966 under a tackling dummy, and were delighted to find that the equipment didn't have to be moved after periods of rain. With artificial turf there was no longer any wear and tear, even after the continued pounding of heavy feet. Two years later, with the Tartan still in great shape, we rolled out a section of Monsanto's Astroturf under our running ropes to give it a similar test.

We probably won't be the first pro football team to install the synthetic grass, primarily because we don't have the pressures of high usage and we have just invested in our heating system. But it probably won't be long before we'll be playing on it in cities where pro baseball, pro football, and college or high school teams tear natural sod to pieces and rain then turns it into a sea of mud. In Detroit last year the downpours floated away strips of sod covering the baseball infield on Thanksgiving Day, and the Lions were up to their ankles in the muck. At the University of Wisconsin, which could no longer afford the luxury of practice fields for the marching band and minor sports when land was needed for parking and expansion, Tartan was the answer. Their football team had an A-1 surface to play on even though it had been used extensively throughout the week before each game.

The Packer organization tends to be quite cautious about

major decisions. We are deliberate in the office as well as on the field. So we are studying very carefully the incidence of accidents on artificial playing surfaces. It has been immediately apparent that the devastating knee injuries have been greatly reduced because the short cleats used on artificial turf do not dig in so deeply, making for cleaner tackles. At the same time, there are more flesh "burns" on the exposed skin of the arms, and at the University of Tennessee, which has the artificial surface, there were five head injuries in the first season of use. Our team doctor has advised us to wait until compatible safety gear is developed before installing pseudograss. Perhaps redesigned helmets and jerseys with "slide guards" on mandatory sleeves will join the soccer-type cleats as the new generation of "Tartan Togs" or "Astro Suits."

Our decision to wait for a second-generation turf instead of being a leader will give us a chance to look at the entire picture of the football field of the future. There's more to it than just spreading out a carpet of synthetic resin compound over your field and topping it off with a fuzzy green carpet. The 3M company, which has the more durable and lifelike of the artificial turfs, suggests a twenty-inch base—layers of soil, crushed rock, two kinds of asphaltic concrete, and finally their surface, to which the "grass" is laminated. Because there is no erosion over the season, the extreme crown of the standard football field (eighteen inches at Lambeau Field; as much as twenty-four inches at the center of the field in wetter climes) is unnecessary.

With time to study this new field, I think we could come up with some pretty exciting developments. First of all, the electric heating blanket could be buried in such a way that it would be effective even to the point of preventing snow accumulation; then all we'll need is a super-sized squeegee roller to remove surface dampness.

Next we can look into the possibility of burying electrical filaments a fraction of an inch below the surface; I've talked to the 3M people, and they say it should be no problem with their surface, which is mixed and poured at the site. Why the filaments? Because this may be a good time to think about replacing the archaic and sometimes imprecise "stakes and chain" system of yardmarking with an up-to-date, electronic system.

"Grabowski breaks a tackle at the thirty-seven and hurls three more yards in a great second effort. He's close to that all-important first down, folks. Did he make it? Let's see. The official is over the ball. He takes out his electronic sensor, points it at the spot, and . . . Yes, there it is on the Forward Progress Panel of the electronic scoreboard. The flashing green light is on, and the Packers have a first down on the opponents' thirty-four."

Did he say "the electronic scoreboard?" And why not? With buried wires and pushbutton control devices like those now available on remote tuning television sets, there's no reason the progress couldn't be visually presented. Proponents of the sticks and chains say the old system has an important element of suspense, but as anyone who has watched the computers at work tabulating, tallying, and predicting on election night knows, electronic systems can be fascinatingly suspenseful, too.

Once the field has been wired, the system could be extended to include the goalposts as well. Remember that controversial field goal against Baltimore in 1965? There needn't have been any dispute if there had been an electronic goalpost, using a combination of surface sensors and electronic eyes to indicate if the ball crossed within the fair zone. If the all-seeing and unemotional "eyes" of the goalpost detected the ball's passage, the three points could be toted up electronically and automatically, accompanied perhaps by three blasts on a suitable scoreboard Klaxon.

Ready for the next logical step? The Computer Animation Corporation of Dallas has programmed a computer to show "live" diagrams of football plays like those used in the space program to chart spacecraft progress. First demonstrated last year on nationwide television during the game between Notre Dame and Michigan State, the device depicts the offensive eleven as squares, the defensive players as triangles, and the ball as a tiny circle. Directions of runs, blocks, and passes are shown with broken lines. As used by ABC Television in its demonstration, the computer screen offered an instant replay that made clear what pattern was used, who performed how, and exactly what the result was. It made the game understandable and exciting to people who had never before comprehended the task of a pulling guard or the route of a tight end. There's no reason why a scoreboard couldn't show what happened electronically for the benefit of the poor but loyal fan occupying a field-level seat in the bowl end of the stadium.

There's even historic precedent, for those purists who don't like to see anything new come along. Back in the 1920s, before there was radio play-by-play or television coverage, the Green Bay fans gathered in a local hall to follow the progress of away games on a huge contraption called the Grid-Graph. News of the game came by private radio hookup through a single large speaker, and monitors at the giant blackboard marked off the position of the ball on the chalk diagram of a football field. The new computerized Forward Progress Panel could be named Grid-Graph II in honor of its predecessor.

If you haven't blown your mind yet, here comes the clincher. What's the fan's favorite pastime? Second-guessing the coach and the quarterback, right? Okay, borrowing a trick from the Czechoslovak pavilion at Expo 67, there's nothing to keep us from installing a certain percentage of "Voting Gallery" seats (for which the ticket scale would be 20 percent higher) equipped with preference buttons connected to the big board. After each play, figures flashing on the board could indicate what percent of the fans predicted the play, and/or what percent of the fans would have tried another approach.

Crazy? Look at what many of the television quiz and game shows are doing these days. Look what happened to organized baseball when it failed to keep up fan interest. Give a thought to the popularity of thumbs up, thumbs down in gladiatorial contests of old. Maybe it's not so crazy after all.

Frankly, I'm not really anxious for this set of electrifying proposals to attract the label "Bengtson's Folly," so I'll lay the blame where it belongs, on my nimble-witted co-author. I've

## PACKER DYNASTY

warned him that his ideas may get him no farther than the fellow who modified the surveyor's mirror system to come up with a more accurate replacement for the chains. The coaches all gave it a look, said, "Gee, it works fine," and completely ignored it despite its merits. Even those who play regularly in stadiums where lines painted across baseball infields are rubbed away after one quarter showed little or no interest.

But any new idea deserves consideration. Football is the number one sport in the country today, but it faces the problems of rising player demands, saturation of television coverage, dissipation of talent by overexpansion, and the ever-present danger of failing to keep pace with the times, as baseball has done.

So we get one coach's idea for variable scoring of field goals: more points for kicking from the forty than for kicking from the twenty. That one will never catch on because it defeats the whole idea of the game. The team that can move the ball to the twenty deserves better odds than the team that could only make it as far as the forty. Pro football isn't about to branch out into the welfare payments business.

And there's the national sportswriter who proposed a soccer-type system for shuffling the divisions at the end of each year, placing the four strongest finishers in the top bracket, and so on down to the four weakest in their own frame. It works great in Europe, where fans get as excited over the prospect of moving up into a higher division at season's end as we do over the NFL championship. But it ignores the important football tradition of regional rivalries such as Green Bay vs. Chicago, Washington vs. Baltimore, and Los Angeles vs. San Francisco. And frankly, it could hurt some franchises to be classed with the stumblebums.

I have one modest proposal that involves no gadgetry, won't cost anybody a cent, and should be warmly received by everyone who owes his daily living to the National Football League. As the league approaches its golden anniversary, it is fitting that the NFL Championship be rechristened the *Halas Cup*.

## PACKER DYNASTY

Our top contest has both an unwieldy label, the NFL-AFL World Championship, and a rather trite one, the Super Bowl. Since the two leagues do not have a common history, and since they have much more important business to attend to during the next few years, I doubt that either of those names will be changed.

But the proud old National Football League owes its very existence to George Halas. He organized the first team in a garage in Canton, Ohio, back in 1920. He coached some of the greats: Bronko Nagurski, Red Grange, and Sid Luckman, to mention just a few of the biggest names. He saved the Green Bay franchise in its darkest years by threatening to pull his Bears out and form a new league if the other clubowners took away the Packer franchise. His Bear teams have won eight NFL championships and have been one of the consistently strong teams throughout the league's history. He was one of the fairest and most charitable men in the coaching profession, active for nearly all of the forty-eight years leading up to his retirement at the end of the 1967 season. "Papa Bear" deserves to see his name on the circuit's top trophy. No other name could ever belong there.

## 26 · CERTAIN THINGS YOU DON'T TAMPER WITH

**F**OOTBALL GAMES, like duels, forest fires, and wars, must be fought to the end, no matter what adversity presents itself. Come to think of it, a sheriff, a good rain, and a treaty can terminate the other three, so that leaves only football and postmen to carry on the tradition of not being deterred by rain, sleet, or snow.

Early sandlot football had that chip-on-the-shoulder showdown quality: "You and your guys be there at one o'clock sharp with the ball, and me 'n' my guys will push you from one end of the field to the other." When colleges and professionals started playing the game in organized fashion, they decided that the "no matter what" element should be an integral part of the game. Nobody questioned it much until the Green Bay Packers started making the NFL championship game a more or less regular Christmas present to their fans.

In 1961 we played New York in Green Bay on December 31, and one Packer summed it up for the press: "The Giants were more concerned about the weather than anything else. They came in tennis shoes, gloves, and scarves. We just came to play." New Yorkers clucked over the "inhuman conditions" for an entire year, after which the rematch was played in forty-mile-an-hour winds on the frozen turf of Yankee Stadium, the Packers won handily, and not much more was heard for a while about Green Bay weather.

## PACKER DYNASTY

The next time our city played host to the game was in the "Fog Bowl" of 1965 against Cleveland, when the grounds crew had the task of removing several tons of fresh snow before the teams could play on the murky field. Our players, slogging through the same mud as the opponents did, gained 204 yards rushing to their 64. Our quarterback, slipping on the same wet grass and tossing through the same dense air as his counterpart did, passed for 128 yards vs. 97 for the Browns. Cleveland, of course, is situated at the wind-whipped end of Lake Erie, smack in the middle of a stretch of white-blanketed countryside the meteorologists call the "Snow Belt." But the topic of conversation in BrownTown for days after was that dreadful Green Bay weather.

The protests became organized, however, after the 1967 championship—the so-called "Freeze Bowl" when Dallas came north in quest of the championship and lost on Starr's brilliant maneuver in the final seconds. In the wake of that game, the league came the closest it has in years to changing its traditional system of alternating the championship game site each year between the Western Conference winner and the Eastern.

Our concern with offering fair and reasonable playing conditions had prompted us to supplement the usual hay and tarpaulin protection with the now-famous (and wrongfully infamous) "electric blanket" beneath the turf of Lambeau Field. There are other heated fields in the country—the Air Force Academy in Colorado has one like ours—but most of them are designed only to promote grass growth in cold climates. Vince "shopped" for ours until he could get a system that would prevent freezing of the turf on midwinter game days.

Installation of our eighty-thousand-dollar unit was completed in the summer before the "Freeze Bowl," supervised by George S. Halas, nephew of Papa Bear. He's a scout for his uncle's team, and he got a kick out of wearing a Bears' cap on our field. But whenever he was questioned about his loyalty, he pointed to a Packer tie clasp and laughed, "I'm playing it both ways until this job is over."

## PACKER DYNASTY

After laying fourteen miles of heating cable 6½ inches below the surface and twelve inches apart, the technicians installed a control panel in a utility room in Packer headquarters so we can keep track of field conditions. When air and turf temperatures dip below forty-five degrees, a thermostat automatically turns on the power in the 780,000-watt system. Lights on the control panel indicate which sections of the field are warm enough and which are still heating. A continuous line on moving graph paper under glass indicates temperatures at the center and the side of the field. The machine automatically brings the entire field to the same temperature. While the system is not designed to melt snow, it usually keeps the grass green and the turf in proper shape for running. The only drawback is that it can't be covered with a tarpaulin unless expensive "breathing canvas" with air holes is used to prevent formation of condensation.

Vince's electric blanket received considerable publicity before the game—so much that he made a point of stating, "Weather won't beat the team that loses this game." He had told people dozens of times before what does beat you: your own mistakes, lack of will to win, superior performance by your opponent. But not weather, for that is the same on both sides.

Another truism is that football is a game where things that "just couldn't happen" usually do happen. The night of December 30, 1967, the temperature in Green Bay plunged to sixteen degrees below zero—so suddenly and severely that our system just wasn't able to handle it. Despite our precautions and our good intentions, we had a field as hard and slick as glazed pavement at game time, and the temperature was still well below zero.

When the frigid encounter was over, the detractors could hardly claim that the weather had given either team an advantage. The statistics on forward progress were virtually identical all down the line, suggesting that if anything the weather had been an equalizing factor:

|  | Dallas | GB |
|---|---|---|
| Rushing yardage | 92 | 80 |
| Passing yardage | 100 | 115 |
| Total | 192 | 195 |
| Offensive plays | 33 | 32 |
| Average gain | 3.2 | 3.1 |

Furthermore, each team scored once on a "bomb" of more than forty yards, so the explosive pass play was not ruled out by the weather.

Nevertheless, the lid was off and all the arguments for and against all-weather football were aired anew. A Dallas *Times-Herald* columnist quoted Commissioner Pete Rozelle as saying, "Under the conditions it was played last Sunday, the game was unfair to both teams," and Dallas sportswriters pressed Rozelle to move the championship games to the South. The same columnist said NFL president Art Modell of Cleveland would push to bring the matter of warm weather sites up at the next league meeting.

Most adamant of all was Dallas Cowboys' president Tex Schramm: "When I saw the four [college] bowl games yesterday which were truly beautiful in great tests of the relative strengths of the teams involved, it was sickening to me that the greatest game of all couldn't have been played under the same circumstances. The resulting comparison was not in keeping with the NFL. It's unfortunate from the Packers' standpoint that the two most crucial games they played this year [the conference playoff against the Rams in Milwaukee and the Dallas game] were not played under proper conditions. This leaves everybody wondering whether the best team is representing the NFL in the Super Bowl. There certainly was no question last year after the Packers played such a marvelous game at the Cotton Bowl."

It takes thirteen votes in our fourteen-member league to change the scheduling of games, and the move led by Schramm and Modell was defeated despite support in some quarters. I think the clamor after the championship game was unjustified, and here are some pretty persuasive arguments:

- For the 1966 championship game in Dallas, we flew from Green Bay to a "warm-weather site" at Tulsa, Oklahoma. We arrived to find a snow-covered field and virtually no facilities to keep it clear. We had to move subsequently to a Dallas high school field, and we were beginning to wonder if we might as well have stayed home and practiced in a local gymnasium.
- On the day of the 1967 game in Green Bay, the weather wasn't all that great in Dallas. The temperature there was a chilly thirteen above, and roads were so icy that several large firms told their employees to stay home for the day because of the rash of traffic accidents and the unsure footing. It was no great day for playing in the Cotton Bowl, either.
- Green Bay's temperature for 1 P.M., December 31 over the past fifteen years has averaged twenty degrees above zero. In fact, 1967 was the first time in that period that it had dipped below zero. In 1965, the high was thirty-nine degrees above; the previous low was seven degrees, in 1953. Both the "Fog Bowl" and the "Freeze Bowl" days were preceded and followed by much nicer days. So blame our reputation on fate, not "typical" winter weather.
- The important matter of tradition and the preferences of the fans who support football must be considered. I like the open letter to Rozelle written by sports editor John Steadman of the Baltimore *News American.* "Dear Pete," he wrote, "don't sell out. . . . There are certain things you don't tamper with. Tradition is one. Nature another. And of course, the championship game. . . . The country club set, the Madison Avenue crowd, those crumbums at Toots Shor's didn't put pro football on the map. The average Joe lined up to buy his season tickets and often deprived himself of a suit of clothes or a couple cases of beer or even essentials for his family so he could see your teams play. . . . Pete, that crowd of 50,861 spectators in Green Bay in 13-degree-below-zero weather was the greatest tribute the National Football League ever received. Even television couldn't have bought all that." At the same

## PACKER DYNASTY

time, *Chicago's American* columnist Brent Musburger was polling his readers, and 81 percent of the Bears' fans wanted the championship played at the site of the conference champion come hell or high water—literally.

• The NFL runner-up bowl (the Playoff Bowl) was played one week after our chilly championship in eighty-plus heat at Miami. I suppose that was a definite advantage to the Los Angeles Rams over the Cleveland Browns. We'll never know for sure, because the Rams were superior to the Browns in their own right and won going away.

I suppose we could balance the argument by refusing to play when it is "inhumanly hot," but I feel Dallas has every right to play its charity exhibition game in the Cotton Bowl in August with the temperature at ninety-seven degrees at field level. And I think the commissioner was right in refusing to call off a game in the Los Angeles Coliseum in 1965 when the rain was so heavy fans couldn't see plays along the far sidelines.

The players, surprisingly enough, don't gripe about the weather. Their attitude is that it is of utmost importance to play the game; weather won't help one side more than the other. Both sides will have to make similar adjustments. The players refuse to use the weather as a crutch. They have been brought by the coaches and themselves to an emotional peak, and they don't want to lose it in an hour of baseball-type rain waits. They know that every disadvantage is offset by an advantage: You can't run fast on a muddy field, for example, but you can't get injured as easily on spongy turf, either. Ram quarterback Roman Gabriel, commenting on the weather in the 23-7 Packer Western Conference victory, said, "I didn't notice the cold until we were 21 points behind."

So I hope the talk of "warm-weather playoff sites" is dead forever. We think the ideal system is the Green Bay Packer Sauna: a bracing, rosy-cheeked scramble in Wisconsin followed by a quick dip in warm, sunny Florida's Super Bowl clime. Until you've tried it, don't knock it.

# PART THREE

# WINNING IS THE ONLY THING THAT COUNTS

# 27 · A COACH WITHOUT PLAYERS

As I headed for our St. Norbert College dormitory on July 10, 1968, I was beginning my fortieth training camp, the first eight times as a high school and college player, the last nine times as a Packer coach. But this year there were two important differences. I was head coach now; the entire responsibility was mine. And I was starting with a mixed bag of thirty-nine rookies and free agents, because the NFL players' association had called a strike of all veterans. To have started the exhibitions with rookies, as some suggested, would have been ludicrous. So, in effect, I was a coach without players.

Negotiations between the association and the owners had broken off late in May. Basically, the players demanded three things: an increase of one hundred thousand dollars per club in contributions to the pension fund, a minimum salary of fifteen thousand dollars, and five hundred dollars' pay for each participant in a preseason game. Under the existing system, players were given a flat ten dollars a day compensation while in training camp, and exhibitions were considered part of the practice work.

Vince Lombardi took an active role in the attempt to reach a settlement, and late in June he, George Halas, Jr., Wellington Mara of the Giants, Rankin Smith of the Atlanta club, and Jim Finks of Minnesota met with player representative John Gordy, the Detroit Lions' guard, in an attempt to iron out the differences. But the talks broke up before the long Fourth of

July weekend at an impasse over the pension plan. The owners refused to make any commitments past 1969 because of the merger with the AFL set for 1970.

The dispute was more complicated than the ordinary labor-management problem. On the surface, pro football is a burgeoning business, fattened by mushrooming fan support and huge television contracts. But the interleague warfare in the early 1960s proved costly, as player contracts were suddenly blown way out of proportion. Eventually the way to merger was paved by a special Congress-approved immunity from federal anti-trust laws. The warfare ended, but the young players with expensive, long-term contracts were still with us.

Veterans began to demand similar treatment, and many threatened to play out their options. Several owners gave star players multiyear contracts, deciding it was easier than negotiating anew every season. This "tenure" situation puts the coach in a strange position, for it hampers the "competition to make the team" that is a vital part of the training camp process. On the other hand, the players argue, it gives them a certain security, which is translated into a happy willingness to perform better.

The worst facet of the problem is that the sport is rapidly nearing the saturation point in terms of exposure. Income and profits show signs of leveling off, while costs continue to mount. After our Monday night game with Dallas last year proved a solid hit in the ratings, the league indicated that the networks would be approached about regular scheduling of weeknight games. That may help for a while—*if* matches of the caliber of a Packer-Cowboy clash can be assured with some regularity. Bolting the networks in favor of community antenna television (CATV) or pay television may be necessary. Presumably the fans, their appetites whetted by twenty years of free, constantly improving professional football, would pay a dollar or two for the privilege. But at this point, it's all a matter of conjecture, especially with many of the details of the merger to be worked out. (How many set owners would pay three dollars to watch the Philadelphia Eagles play the Buffalo Bills if they were in their doldrums of recent years? That's the kind of question the owners must consider.)

It became apparent over the Fourth of July weekend that the strike would be on: The association's poll of its members showed most of them in favor of a walkout. So the owners took the initiative and closed the camps to veterans. Although I was chagrined, I was happy that our players were spared the agony of individual decisions of loyalty. I'm sure most of them wished to see the pension benefit and exhibition game pay demands met; they worry about their futures as much as any players. But their championship years had molded them into a contented, richly rewarded, and proud unit, and they hated to see the league dispute ruin it. (As recently as 1965 there hadn't even been a Green Bay Packer in attendance at the players' association annual meeting, at least partly a reflection of their contentment.)

The day scheduled for the opening of our camp was warm and brightly sunlit. Coaches, trainers, and the flock of rookies and free agents began the ritual workouts on the Oneida Avenue practice field. Across town, at the well-equipped training facilities of Premontre Catholic High School, Bart Starr was calling the veterans together—more than a dozen of them who lived in town and several more who had come to Green Bay unsure of what would develop. Forbidden to show up at club headquarters, they went through the same calisthenics, wind sprints, blocking exercises, and pass drills that they knew occupied us at the same moment. Their discipline would not permit them to sit out the dispute. And they were mindful that the delays would hurt us more than any other team, because we were scheduled for the All-Star game on August 2, a game they had fought all last year for the privilege of playing in—and a game that provides a sizeable extra paycheck. It was probably the worst-kept secret in Green Bay that the first string was hard at work, but I was forbidden by the circumstances to even acknowledge the fact.

Fortunately, a compromise settlement was reached after a week, with the clubs satisfying all the players' demands in part.

## PACKER DYNASTY

In the long run, the Packers were not hampered as much as those clubs which had to face better-prepared AFL teams in the early preseason weeks. But that didn't comfort me much as I belatedly began the toughest job of my life: our attempt to capture an unheard-of fourth straight championship.

## 28 · FOOTBALL WITHOUT THE FOOT

THE 1968 STORY boils down to two distinct elements: Kicking, and everything else. If we had it to do all over again with just one thing changed, I think my only option would be to kidnap Don Chandler.

Ironically, in a year when training was delayed over the players' gripes about pay, Chandler decided to quit football and devote full time to his real estate interests in Tulsa. Even the memories of three straight years of championship pay plus two years of Super Bowl earning were not enough to change his mind. Nor would the personal urgings of Bart Starr and his other teammates dissuade him.

Is the placekicking specialist—a guy who plays maybe seventy-five seconds a game by the official stopwatch—all that important? Well, in 1965, Chandler's first year with us, we won two regular-season games with fourth-quarter field goals. And it took his fourth-quarter field goal to tie Baltimore, and his "fifth-period" boot to win the playoff. We lost our first 1967 meeting with the Vikings by a margin of 10–7 when a Chandler attempt went awry; he came back in the rematch to win it for us, 30–27, on a field goal with eight seconds remaining. Earlier that season he had pulled out the first Chicago game, 13–10, with a forty-six-yarder in the last period. Don kicked a total of nineteen field goals in 1967 regular-season play and went on to kick four in the Super Bowl. Yes, he was all that important to us.

## PACKER DYNASTY

The idea of a kicking specialist is relatively new to football. When the player limit was thirty-three per team, they were unheard of. After the figure was raised to thirty-six, some teams afforded the luxury. Now, with the rosters at forty, teams like the Rams and the Vikings have two kickers, one for placekicking and another for punts. The kickers have their special flat, square-toed shoes, their own vocabulary, their peculiar perspective of the game, and their own repetitious training regimen. Few have the physiques of football players, which is especially obvious because they wear little or no padding. Rhythm and readiness are their principal attributes. Consistency is what makes or breaks their reputation. Mighty Lou Groza was so consistent in his lifetime of kicking for the Browns that we could sense a certain complacency on their offensive squad whenever they got within field-goal distance; we coaches agreed among ourselves that the Browns would probably be a better team if they didn't count so heavily on The Toe.

Finding kicking specialists has become the number one personnel problem in pro football, even more critical than the development of experienced quarterbacks. Although the game has come to emphasize kicking more and more in recent years, colleges just don't turn out men who can say, "Draft me; I'm an All-American kicker." So we must look in many directions for kickers, including to other sports and other countries.

Two years ago Dallas, faced with the imminent retirement of tiny Danny Villanueva, launched a now-famous "Kicking Karavan." At the expense of one hundred thousand dollars, they sent a coach, one-time Packer Ben Agajanian, and a holder around the country, preceded by advertisements in the local papers. For all their trouble, they didn't sign a single man, although two who tried out eventually found places with the Bears and the Falcons. Again last year Dallas made a supreme effort when Villanueva announced he wouldn't return. They brought about twenty men into camp, and I noted on the first waiver list circulated to all teams by the league that over half of them were cut after the first look.

## PACKER DYNASTY

Chandler had indicated to me early in the spring that he would defer his decision for a while. Just a few weeks before training camp opened, he received his approval on a business loan, and I was without a placekicker. It was the first time the Packers, in Lombardi's and my regime, had ever experienced the early retirement of a veteran owing to business pursuits. (At thirty-four, he could have kicked for a half dozen more years.) Suddenly I had to put our search into high gear. We sent out the word that we were in the market, and things weren't the same around Packer headquarters for three months. We were deluged.

The first wave consisted primarily of soccer players. I received a telephone call from one in Ireland and a letter from another in Australia on the same day. I don't know how they'd heard, but they wanted to try out. We decided to restrict our recruiting to people on the North American continent, so we satisfied ourselves for the time being with a Swedish soccer-style kicker we brought in at our expense from a college on the West Coast. He turned out to be awful, and we sent him back the next day. We had no qualms about looking at the soccer-type kicker, but neither Vince nor I feel any preference for them. The soccer technique is easier to develop than the traditional football technique. Soccer kickers use a different set of muscles in a sweeping motion rather than a snapping motion, and they have the advantage of suffering fewer injuries. They also can control the ball better when attempting on-side or squib kicks—neither of which we employ.

The problem is that most of the soccer fellows just don't belong on the same field with football players. They're usually smaller and not aggressive in the same way that a football player is. We insist that the kickoff man run downfield, because we can't afford to show ten men against an eleven-man return rush. Often smaller or older kickers add absolutely nothing to the coverage: Agajanian didn't even go through the motions in his twilight year at Green Bay. Lou Groza, on the other hand, used his ample figure to fill up some of the space as he ran downfield, and many's the time he made a saving tackle on the runner. Chandler made some pretty good tackles in his day, and in 1967 he prevented a touchdown with a block that earned him a painful jammed neck.

Just before the Fourth of July weekend, I got a letter from a twenty-three-year-old in Saskatchewan, Canada, who had failed to win his competition with the veteran kicker on the hometown team. Canadian rules prevented him from trying out for a team outside the province, so he asked us for a special audition. He mentioned in the letter that he especially wanted to run downfield and tackle after the kickoff, hoping to impress us with his aggressiveness. We told him to come ahead.

He arrived wearing a green-and-yellow tie, the Packer colors—another sign of desire. But he also had a Groza-like midsection. We took him down to the practice field where our center, Ken Bowman, snapped, assistant coach Tom McCormick held for him, and my son Brian shagged the ball. His first few kicks from the twenty hooked wide. He not only was out of condition, he lacked the rhythm a kicker needs.

"I can get in shape," he pleaded when he realized we were discussing his condition and moves. "And I can kick better from far out." Since he hadn't hit anything from the twenty, we moved him back to near midfield. Whomp! One, two, three balls sailed through the uprights dead center. Next he tried a few kickoffs. They were rather low, but they had great distance. Suddenly McCormick was more enthusiastic. "He's the best we've seen so far," he told me as I watched from the sidelines. "I know he doesn't look too great, but he feels solid when he comes at the ball. He's got real strength on the long ones."

McCormick talked me into keeping the man around another day or two—his poor conditioning meant we couldn't work him too hard for a while. I gave my approval, and the kid was heading for the showers when Dave Hanner commented loudly enough for everyone to appreciate: "Geez, he looks like a coach—fat belly and ugly legs." The next day the boy got a second tryout, with Bart Starr himself holding. Again, he hit the long ones, but was frustrated on short attempts. I shook my head, and we let him go.

## PACKER DYNASTY

We had a look at a left-footer, which meant that the entire process was reversed—Starr had to take the snap from Bowman with his hands crossed, because the holder must put his "preferred" hand on top. After a few practice snaps, they got it down pat, and the left-footer took his turn. The left-footed kicker is no joke in professional football. His toe puts a reverse spin on the ball, and the receivers have to be primed for the effect. Donny Anderson, who does our punting, uses his left foot, and we've picked up more than one fumbled catch because the deep men couldn't hang on to it. The change in kicking foot even affects the drift of the ball, which is a receiving consideration on kickoffs, and a spotting factor on field-goal attempts. One of the ideas I've dreamed of on lazy April afternoons is the kind of fun we could have with a switch-hitting kicker who could decide at the last instant what spin to deliver. But the matter at hand was the current bidder, and he wasn't very hot. The front office cut another expense check and made another plane reservation.

One fellow who called for a tryout drove all night long with his wife and arrived in our camp at 5:30 A.M. He was a roly-poly little man who had kicked for a midwestern college and had high recommendations from his coach there. When we arrived on the practice field at nine-thirty, he had been there practicing, sleepless, for four hours. He wouldn't suit up, shower, or eat with the team, and he wore his own uniform and shoes. He showed up for three succeeding practice sessions and kicked exceedingly well for such a small man. Finally the assistant coaches decided there must be something odd about his shoe, so they asked to look at it. It was specially made by the Wilson sporting goods company so that he could get the same lofting effect as a bigger man from his much smaller leg —legal, but strange. By then the other players were beginning to ask about the man's habits, his personal uniform, and his massive brogans, so I told the personnel director to send him on his way. About that time the poor fellow's wife had an auto accident, and he didn't even stop by to pick up his expense check. We didn't have his address, but a few weeks later his family called and asked for the names of other teams that might need a kicker. I don't know who else looked at him, but he never showed up on anybody's roster.

In the second week of training, Hanner came to the lunch table and told me, "You've got a call from the commissioner." I hurried to the phone to find that it was a collect call from a father whose son wanted to try out as a kicker. I took his name, asked him to write a letter, and went back to give Hanner a piece of my mind. We were getting collect calls three or four times a day; the commissioner, as a matter of fact, was about the only one in the entire country who didn't want to kick for us.

As the All-Star game approached, our plight was gaining national attention, but I had about decided we couldn't rely on *The Ted Mack Amateur Hour* for help. So we called Atlanta and worked out a trade for their backup kicker, Wade Traynham. We had only a few days to work him in with our center and holder, but we felt he had good potential. Taking over at Atlanta the previous year when the regular kicker was injured, he had drilled some impressive field goals from far out. We had a fair indication that Jerry Kramer and fullback Chuck Mercein could handle the close-in attempts, but Traynham could be expected to kick effectively anywhere from midfield on in.

Two days before the All-Star game, I got a call from a man in New York who spoke with a heavy accent. He said he was the interpreter for a Brazilian who was trying out for the New York soccer team, and would we be interested in giving him a tryout? I said our situation had firmed up somewhat since we had traded for a man who could hit well from the forty. "My man, he can kick from sixty yards," came the reply, from what turned out to be the player's "manager" as well as his interpreter. That caught me by surprise, so I then asked how we could communicate with the man if he needed an interpreter. "No problem," was the reply. "He learn very quick. You just tell him names for what you want, he put ball where you say, right?" Slightly flabbergasted, I suggested that he wait until after we saw our new man in action. I told him we'd call back the next week if we wanted to see his man.

In our pregame warmup that Friday night, we had everyone who could bring his leg through an 180-degree arc warming up for possible kicking duty: Traynham, Kramer, Mercein, Anderson, and rookie defensive end Francis Winkler, who'd done some kicking at Memphis State. Suddenly Traynham went limp, and the trainer ran to his side. He had pulled a muscle. The trainer went to work on it, and Traynham said he would be ready to kick. It meant he had to pace the sidelines constantly to prevent the muscle from stiffening up.

Our first drive faltered before we could penetrate the All-Star defense, so we called on our gimpy kicker. His attempt was wide. Fortunately, our next three drives resulted in touchdowns, and we had twenty-one points without relying on field goal kicking. Late in the first half, Traynham came in to kick a successful thirty-yard field goal. But the real kicking excitement on our way to a comfortable 34–17 victory over the rookie stars came in the second half. We ground to a stop just across midfield. A field goal was called for, but because Traynham was stiffened up by then and we had a fairly healthy lead, I sent Kramer in to do the job. He booted a forty-seven-yarder to break the All-Star game record. Earlier he had missed from the forty-five, but now he gave our kicking hopes a real shot in the arm, or I suppose I should say leg.

The next day the Brazilian was on the phone. I told his interpreter we thought we were in good shape after seeing what Kramer could do. I heard some furious Portuguese in the background, and then the voice said firmly: "He says he watched the game on television, and he can do much better. Yesterday he kicks it over the soccer net and across the street." At that point another man got on the phone—an American member of the soccer team—and insisted that it was true. He said the Packers were crazy not to look at the man. So finally I relented and told the man and his interpreter to come out to Green Bay. When I got back to camp a little later, Hanner came into the coaches' room and sighed, "Cancel our advertisement for a kicker; we've had two more calls here since the All-Star game, and the janitor says one guy even came to the door last night."

The next day Fernando Souza hit camp.

Souza, twenty-eight, was accompanied by John Bertos, manager and part owner of the Fall River, Massachusetts Astros of the American Professional Soccer League. Before heading for Green Bay, the pair had stopped at Hartford, Connecticut to show Souza to the coaches of our Atlantic Coast League affiliate there, the Hartford Knights. The Hartford people sent him on after certifying that he could, indeed, kick the ball more than sixty-five yards from a tee. Bertos assured us that Souza was one of the high scorers in soccer, although he had only tried kicking a football once or twice before.

When the Spanish- and Portuguese-speaking Souza and his interpreter came on the practice field Monday morning, the six-foot, dark-haired Brazilian looked more like someone you'd run across jogging in a city park than a professional athlete. Wearing the low-cut soccer shoes with flappy tongues and a loose-fitting sweatsuit that twisted about him like wrinkled elephant skin when he ran, he took a warmup lap before he was introduced to kicking coach Ray Wietecha and the center-holder team of Bowman and Starr.

We started him off with kickoffs, and every single one went from the thirty-five to five yards deep in the end zone. (Kickoffs normally go from the forty, but we have to move around in practice so we won't wear out one spot on the field.)

The sight of the unorthodox kicker running in a crazy, sweeping arc and kicking on the bias caught the other players' attention. When they saw the long, soaring kicks, those who weren't drilling gathered around to watch. Next Bart moved up and we started the field-goal attempts from the thirty. Every one went through dead center, and most carried another thirty yards beyond the goalpost and over the fence, out of the practice field. From out in the vacant lot where he was shagging the balls, Boyd Dowler yelled: "Good grief, move him back or I'll have to go across the street." So we moved him back five yards, and then five yards more. Still they split the uprights and sailed over the fence. By now everybody was watching, and Ron Kostelnik asked defensive secondary coach Wayne Robinson, "Well, when do we start taking Spanish lessons?"

We stopped after he had put three forty-two-yarders through. He was tired from the travel and the excitement, but Bertos assured us that within two weeks Souza would be kicking field goals from the fifty on demand. He spoke a few words of one or the other of Souza's languages to him, and then corrected himself: "He says maybe in *one* week."

It was just a day short of a week when we first used Souza. He gave us two points after touchdowns as well as a couple of very deep kickoffs against the Giants in our home preseason opener. But then, like Traynham the week before, he pulled the muscle in his leg. Leading 14–9 in the final period, we called instead on Traynham to try a forty-one-yarder, but it drifted to the left. I decided to try Kramer if we had another such situation. The Giants, hammering away at the reserves who had been brought in when both our defensive tackles were hurt, put together a late drive to go ahead, 15–14, with less than half a minute remaining. With one second left, we were just barely in Giant territory. A winning field goal would have to come from fifty-six yards out. That meant Souza, if his boast was to be made good, but he had a huge ice pack on his swelled leg. I turned to Kramer, hoping he could beat his record performance of the previous week, but he couldn't get the right kind of shoe on fast enough. So Traynham got the call again. His attempt was blocked. We lost by one point.

Preparing for the exhibition game with the Bears, I had to wait all week to decide who would do the kicking. Both Traynham and Souza were limping. Two days before the game, Souza hit on five forty-seven-yarders in a row during practice, so I was inclined to give him the nod. In the pregame warmup, we had Souza working out, and he hit on seventeen of nineteen tries. One of the two near-misses came from midfield. I had made up my mind that in order for him to make the team, he'd have to prove he could hit the record-length shots. If he could, he'd be a potent weapon for us. But the game was one of those

## PACKER DYNASTY

where practically nothing seems to go right. I gave Souza a chance from fifty-two yards out, but the snap was poor, the ball was crooked on the tee when he connected, and it wasn't a real test. To make matters worse, he also missed an easy shot from the twenty. Traynham then missed a forty-two-yard attempt. Both tries should have been good. We lost, 10–7.

Two days later, I cut Souza. Our experiment with soccer-style kicking produced some exciting moments in practice, but nothing when it counted. He wasn't able to get the ball up fast enough. And he just didn't seem to be able to perform under the intense pressure that a kicker faces in actual game play. Getting ready for the Cowboys, who were trying out kicker Mike Clark, formerly of the Pittsburgh Steelers, I decided to make Kramer the prime placekicker, with Mercein ready and Traynham recuperating. In 1963, when Paul Hornung was suspended, Kramer had handled the placekicking, connecting on sixteen of thirty-four field-goal attempts and forty-three of forty-six extra points to lead the club in scoring. Now during practice we also had Winkler and veteran linebacker Lee Roy Caffey working on kickoffs. If Bart Starr, Vince Lombardi, or Governor Warren Knowles had shown the slightest indication of being able to kick, I think I would have given them a chance to try out.

One of the fans in the stands for our nationally televised game with the Cowboys was Don Chandler. Pressed by newsmen, he assured them his decision was final, although he did add, "I felt bad last week, watching *us* lose to the Bears." With Don watching on, Jerry kicked four conversions and a fifteen-yard field goal as we defeated Dallas by what has become a "typical" margin for the two teams, 31–27.

The next day we put Traynham on waivers as we trimmed our roster to meet the next league cutdown limit. At the same time the new AFL expansion club, the Cincinnati Bengals, cut one of their kickers, a stocky first-year man from Sacramento College named Mike Clemons. We decided to take a look at him because he had kicked several field goals in college while playing at fullback and linebacker; if he did well, we might be

## PACKER DYNASTY

getting more than a kicking specialist. Coincidentally, he is the son of Ray Clemons, a former Packer linebacker of the 1940s. Unfortunately, he didn't have quite the accuracy and reliability we expected, so we took advantage of the revised league rules to put him on our taxi squad.

We won our last two preseason games without much footwork: Three touchdowns were enough to beat Pittsburgh, 21–17, in the rain, and Kramer's stupendous repeat of a forty-seven-yard field goal was hardly needed in our 31–9 victory over the Browns. Right after that game Cleveland released kicker Errol Mann after deciding that Don Cockroft (who had produced all nine of their points) could pick up the mantle of Lou Groza. Still feeling a bit insecure over our lack of a genuine specialist, I made arrangements to bring him to Green Bay for a last-ditch tryout—for him and us both! He, too, was good enough to carry on the taxi squad.

In our opener against the Eagles, Kramer connected on three field goals in three attempts in the second half, from seventeen, twenty-two, and thirty-five yards in that order—just as if he were sharpening up in practice. A week later, he had no field goal, and one of his conversion attempts ricocheted off the upright for a miss. The third week he made one thirty-eight-yarder. In the fourth game, he missed his first three attempts—two of them from the twenty—and in the second quarter I had to call on Mercein, who made a twenty-one-yard placement. I felt that Kramer's failures, all of them near-misses, were the result of a head cold he was nursing, so I assured him he'd be the kicker against the Rams in our fifth game. As it turned out, we didn't call on him, because we elected to punt both times we stalled near the Ram forty. Anyone who watched the Rams last year knows how many field-goal attempts their exceptionally tall defenders blocked, and with every chance of winning without a field goal, we didn't want to risk a disastrous runback. The gamble didn't pay off, however, as the Rams added a three-pointer in the final minutes to beat us, 16–14.

In our sixth game, Kramer was injured. Chuck Mercein performed admirably on conversions, but he was unable to connect on his one forty-yard field goal attempt as the ball drifted to the right. We suffered a 14–14 tie with our field-goal threat nullified. So we reactivated Errol Mann in time for the nationally televised Dallas rematch. The sportswriters and television color men were preoccupied with our supposed "jinx" over Dallas, but I was beginning to wonder about the "jinx" on our kicking.

The Cowboys had run up a 10–0 lead before we finally began scoring. But as most every Monday Night at the Movies fan knows, we produced four touchdowns for a 28–17 victory, and Mann converted after all four. Our first drive ended when a thirty-seven-yard field goal attempt by Mann was inches wide to the left. Reviewing the films, we saw how close Mann's field goal try had come, and we were convinced that with a little coaching he could become more accurate. He also needed work on kickoffs; some were erratic in the Dallas game. And believe it or not, Mann pulled a muscle late in the Dallas game—that was beginning to be the standard operating procedure for anyone who joined our kicking ranks. But with Kramer on the mend, I didn't worry as much as I might have.

I guess I should have gone on worrying. Beginning the second half of the season, the Bears beat us, 13–10, in what can only be described as a kicking nightmare.

It was a hard-hitting, defensive grudge match with the Monsters of the Midway. One touchdown was the most either side could muster, which is typical of our rivalry—they had clipped us, 10–7, in the preseason game, and we had beaten them, 13–10 and 17–13, the previous year. We had plenty to kick about, but the toe just wasn't there. Mann missed a difficult try from the forty-four. But then he missed from the twenty-nine, and I began to have second thoughts about starting him. When we came up with a fourth down on the nineteen, I gave Mercein the nod, and he scored. But shortly after, from the twenty-two, he missed. One field goal out of four tries wouldn't win it for us.

Locked in a 10–10 tie, and still alive despite the 205-yard performance of Gale Sayers, we fell victim to Rule No. 4 in the NFL book: the free kick. "When receiving team fair catches the ball," goes the rule, "captain has option on how he wishes to put the ball in play." Normally, of course, you line up and run a regular play. But the rule continues: "Free kick (punt, drop-kick, or place-kick without tee). . . . If place- or drop-kick attempted and ball kicked between uprights, field goal is awarded for successful kick (3 points)." The situation also calls for a restriction on rushing by the defensive line. We were perfectly familiar with the rule; we'd used it in our opening game against these very same Bears in 1964. That time it was a successful fifty-two-yard boot by Paul Hornung in the final minutes of the first half.

We hardly expected the Bears to have the opportunity to invoke the free kick. We would be punting from our fifteen, and Donny Anderson had been averaging forty-two yards. But fate was not with us. For some inexplicable reason, Anderson punted a meager twenty-eight yards, and not out of bounds. The Bears were ready for just such a miscue. They made the free catch, and immediately kicker Mac Percival came in to make the attempt. Mac Percival, a product of the Dallas Cowboys' infamous Kicking Karavan of the previous year. Mac Percival, Chicago's answer to three years of kicking woes. Mac Percival, who had beaten the Vikings just the previous week on a forty-seven-yard field goal with three seconds remaining.

The officials reminded our players that the special rule forbade them to move from their alignment, and they had to just stand there helplessly like chorus girls waiting for the downbeat. As I stood on the sidelines, all I could hope was that holder Richie Petitbone, who had been shaken up earlier in the game, would be woozy. Or that the wind would spring up. Or that Percival would clutch. But the ball traveled forty-three yards straight and true. With only seconds left, the game was theirs. "We didn't forget," Bear coach Jim Dooley said at midfield. He was not being vindictive about the revenge for 1964. He was just playing exceptionally cool and intelligent football.

As I walked off the field, I pondered the importance of another fourth-period kicking play. Kramer's kickoff after our field goal had touched a Bear, and the opponent had subsequently fallen on the ball in the end zone with one of our players on top of him. Two officials signaled a safety, which would have given us a 12–10 lead at that point and forced the Bears to kick off to us. But the referee overruled the other two officials and called it a touchback, bringing the ball out to the twenty. I didn't dispute the official call, but I couldn't help wonder what forces were at work to make the kicking decisions all go against us.

Despite our losses, the Central Division's race was still open, and Vince agreed with me that we should be able to find a kicker to replace the bruised Mann. Since the league trading deadline was past, it would have to be a free agent. We had looked at approximately fifty men so far, and each day's mail brought a few more letters requesting tryouts. After looking over the choices, we called Mike Mercer at his Lafayette, California home and asked him to report at once.

Mercer was no stranger to us. He had been the Vikings' kicker for a couple of their earlier years, and then he went to the AFL, where he moved around from Oakland to Buffalo to Kansas City and back to Buffalo. It was he who kicked the field goal that brought Kansas City so close at halftime in the first Super Bowl. Cut by Buffalo, owing to a pulled left hamstring muscle in training camp, he had been practicing at home and waiting. Since we hadn't used an uninjured kicker yet, we were willing to gamble that he had mended sufficiently to work for us.

Mercer arrived in Green Bay a few days before our second Viking game, and as soon as we determined he was fit and could still kick, we activated him and cut Mann from the regulars. Mercer connected on five straight attempts from the forty-two on his second day of practice, and soon after, he made a few from midfield. Against the Vikings, he opened the scoring with a thirty-two-yarder, and it looked like we were back on the track. Fumbles and other errors prevented him from trying again until early in the fourth quarter. Penalized for clipping at the Minnesota five, we were pushed back to the

## PACKER DYNASTY

twenty, where we stalled. So Mercer came in to try from twenty-five yards out. The Vikings' Carl Eller, who moments earlier had rushed in savagely to knock Starr practically senseless, tore through to fling his hands up and block the attempt. Mercer's kick had been fast, straight, and high, but Eller was in there just too quickly. We lost the game, 14–10, because of crucial fumbles and penalties, but the failure of a sure kick was as nagging as any factor. A blocked field goal, if nothing else, is a bad psychological blow to the kicker's protectors.

The next week, against the New Orleans Saints, Mercer again started off the scoring with a thirty-plus placekick. And again he had an attempt from medium distance blocked later in the game. Two blocked field goal attempts in two successive weeks: nothing to give a coach encouragement. The day after the game I received a call from Bill Kiss, sports director for an Appleton, Wisconsin radio station and kicking coach of the Lawrence University team. He has been a kicker himself and is one of the better specialist coaches around.

"I think I know what Mercer's troubles are," he said. "It kills me to see him get blocked; how about if I come up and give him some suggestions—we're through with our season, and I'd be more than happy to volunteer."

So he came to Green Bay and began working with Mercer, showing him how to shorten his stride and connect with the ball lower to give it more altitude. Kiss managed to find the formula within about a half hour of working with Mike, but he didn't leave then. "A kicker has nobody to talk to," he explained to me. "Everybody else on the team has two or three counterparts to exchange ideas and information with, but the kicker is all alone. I'll stay around and talk with him as long as I'm needed."

So Kiss, who kicks every day of the year like some people jog or play golf, stayed on. And Mercer improved. He hit two out of three in the Washington game, made two identical forty-four-yarders in the San Francisco game, and produced our only score in the Baltimore game with a forty-five-yard shot to the right upright which bounced to the left and looped over the crossbar.

But our bid for the division title was now dead. A total of just thirteen points would have given us four more victories. After nearly twenty frustrating weeks of searching for a kicker, we had a respectable one, but nowhere to go with him. The long quest had drained us of more emotion than any other problem in the long, difficult season. Our only consolation is that perhaps it has cost us just *one* season.

When I read in the papers that another coach is faced with the dilemma of replacing his Toe, I'll know just what kind of agony he's going through. Like gout, it's a foot condition I wouldn't wish on anybody, not even my worst enemy.

## 29 · WITH A LITTLE HELP FROM OUR FRIENDS

"**I** feel sorry for people with backs."

It was the day after our preseason game with the All-Stars, and offensive line coach Ray Wietecha was commiserating with tackle Henry Jordan, who was in such pain from muscle spasms after his collision with a teammate on an attempt to block a kick that he was practically ready to retire on the spot.

Before the season was over, we would have ample opportunity to feel sorry for people with backs. And ribs. And hands, and legs, and heads. It was a year when practically everybody else in the league had the Hong Kong flu. Never ones to get exotic, we merely had simple fractures and general bruises. For the Packers, 1968 was an unmitigated medical disaster.

Jordan, who had started every game for five years without being sidelined, was just the first member of the defensive line to be taken out of action. Next it was our other first-string tackle, Ron Kostelnik, who was out for two weeks with a knee injury. The "backup" men for these two vital members of our bulwark? Bob Brown broke his arm the first week of training camp. A few weeks after he came back, he broke his leg. Jim Weatherwax was out with an injured knee all season. Through most of the preseason games and several during the first half of league play we had to use third-string men at tackle, and of course our opponents took every advantage of the situation.

From backs and knees, the injury bug moved to hands. Bart Starr injured the little finger on his passing hand and had to tape it during preseason and early-season games. The same problem afflicted Willie Davis. Of all the people you don't want to work with bandaged hands, the quarterback is number one, and a defensive end is close to number two.

We came out of our last preseason game with no new injuries, and men like Elijah Pitts and Bob Jeter, who had been out of some exhibitions with bruises, were ready to go. I pronounced the team in good physical shape for the opening of the season.

Even though we defeated Philadelphia, 30–13, in the opener, I could see what the debilitating exhibition season had done to our defensive line. They just weren't playing as a unit, and the reason was they had never all been well at the same time. We were short of desired form, and it would show against stronger opponents. In the next two games, division foes Minnesota and Detroit both beat us by two touchdowns. Kostelnik and Jeter were reinjured against the Vikings, and in both of the games Jordan just wasn't sufficiently restored to prevent the strong short rush.

Kramer and receiver Carroll Dale came out of our Atlanta victory with injuries, but it was in the warmup drills for the fifth and vitally important Ram game that adversity struck its cruelest blow. Bart Starr walked over to me after lobbing a routine practice throw and said, "Something just snapped in my passing arm, coach." In the dressing room the doctor diagnosed it as a pulled tendon in the bicep. As we headed for the playing field, Zeke Bratkowski learned that he would have to go the entire game. He did a magnificent job, but we lost in a squeaker.

We activated inexperienced rookie quarterback Bill Stevens from our taxi squad, but when Bratkowski was injured in the next week's game with Detroit, I sent Bart in for one play. He threw a touchdown pass with his injured arm to secure a 14–14 tie and keep us halfway alive in the division.

We experienced a "well" night at the midpoint of the season in order to triumph over Dallas, just as we had in preseason play. It wasn't a matter of the Cowboys being "jinxed" by us. It's just that they're apparently a tonic—a wonder drug—for us. Both Starr and Bratkowski performed well in our 28–17 victory. Jerry Kramer sat out almost the entire game, but he managed to come in for two plays, stimulated by the fierce competition and an unwillingness to be sidelined.

After losses to Chicago and Minnesota by three and four points respectively, we beat New Orleans. Because they were weaker? No, because we had our entire first-string playing together relatively uninjured for the first time in as long as anyone could remember. But even that win was a Pyrrhic victory. Bart, nursing sore ribs from a tackle by Minnesota's Carl Eller, was reinjured when he was forced out of the pocket and had to scramble. Bratkowski finished the game and played the entire next week against Washington in our 27–7 win.

For all our woes, we moved to within half a game of the Minnesota Vikings with just three games left to play. We were ahead of the Bears, the only team in the league with worse injury problems than ours, and the Lions, who had fallen on hard times when their ace runner, Mel Farr, was injured. All we had to do was win our remaining three games—against the 49ers, the Colts, and the Bears—and with a little help from our friends we'd win the frantic Central Division title. We all felt that our big-game mentality could carry us through the postseason money games. Hadn't it already showed itself in the big Dallas game?

But in the NFL you don't get much help from your friends. Whatever favors anyone in San Francisco owed us, they were forgotten. After we moved to a 10–0 lead in the second quarter, Bart was felled twice in succession and left the game with reinjured ribs. Zeke moved us ahead, 20–7, at the end of three periods, but with the 49ers finishing strong, he, too, was knocked out of action. I turned to Bart, but he had stiffened, and his chest was so pained that he couldn't go in. So, deep in our own territory, we had to use Stevens. Zeke came back to finish the game, but the damage was done: the 49ers defeated us, 27–20.

Lombardi's words to the press following the Dallas game

suddenly sounded more prophetic than ever: A 7–7 record might win the division title. Minnesota's loss to Los Angeles made it possible. Added to all that was Bratkowski's record substituting previously against our next foe. He had beaten the Colts twice in 1965 and once in 1966 to help us on the road to championships.

But prophecies, percentages, and precedent were not enough to overcome the league's best football team. We lost to the Colts because they were superior, not because of injuries. The Rams, the Vikings, and the Browns can bear us out on that.

In our final game, with the Bears, Starr was soon joined on the sidelines by Bratkowski, both of them now suffering rib injuries that made it impossible for them to play. By a twist of fate, second-year man Don Horn, who had been called to military service the day training camp opened, was released from duty. We activated him the day before the game, and he came from nowhere to be its hero. Although he had not worked out with the team all year long, had not spent the thousands of hours studying, had not even met some of his new teammates, he came in to toss two touchdown passes, set up another score, and lead us to a 28–27 victory.

What was his secret? Well, he is a fine, smart, young quarterback. He benefited greatly last year from working with Bart and Zeke.

And, of course, he was healthy.

## 30 · THE PACK WILL BE BACK

It was Grantland Rice who wrote the memorable line about that One Great Scorer marking down "not that you won or lost—but how you played the game." Heaven only knows how many high school coaches have invoked it after a losing effort, and how many Hollywood scriptwriters have injected it in their locker room pep-talk scenes.

But in professional football, winning is the only thing that counts. Purchase of a ticket implies that the holder is entitled to see a well-played game. Most fans feel that a good game is when their team wins. So we must win. We can't settle for less any more than the man who sells cars can say, "I know they're all lemons this year, but we really tried hard to build them right, and we think we did a tidy job of polishing the hubcaps."

Why couldn't we deliver in 1968? Any explanation sounds like an excuse. Other teams have gone through kicking letdowns; everybody has a certain number of injuries. Wasn't there something more?

Yes. We tried too hard to live up to the legend. We had pushed ourselves to the limit the previous year to win an unprecedented third straight championship for a beloved, demanding coach, and we had succeeded. Now the players were trying to dream an even more impossible dream. "We're going to win them all for you, Phil," Ray Nitschke told me the day I was named to take over the club. Three or four games into the season it finally hit some of the veterans who had been living in what Jerry Kramer called "Camelot": It's impossible to play football any way except one play, one game at a time.

## PACKER DYNASTY

Once, twice, three times during the long, hard season the veterans tried to pull everything together again, and after one or two games it seemed we had the formula once more.

But there were mistakes. Costly mistakes. It was as if the law of averages had finally caught up with us: fumbles, interceptions, interference calls, personal fouls, one-yard plunges to the goal line that the officials did not judge to be touchdowns, footballs hitting uprights, blocked kicks. Suddenly we were making mistakes, just like everybody else. And it hurt. In *the* big game with the Colts, Anderson and Grabowski both lost critical fumbles, not on poor execution, but on all-out extra effort. They were playing their hearts out.

And there was that incredible pressure of just being the Packers. It was responsible for our big-game mentality, of course. But it also meant that the lowliest teams in the league were preparing to make their best effort against us after watching us on television in game after championship game. It gets to be a downright nuisance, being the big guy that everybody would just love to knock over in order to prove his own power.

The All-Star game and the Super Bowl had become "no-win" situations for us. If we came out on top, people said we should have. If we lost. . . . Well, that's the price I had to pay. I said before the season that we would win the fourth championship in a row. And I believed it. I really did, because in this business you must believe in yourself or you can't go out there week after week and give everything you have.

So the string is broken. Now we must start all over again. As Nitschke told the nation in the postgame show from Chicago last December 15, there's a saying in Green Bay: "The Pack will be back." We know it, and the fans know it: Martha's Coffee Club has printed twenty thousand bumper stickers carrying the message. When our fans stood and cheered their heads off in the final seconds of the disappointing game with the Colts, it was the biggest vote of confidence we could have received.

We'll have to do it in the league's toughest division. Some writers have branded the Central a weak division because of the unimpressive won-loss records and their performances last year against outside contenders. But don't believe it. Ours is the most evenly balanced quartet in the four-division setup, and all four clubs are no-nonsense outfits that stress strong defense and basic offense. We play football the way it was meant to be played, and we deliver some of the most exciting Sunday afternoons to be had. Our various divisional rivalries make every game unpredictable. Chicago, Detroit, and Green Bay have won more than half of the league championships in the thirty-five years the NFL has crowned a winner. Our division shows signs of continuing to offer the tightest races for the next few years, and it will be a sign of strength all around, not weakness.

What will we do when Bart Starr is gone? When Nitschke retires? And so on and on?

Well, we made the transition in the backfield from Hornung and Taylor to a combination that won for us in 1967. And we'll be able to continue when Bart and Ray bid us farewell. Just look at who we have coming along:

At quarterback, Don Horn is destined to be as great as Bart Starr. Those are Lombardi's words. And Starr, while not measuring Horn against himself, has made every bit as complimentary an evaluation. Horn came of age in the final game with the Bears last year. Not many of the sportswriters have noticed him, but there is going to be a new wave of sensational young quarterbacks in another year or so, and Horn will be riding the crest.

At middle linebacker, Nitschke will hold forth as the best in professional football. Coming up behind him is young Jim Flanigan, a tough specimen whom Vince described after the second Super Bowl as "a young Irishman who'll make them forget the Ancient Order of Hibernians." He'll be flanked by Robinson and Caffey, who have already come into their own.

Our backfield is so rich with youthful talent that we frankly came very close last year to making a trade that would have astounded the football world. Anderson and Grabowski have begun to mature, and they are at the same stage in their professional development as Hornung and Taylor were when we began our rebuilding. Like all huge investments, we expected to wait a while before the payoff began. The time for clipping coupons is now, and it can last for years.

Travis Williams, after an amazing rookie season, suffered the pangs of reality last year. Many teams refused to kick to him, denying the long run. And when he did take the kickoff, he couldn't seem to go with it because, as he finally realized, he was thinking a hundred yards ahead instead of just five or ten. He fumbled a few, too, and he failed on some attempts at one-yard plunges for first downs. Now he has the humility and character to go with the attributes uncovered as a rookie. He'll be working harder than anyone this year, and he'll be a success. Pitts, Mercein, and Wilson in the backfield corps make it a problem of too much talent rather than too little.

Laboring behind Dowler and Dale at flanker is Claudis James. He dropped a few in clutch situations last year, but with experience he will be a genuine threat. Marv Fleming at tight end has begun to deliver when the chips are down, and he has a strong, authoritative build as well as the ability to snare passes in a crowd.

In another few years there will be retirements in the defensive backfield. But we're not lacking there. When Bob Jeter was injured in a late-season game, the opposing quarterback soon found that he couldn't gain much by picking on young replacement John Rowser, who can hold his own at either safety or cornerback.

And in the lines—the place where the trench warfare opens up holes and determines if the aerial battle will succeed—we have a crop of youngsters who will do well in years to come.

It's the same all around the league, of course. Other teams are making orderly replacements and training the superstars of the future. But we have to convince people of it, because they think the trading of a Hornung is disaster, the retirement of a Bart Starr tantamount to catastrophe. They forget that we have made an orderly transition at almost every position in the past decade without serious harm to the team's record. So it shall be in the years to come. What makes the picture even more encouraging is that the men who are coming up within the system have been groomed by today's veterans. They should be able to assimilate their predecessors' knowledge and add to it with newfound abilities of their own.

Yes, the Pack will be back. And if we come out on the short end of the score for a while, it's because the gun went off early. We have always played right down to the last second firmly believing that we are going to win. That is the mental attitude of a winner. As Colonel Blaik wrote on the blackboard at West Point: "There never was a champion who to himself was a good loser. There is a vast difference between a good sport and a good loser."

And Vince Lombardi wrote on our blackboard: "There is no laughter in losing."

My contribution to the list of variations on the theme by Grantland Rice is probably the least literary, the least charitable, and most to the point. It's going to be our slogan from here on in: *Winning is the only thing that counts.*

At the end of the first week in February 1969—one year after his retirement as head coach—Vince Lombardi asked for release from his Packer contract so that he might accept an opportunity to become head coach, general manager, and part owner of the Washington Redskins. A month later, I took on the Packer general manager's job. During that period I also named two new assistants: retiring offensive tackle Forrest Gregg and quarterback Zeke Bratkowski.

Lombardi had made good on his promise to leave the coaching to me, but he began to realize as early as July that he wouldn't enjoy his "retirement." On February 21, 1969, he had told a *Press-Gazette* reporter, "I will be very much disappointed if I do not have enough self-discipline to stay away." On July 11, the morning of our first workout, he appeared on the field at 9:38 A.M., smiled limply at the newsmen, and sat quietly and forlornly on an upended tackling dummy at the far side of the field. Eight minutes of self-discipline. He was miserable.

The evening of our first exhibition, he took his new season seat high in the press box. After the game he drew me aside and demanded: "Who were all those people on the sidelines? There was a whole crowd of people standing around the bench."

"It was the same people as always," I replied. "Bud Jorgenson, Dad Braisher, Dave Hanner, Vern Biever taking pictures, Brian (my youngest son) helping with the equipment, Dr. Nellen—"

Vince shook his head. "Yeah, yeah. I guess I just never noticed. It looks different from up there."

It does look different from up there. It sounds different. And it feels different. It's no place for a football coach to be. George Halas couldn't stand it up there. Vince Lombardi couldn't. And I don't think I could either.